SOCIAL MOVEMENTS
AND CULTURAL CHANGE

SOCIOLOGICAL IMAGINATION
AND STRUCTURAL CHANGE

An Aldine de Gruyter Series of Texts and Monographs

SERIES EDITOR

Bernard Phillips, *Boston University*

Leo d'Anjou
Social Movements and Cultural Change
The First Abolition Campaign Revisited

SOCIAL MOVEMENTS AND CULTURAL CHANGE
The First Abolition Campaign Revisited

Leo d'Anjou

ALDINE DE GRUYTER
New York

About the Author

Leo d'Anjou is Associate Professor of Sociology at Erasmus University in Rotterdam, The Netherlands. Dr. d'Anjou studied law and sociology at Erasmus University and received his Ph.D. from Rijks Universiteit, Leiden. His fields of professional interests are sociology of law, social justice, and social and cultural change.

ALDINE DE GRUYTER
A division of Walter de Gruyter, Inc.
200 Saw Mill River Road
Hawthorne, New York 10532

This publication is printed on acid free paper

Library of Congress Cataloging-in-Publication Data
d'Anjou, Leo, 1937–
    Social movements and cultural change : the first abolition
campaign revisited / Leo d'Anjou.
        p.   cm. — (Sociological imagination and structural change)
    Includes bibliographical references and index.
    ISBN 0-202-30521-X (alk. paper). — ISBN 0-202-30522-8 (pbk. :
alk. paper)
    1. Antislavery movements—Great Britain—History—18th century.
2. Slave-trade—Great Britain—History—18th century.   3. Slavery—
Great Britain—History—18th century.   4. Abolitionists—Great
Britain—History—18th century.   5. Social movements—Great Britain—
History—18th century.   6. Social change—Great Britain—
History—18th century.   I. Title.   II. Series.
HT1163.A55   1996
326'.0942'09032—dc20   96-1030
                                                            CIP

Manufactured in the United States of America

10 9 8 7 6 5 4 3 2 1

For Fogi

Contents

PART III CONFRONTATION

8 Social Movements and Social Construction of Meaning

Acknowledgments

"You'll Never Walk Alone" is not only true for soccer fans but for authors as well. Looking back, it is amazing how many people have—in one way or another—contributed to this book. Now is the time to give them credit.

Three of those have been essential and I will therefore mention them first. The late Guus ter Hoeven, Professor of Sociology at Erasmus University Rotterdam, not only put me on the track of sociology when I entered law school in the seventies, but also led me toward abolition at a later date. When discussing my early ideas concerning social movements and cultural change, he told me that if I wanted to test those ideas I had better take an "impossible" case like abolition. If the ideas would hold there, they would hold anywhere. Guus, my thanks for that suggestion as well as the many others.

John van Male is the second of these indispensable people. He has been indefatigable in reading every draft (and there have been many), criticizing my unclear thinking and writing, bringing forward all kinds of useful suggestions and proposals, and encouraging me to go ahead when I doubted. Most importantly, his unremitting zeal in convincing me to skip needless digressions and frills has, I hope, saved the reader from unnecessary aggravation. John, thanks for being such a great pal.

The last but not the least of these pivotal people is my wife. She enabled me to indulge in this adventure of idle curiosity. She (and with her all partners of authors) knows what it takes to set one free. Words are not enough to express my gratitude; perhaps the dedication of this book to you will help.

There are many others who contributed in important ways. I would like to mention first the members of the research group of which I am proud to be a part. I thank them all for their support, for the discussions we so often had, and for their companionship; it is and has been wonderful to work with you guys. Those who deserve special mention are Professor Jan Berting for allowing me my own space for so many years; Els Hoeffnagel, Kees Molenkamp, Dick Houtman, and Peter Oeij for their valuable assistance in the search for literature; and Bram Steijn and Dick Houtman for their comments on the final concept draft of the manuscript.

I would also like to thank those outside Erasmus who commented on earlier drafts, parts of the manuscript, and/or the final concept draft of the manuscript. In alphabetical order, Professor Seymour Drescher of the University of Pittsburgh, Professor Stanley L. Engerman of the University of Rochester, Professor William Gamson of Boston College, Professor Sidney Tarrow of Cornell University, Professor Charles Tilly of the New School for Social Research in New York, Marga de Weerd of the Vrije Universiteit Amsterdam, and one anonymous reviewer. You will see that I have often—or perhaps, in your opinion, not often enough— heeded your suggestions and advice.

Finally, I would like to thank those who have been involved directly in producing this book. First, Professor Bernard Phillips of Boston University, editor of this new series, who believed in my book from the moment he laid eyes on only a part of it. His trust, enthusiasm, and many suggestions made this book possible. Second, Michael Krass, with his talent for both the English and the Dutch language, has assisted me greatly in producing a readable text as far as the English is concerned. At this point I would also like to thank Lisa Sove and Brigitte d'Anjou who assisted me with this in earlier stages. Third, Wil Bouwman and Paul Van Wensveen aided me in finding my way in the sometimes incomprehensible world of WordPerfect, Harvard Graphics, and other computer programs. Fourth, Dr. Richard Koffler and Mrs. Arlene Perazzini of Aldine de Gruyter, who guided me through the unknown territory of international publishing.

It goes without saying that I remain responsible for all the errors that remain. Thank you all.

I

Theory

1

Introduction

1.1 THE FIRST PROBLEM

On the twenty-eighth of January 1986 the space shuttle *Challenger* exploded. At that time shuttle launches had almost become a routine matter. A few hours later on that same day, a barge, the *Searan II*, sank after a collision with a seagoing ship in the harbor of Rotterdam. In both cases, the fatal accidents were due to a failure of the craft involved. In both cases, the crew died. The way both accidents were treated, however, differed enormously. The explosion of the space shuttle was a drama that shook the world. The sinking of the barge got a few lines in the newspapers and was only a drama for the families of the victims.

The vast difference in the treatment of the two accidents—in both cases involving people just doing their job in a more or less routine way—gives rise to the question, Why? Part of the answer to this question is naturally to be found in the kind of job the victims were doing. Space transport is less common than transport by barge. However, this does not fully answer the question. What, for instance, would have happened if the particular barge had been loaded with dangerous toxic chemicals (not an extraordinary situation in the harbor of Rotterdam)? The exposure of the accident with the barge would then have been much greater. Not only would the media in the Netherlands and in neighboring countries have gone into the causes and consequences of the accident, but so would politicians and environmental groups. Chances are that a large part of the discussion would have centered on governmental policies on safety regulations and the need for official action on that issue. It seems that a relatively small change in the circumstances of an event can make a big difference as to how an event is defined and treated.

One of the outstanding characteristics of the process in which events are defined and portrayed in the media is that the "defining" occurs almost automatically. The way an event is defined is often not the deliberate choice of an individual (a journalist) or of a group or organization (an interest group or a social movement organization). Labels such as "disaster," "accident," or "inadequate safety regulations" seem to belong quite naturally to certain happenings or occurrences. They are part of the everyday taken-for-granted world. We can say that in every society there is a stock of labels or definitions available and that rules exist that stipulate the way occurrences are defined and thus transformed into events (cf. Molotch and Lester 1974). These definitions are common or collective definitions and together they form society's codebook.

These collective definitions do not only function as guidelines telling people how to look at events in their environment. They also inform people how to act, which makes these kinds of definitions real in their consequences, the famous Thomas theorem (Coser 1971). A fatal event described as an "Act of God" leads to prayer and penitence. The same event defined as a consequence of failing management may lead to the dismissal of the manager or a suit against the company. More sociologically stated: collective definitions structure the way to act.

The relationship that exists between the way an event is defined, the way people look at that particular event, and the way they act toward it means consequentially that in every society there will be actors who have an interest in the way "things" are defined or are not defined at all. For instance, defining a flood as a punishment by God will probably lead to the filling of churches but not to the building of dikes. Defining the same event as a consequence of incorrect policy choices in the past will most definitely lead to the reformulation of policy on controlling the sea and to the building of new and higher dikes. (Witness for instance what happened after 1953 and again in 1994–1995 in the Netherlands[1]). The first definition is in the interest of clergymen and the second in the interest of organizations who design and build dikes.

The importance of the way events are defined leads to the question of the relationship between interests and the process by which the content of the societal codebook is determined, or more precisely, to the question of how to understand

> the formation, continuity, change, survival and disappearance of common interpretations, reference schemes, beliefs, worldviews, etc. (the collective definitions of the situation) in relation to actions of the "definers." These are social movement organizations, interest groups, bureaucratic (governmental and nongovernmental) organizations, politicians, etc.

This question, which is phrased quite generally, forms a useful starting point for devising research projects, but is far too broad to function as an actual research question. One way to come to such a question is to narrow down the field of actors involved in the "defining" activities, i.e., in the process of constructing meaning. We have chosen this strategy and have opted for social movements as the focus of our research. This choice is influenced by the fact that social movements are of prime importance in the process of social change in modern society (Garner and Zald 1987). Moreover, movements play a central role in processes of cultural change because they function "in part as signifying agents. They frame or assign meaning to and interpret, relevant events and conditions" (Snow and Benford 1988:198).

At this point some clarification is needed. The way the term *social movement* is often used suggests at least that social movements are taken as purposeful actors. This usage easily leads to reifying social movements and to putting them in the place of the actors acting in the context of a movement. As Tilly (1993–94) rightly points out, a social movement is not a group or a grouplike organization and thus not an actor. The term refers, on the contrary, to a relational network of actors produced by actors who are collectively involved in conflicts and which as such is a condition for these contentious actions (Tilly 1982; Diani 1992; Tarrow 1994). At the same time, it is difficult to avoid using the reifying term *social movement* when alluding to the activities of the contending actors comprised in a movement. In many cases it is a useful kind of shorthand for keeping a text readable; this is in any case the way the term *social movement* is regularly used throughout this book.

Movements play this role of signifying agents in interaction with the media, the state, countermovements, and other actors in society and are thus part of the social processes in which meanings are constructed. This focus on social movements as agents active in defining situations brings us to the first theme of this book, namely the question, *Which role do social movements play in the social construction of meaning?*

1.2 THE SECOND PROBLEM

The interest in cultural topics has been surging in sociology in recent years, or as Dubin (1992:719) has it in a recent book review: " 'Cultural studies' has become an academic buzzphrase." This surge can also be detected in the field of social movement research where the social production and construction of meaning has become a focal point (see, for instance, the recent "stock-taking" of the developments in social movement research in Morris and McClurg Mueller 1992). The focus is directed at the following three aspects of the movement process:

• the role that cultural elements such as movement ideology and collective action frames play in the mobilization of resources and the organization of support (Snow and Benford 1988, 1992);

- the creation of new collective identities by movements as a goal in and of itself, as a "defensive . . . refusal of reification in family, publics, mass culture, etc. [and as an] offensive . . . identity" oriented at structural reform (Cohen 1985:715);
- the effect of the symbolic struggle—an important aspect of the activities we call a social movement (Gamson 1988)—on the consensually held meanings in society: the theme of this book.[2]

A pressing problem that confronts the researchers of cultural change and social movements pertains to the elusive character of meaning and meaning production. The notion that meanings are socially produced implies that meanings are not made to last an eternity; they are not inherently stable and unchangeable, and they do not "lead" an objective existence independent of the actors who use them. It even denies, in principle, the existence of an objective social reality because all social "things" are constructions, the social science concepts included, and are the result of negotiation and communication processes.

As Hunt and Benford point out, the constructivist position—strictly maintained—leads to an infinite regress and traps the sociologist "in a post-modern quagmire" (1992:37). In fact, as Berger notes, the switch to the reflexive, interpretive point of view in, for instance, ethnography, historical sociology, and the sociology of culture has already led ethnographers, anthropologists, and sociologists to give up the original rationale of the sociological approach, i.e., making causal generalizations and giving explanations through empirical research guided by concepts and hypotheses. Instead, the emphasis in their research has shifted toward the richness of descriptive detail and the depth of insight into the unique (Berger 1991:2).

Dealing with social construction of meaning *and* maintaining the rationale of the sociological approach, making generalizations and giving explanations, as we intend to do in this book, poses therefore a fundamental problem. This problem is further augmented by the fact that research into the role of social movements in producing meaning is almost only possible in the form of qualitative case studies. In practice, however, the qualitative research tradition leans strongly toward the reflective interpretive position of the constructivists. Here we also find a preference for the interesting and appealing particulars of the case studied and a neglect of the generic properties and underlying dynamics of social life, and we see that qualitative case studies often explain little and that their results are difficult to generalize.

In our view, the only way out of this problem is—while recognizing the constructed character of social life and thus accepting its inherently provisional status—to bracket this provisional status for the time being. Social science has to treat social life as an objective or at least as an intersubjectively agreed-upon reality in order to conduct empirical research. For their explanations of the phenomena of social life, sociologists need to know "what causes what" and sociology therefore "*must* be deterministic [and it] must also be reductionistic if it wants to wrest some relatively simple generalization from the infinitely complex data of lived life" (Berger 1991:9).[3]

We agree with Berger when he states: "That's why we need concepts, abstractions, and why we study the empirical relations among their indicators" (ibid.). This statement also converges with Turner's ideas on analytical theorizing. Important in his viewpoint is that "the main task of all theory [is] to understand how the social world operates" (1987:156) and that this understanding is only possible if sociologists develop their conceptual tools first and then confront them with the empirical reality of social life expressed in the data they have assembled.

More specifically, the line of theorizing advocated by Turner consists of a synergetic combination of three types of approaches utilized in sociology:[4]

1.   The approach proposed by Blumer (1969): the use of sensitizing analytical schemes. In this approach the emphasis is placed on the sensitizing function of concepts, which is an essential property of concepts as it directs the attention of the researcher and guides his[5] research.

2.   The approach propagated by Willer (1967): the use of analytical models. In this approach it is stated that concepts employed in sociological research must be context free and must be related to each other in causal terms. The concepts, moreover, are often presented in a visual picture. This approach makes generalization possible even in qualitative research.

3.   The approach taken by Homans (1974): the use of abstract formal propositions. Here, the underlying dynamics of social life are set down like laws and from those laws "in what is often a rough and discursive manner 'deductions' to empirical events are made" (Turner 1987:163). Empirical instances—among them those resulting from qualitative case-studies—are considered to be explained if they can be deduced from general statements about the generic properties of social life.

At this point, it is possible to clarify our position vis-à-vis the construction of social meaning by stating our conclusions regarding the foregoing:

•   We agree with the constructivist position that social reality is basically a social construction.
•   We follow Berger as he posits that the bracketing of the constructed character of this reality and its inherently provisional status is necessary.

• We accept the basic assumption of Turner that social reality is actually capable of "talking back" and may so defy our conceptualizations.

• We think that social science is possible—even with regard to such an elusive phenomenon as the social construction of meaning—but only if adequate conceptual tools are used. This means using theoretical models in which concepts are sharply defined and the relations between them clearly and unambiguously formulated.

The latter, moreover, enables us to master the bewildering complexity of social movements. Here we are confronted with yet another problem. Most recent work on social movements is based on a view of human nature in which the actions of men are seen as being regulated by the environment.[6] Action is mainly a rational reaction directed at getting the rewards one's environment offers and at avoiding its punishments. This view of man as a rational actor mechanically choosing between the good and the bad in his environment is the transposition of the "machine" metaphor of the classic natural and physical sciences (Dijksterhuis 1986) to the social sciences. In the latter, man is primarily portrayed as an object kinetically moved into action by outside influences: man metaphorically depicted as a billiard ball.

The problem with this view is not that it is entirely wrong but that it is incomplete and thus inadequate for explaining human action. Being human entails more than being rational and self-interested (cf. Buechler 1993:227–28). Therefore, a more adequate view of human nature is needed alongside the aforementioned adequate conceptual tools. For the former, we will use the view in which man is seen as an agent acting on the basis of his internal drives and resources *and* in accordance with the facilities and constraints that his environment contains; in terms of the metaphor, man as a player shooting a game of pool in the context of the (im)possibilities of rules, material, and other players. This way, moreover, the Scylla of the undersocialized conception of man may be avoided without hitting the Charybdis of its opposite, the oversocialized conception of man (Granovetter 1992).

Much work in developing conceptual tools has already been done; see, especially, the work of Gamson and his associates (for instance, Gamson and Lasch 1983; Gamson and Modigliani 1989; Gamson 1988, 1992a) and that of Snow and others (for instance, Snow, Rochford, Worden, and Benford 1986; Snow and Benford 1988, 1992). One of the problems with this work, however, is that it is still piecemeal and the propositions and concepts used in it have an ad hoc character. It seems time to move somewhat further and to bring the concepts, propositions, and other ideas concerning the role social movements play in meaning construction together in a conceptual model. Devising such a model necessitates (1) choosing between competing conceptual formulations; (2) filling the gaps in the theoretical reasoning; and (3) bringing coherence to the model as a whole. *The development of a conceptual model as an instrument for the study of the role of social movements in the social construction of meaning* is the second problem this book will address.

1.3 THE STRATEGY

The purpose of this book is to understand the role social movements play in the construction of meaning in society. As we will see in Chapter 3, meaning construction by social movement actors always implies changing meanings because social movement processes are invariantly involved in change.[7] Therefore, this book is actually about understanding social movements and cultural change. To enhance this understanding we will employ a double-edged strategy consisting of a combination of (1) an explicit conceptualization of movement and cultural change processes and (2) the use of Zaret's analytical strategy of distinguishing between the context of movement activities and the context of foregoing and concomitant events (Zaret 1989).

The Conceptual Strategy

We have made clear above that understanding the role of social movements in meaning construction processes (and, more generally, in cultural change) depends on adequate conceptualizations. At the same time, this understanding must, like all sociological insights, be firmly rooted in the empirical reality of social life. This can be reached through a dual process of conceptualization and empirical research in which concepts inform and guide research *and* in which the latter corrects and shapes the former. This process implies alternating between going to ever higher levels of abstraction and going down to the level of concrete data and particular historical situations. As Phillips (1990), inspired by C. Wright Mills, calls it, going up and down ladders of abstraction.

The conceptual model needed for our research will be developed in three steps. First, we will use the existing literature—especially books and articles with a firm empirical base—on social movements and social construction of meaning to devise a provisional conceptual model. Second, this provisional model will be examined on the basis of a secondary analysis of the data of a case study. This case study concerns the social movement directed at the abolition of the slave trade that occurred in Great Britain between 1787 and 1807. This movement did not only lead to the abolition of the slave trade but changed the social meaning of slavery and the slave trade as well. The latter aspect will be the focus of our study. Third, the results of this secondary analysis will serve to adapt the conceptual model and thus improve it. This will make the model more useful for future empirical research.

Zaret's Analytical Strategy

In a comparable study, Zaret (1989) proposes a specific strategy for analyzing these kinds of changes. He conceptualizes the activities of social movements as an organizational context that mediates the influence of cultural and structural factors on ideological changes. He also distinguishes another mediating context in this regard: the episodic context or the context formed by historical events. An important part of these events antedates the movement actions and as such conditions the organizational context of the movement. The importance of these kinds of foregoing events also became evident from a first look at the studies we selected for our secondary analysis (see note 1, Preface to the Case Study). This made clear that several long-term developments (and not only the type of historical events that Zaret mentions) in British society prior to the abolition movement were of prime importance to the origin, development, and impact of the abolition movement. The notion that foregoing developments are important in understanding movements and change came, moreover, strongly to the fore when the conceptual model was further elaborated.

The importance of these historical developments has changed our initial idea on how social movement processes function in constructing new meanings and in changing extant ones. Studies show that actors involved in social movements do not "invent" these new meanings nor do they produce them wholly on their own. Meanings are constructed in contentious discourses in which actors try to mobilize resources and support and to convince "others" that they are right. In these attempts they use existing ideas, beliefs, and other cultural elements that come forth from these foregoing developments. Moreover, they operate within circumstances shaped by historical processes and are deeply influenced by them. Movements seen as conflictual processes mediate, as it were, between ongoing cultural and structural processes and specific cultural changes.

The first introduction into the studies of the abolition movement combined with the strategical proposals of Zaret and the later elaborated theoretical notions brought us to the following conceptual distinctions that we will make in our case study of the abolition movement. In this study we will distinguish between:

1. the long-term developments in British society antedating the abolition movement that shaped the general conditions and circumstances for the movement;
2. the episodic context of the specific historical events that conditioned the specific situation in which the abolition movement originated and that influenced the conditions in which the movement operated;
3. the organizational context or the activities that the abolition movement applied in order to reach its ends.

The chosen strategy poses two problems, however. The first is whether theoretical notions concerning social movements that are clearly tied to the present-day period are also valid for studying events of two hundred years ago. Tilly's work (1982) shows that this is the case, because the social movement as we know it now arose at that point in time. Second, there is the problem of studying only one case. This restricts the possibilities for validating the model because direct comparisons with other cases are not possible. This problem is solved as far as it can be by incorporating an internal and an external comparison in our study . The internal comparison is that between the characteristics of the campaign, which was successful, with those of the anticampaign, which was not. The external comparison is a longitudinal one. As we explained above, the model in this book is part of an ongoing project. It is based on earlier empirical research; it is itself probed in this study; and it will function as a starting point in future studies in which further adjustments will be made.

1.4 THE PLAN OF THE BOOK

As we stated above, social production of meaning by social movements comprises the ongoing cultural and structural dynamics in society, the dynamics of the social movement, the interface between them, and the changes in the collective definitions of the reality in which people live. The conceptualization of this meaning construction process will be executed in two stages. The first stage will consist of the development of the basic outlines of the process of social change in which collective actions play a central role. The second stage will involve the transformation of these basic outlines into a conceptual model in which the elements described above are assigned their place.

The basic outlines of the social change process will be elaborated in

Chapter 2. Here, we will use Weber's vision on social change as a guideline for this elaboration, especially the notions he developed in his sociology of religion. In this chapter we will combine Weber's conception of the dynamics of ideas and of the importance of actors and their actions relative to these dynamics with recent notions on social action, structure, and agency in order to reach a basic theoretical scheme of social change. In this scheme the emphasis will be placed on the relation between collective action and transformation. This scheme will form the foundation of the conceptual model in Chapter 3.

In Chapter 3 we will develop a conceptual model concerning social movements and the social production of meaning. Here we will employ the literature on social movements, especially the studies on the role movements play in framing discourses on contested issues. Special attention will be given (1) to the structure of opportunities and power as the interface between historical developments and the rise and the activities of social movements *and* (2) to the activities of movements as the interface between the social movement and the change in collective definitions.

The conceptual model in Chapter 3 will subsequently be examined on the basis of the aforementioned case study of the first phase of the campaign waged by the movement directed toward the abolition of the trade in slaves by Britons. This first phase ran from 1787 to 1792. I choose 1787 as the beginning of this first phase because in that year the Abolition Committee that started the campaign against the slave trade was founded. I take 1792 as the closing year because by that year the collective definition of slave trade and slavery was definitely changed. In the words of Drescher, "What had changed, and permanently so, was a cognitive world-view, whether one deals with it in terms of its psychological or its political dimensions" (1986:87). The final legal abolition of the trade was, however, not reached until 1807.

The secondary analysis of the historical studies on the abolition of the slave trade will be executed and presented in the three phases we distinguished before.

1. The—more long-term—developments in philosophy, religion, literature, politics, and economics in the first seventy to eighty years of the eighteenth century that created a situation rife for change. These developments are described in Chapters 4 and 5.

2. The episodic context of the change process. This consists of the historical events that proved to be essential for turning the potential resulting from the long-term developments into an actual opportunity structure that made the takeoff of the abolition movement possible. These events are the subject of Chapter 6.

3. The organizational context—the campaign executed by the abolition movement between 1787 and 1792 that resulted in the change of the way slave trade and slavery were—collectively—defined. The movement campaign is presented in Chapter 7.

The following step involves the confrontation of theory and data. This is done in Chapter 8. Here the proposed conceptual model will be reexamined and, where necessary, adapted in light of the results of the abolition study in order to reach a model that better fits the empirical reality of social movements engaged in the social construction of meaning. This model will subsequently be placed in a more encompassing theoretical view with regard to processes of cultural change. The book concludes with an epilogue, Chapter 9. In this chapter, the choices we made in this book are evaluated and the chapter ends with a brief and tentative excursion into the future of social movements and cultural change.

NOTES

1.   The 1953 flood painfully showed the Dutch people how defense against the sea had been neglected and led to an enormous program, the Deltaplan, of building new dams and dikes and of raising the existing ones. The events of 1994–1995—the threatening dike bursts inland and the ensuing evacuations—made clear that the legal and administrative procedures of this Deltaplan had delayed the strengthening and raising of the river dikes. As a consequence, an "emergency" law was devised that made quick action possible.

2.   In our first research question, the focus on the effect of movement processes actually results in introducing the notion "social" two times—each time with a different meaning (a double meaning that is easily obscured by the current use of the phrase "social construction of meaning"). This means that—more precisely formulated—the question concluding Section 1.1 runs as follows: Which role do social movements play in the social (i.e., interactive) construction of social (i.e., consensually held) meanings? We will, however, maintain the wording of the question in the text, because this concurs with convention.

3.   Emphasis in the original. Whenever italics are used in citations, they are used in the original unless otherwise stated.

4.   Turner's argument is essentially an adaptation of the strict precepts of logical positivism to the reality all empirical sciences have to cope with outside the "purity" of the experimental setting. As Turner points out, this realistic adaptation is quite common in the (so-called hard) natural sciences, too. See as examples the evolution theory and the big-bang theory. As Turner states: "Much of what constitutes a "deductive system" in all scientific theory is folk-reasoning, and highly discursive" (1987:158).

5.   In order to avoid awkward combinations like his or her; her/is; or s/he the terms *he, his,* etc., are meant in a neutral way.

6.   This is different with the theories regarding the so-called identity-oriented movements (see, for example, Cohen 1985).

7.   In the social movement literature there exists widespread agreement on the fact that social movements are directed at changing aspects of the social order and sometimes of the order itself or at preventing that. See, for instance, Blumer (1939)—to establish a new order of life; Heberle (1951)—to bring about fundamental changes in the social order; Smelser (1962)—to modify norms and values; Gusfield (1970)—toward the demand for change in some aspect of the social order; Wilkinson (1971)—to promote change; Turner and Killian (1972)— some established practice or mode of thought is wrong and ought to be replaced; McCarthy and Zald (1977)—directed toward social change; Marwell and Oliver (1984)—wanting or trying to promote or resist some kind of social change.

2

Collective Action and Social Change:
The Basic Outlines

2.1 INTRODUCTION

"Interests (material and ideal), and not ideas, directly govern actions of men. But the worldviews which were created by ideas have very often, as switchmen, determined the tracks in which the dynamic of interests propelled the action. The worldview informed one "from what" and "for what" one would and—not to forget—could be saved" (Weber [1920] 1986:252). This typical Weberian statement—brief, to the point, and more or less concealed in a detailed exposition of some point—expresses Weber's vision on social change very succinctly, a vision that is among other things the foundation of his sociology of religion and of his analysis of the Reformation in the *Protestant Ethic* (Weber [1920] 1975, [1920] 1976).

In this vision three central elements may be discerned:

1.   The dynamics of social action. These originate, on the one hand, in interests but are, on the other hand, shaped by cultural elements like worldviews, which indicate how to promote these interests.

2.   The dynamics of the cultural realm; the creation of worldviews by ideas. These refer to processes of signification and meaning construction that have an autonomy of their own (*Eigengesetzlichkeit*).

3.   The actors, i.e., those who initiate and sustain both dynamics.

The role that ideas play in processes of social change is of prime importance in Weber's view, a role that is typified by Marshall as follows: "Weber was insistent that ideas become significant in history and are causally effective in shaping social conduct because, at certain points, a class or status group with special material or ideal interests takes up, sustains, and develops these ideas, and is influenced by them. He accepts . . . that ideas are both shaped by and, in turn, help shape interests and action. As a general principle, however, the 'inner logic' of their

15

development does not proceed independently of all other spheres of social reality" (1982:161).

In this chapter Weber's vision on social change is used as a guideline for developing the basic outlines of the way collective action and social change will be conceptualized. These will form the foundation of the conceptual model in the next chapter, which concerns social movements and cultural change with particular attention to the social construction of meaning. The conceptualization starts with the elaboration of the dynamics of social action in Section 2.2. In this we will employ recent notions on action, structure, and agency. Following, we proceed in Section 2.3 with the transformation of the action scheme from the foregoing section into a theoretical model of social change. In this model, the actor as well as the notion of relative autonomy receive an important place. The chapter concludes with a section in which the threads that we have spun in the foregoing sections are drawn together. This results in a schematic model of social change as a product of action and reaction in which collective action occupies a central place.

2.2 ACTION THEORY

"[A] theory of action is a conceptual scheme for the analysis of behavior of living organisms" (Parsons and Shils 1990:39). Here we are only interested in the behavior of human beings insofar as one human being orients his actions toward the actions of one or more other human beings, i.e., we are interested in social action. Action, when we take its kernel, is *to relate to something* (Nuttin 1984). In the case of social action, this means first of all *to relate to somebody*. The motivation to do so may—in Nuttin's view—arise from within the actor (from drives, impulses, needs, etc.) or originate in objects (social, cultural, or physical; Parsons and Shils 1990) in the actor's environment. Nuttin's notion of action is schematized in Figure 2.1.

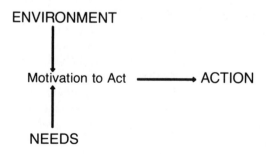

Figure 2.1. Nuttin's action scheme.

Environment, Needs, and Social Action.   Action, however, is not a simple product of either an internal need (a push) or an external signal (a pull). Needs and environment are related in a complicated way, a relationship that can only be fully understood if we take into account two basic characteristics of both the environment and the needs. First, the environment in human action is always a social environment. This is obvious when we think of the environment in terms of other actors—the social environment—or in terms of cultural objects—the cultural environment. It is, however, also social in relations with physical objects, because these objects are only relevant for human action when they mean something to acting individuals, i.e., when they are culturally mediated, and when they are used within social relationships; in other words, when they are socially imbedded.

Second, needs are diffuse feelings of *manqué* (Heller 1978, using a concept of Sartre). This diffuseness, however, does not mean that needs do not provide any direction toward action. A feeling of hunger is quite different from the need to distinguish oneself from others or the need to make sense of one's existence. In the past, copious attempts have been made to devise catalogs of needs, drives, impulses, etc.[1] For a sociological theory of action, such extensive catalogs of needs are not necessary. Weber's distinction between material and ideal (immaterial) needs[2] will suffice here. The material needs concern "the 'happiness' of human beings, their well-being, health and longevity" and the ideal needs concern "[the] search for meaning" (Schluchter 1981:25).

As needs are diffuse they demand social arrangements to make fulfillment possible. They can only be satisfied when they are "translated" or "transformed" into cultural forms and when structural opportunities and possibilities for need-fulfillment are created. This, moreover, makes the relationship between environments and needs a dialectical one.[3] On the one hand, the social environment shapes a person's needs, creates possibilities for need-fulfillment, and—what is more—appeals to a person's diffuse needs with its opportunities and promises for satisfaction. On the other hand, needs are the dynamic force behind the creation of social and cultural forms of need-satisfaction and they press for changes if existing forms are not adequate.

Up till now we have emphasized the "recipe" character of the social environment of acting persons (telling people how to act) and the enticing properties of it. Objects (again, other actors, cultural or symbolic objects, or physical objects) in one's environment may also compel actors into action, e.g., by way of precepts, sanctions, or sheer force. Thus, the social and cultural environment of an actor (1) offers facilities and resources for action, (2) guides action by rules or norms that function as recipes and precepts, and (3) demands or constrains action, especially by actions of other actors. This relationship between environ-

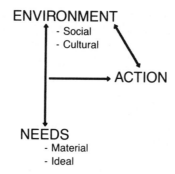

Figure 2.2.   Dialectical model of action.

ment and action is, moreover, not a question of one-way traffic. The environment functions as an *action-structure* that, for an actor, is at the same time a given *for* and a product *of* his action. Every act is the enactment of a text that is already written *and* the (re)production of that text that would not exist if not enacted. This means that the relationship between environment and action is dialectical as well. This conceptualization of action as the outcome of two kinds of dialectical relationships is graphically depicted in Figure 2.2.

The Action-Structure.   The notion of action-structure we introduced above is more or less the same as Giddens's concept of structure (1982, 1984), which he refers to as the set of rules and resources people draw upon for their actions.[4] It is—seen from the viewpoint of action—an action-potential that, however, comprises more, as Sewell (1992) and Thompson (1989) rightly contend, than rules and resources in the strict sense of the word. The foregoing implies this as well. First, rules are more than recipes for action. They embrace a great variety of cultural schemas such as "conventions, recipes, scenarios, principles of action, and habits of speech and gesture" (Sewell 1992:8). Second, resources, both nonhuman and human, must be seen as media of power that are unevenly distributed (ibid.). Third, this potential not only enables people to act: it constrains their actions as well. As Thompson (1989) states, it involves constraints following from the semantic and moral aspects of rules as well as from the way society is socially structured.[5] This last aspect refers to the range of options of acting (e.g., power, life chances, etc.) that are differentially distributed and social-structurally circumscribed.

A comparable description of this action-structure can be found in Sztompka's interpretation of Merton's concept of social structure (1986b). Merton's concept encompasses the norms directly governing behavior, such as shared expectations and role sets; the life chances people have or their chances and opportunities of realizing their goals and fulfilling their wants; and the shared beliefs and ideas concerning the world in which people live, the values to which they adhere, the norms to which they subscribe, the structure of opportunities, the legitimacy thereof, etc. Together, these norms, rules, values, ideas, beliefs, resources, etc. (organized in sets), form the action-structure. In this they function as facilities, they *enable* action and *entice* people into action, and as constraints, they *guide* action and *limit* it.

The Actor. So far, we have treated action-structure as a concept comprising all that is pregiven in the situations where action takes place. It has been used as a catchall phrase for all features of any particular action-situation that "generate, define, and determine the course of a [specific action] process" (Berger, Eyre, and Zelditch 1989:21), i.e., everything that structures action, gives action its form, and more generally makes one action more probable than any other action. Moreover, we have more or less reduced the actor to his needs. This is obviously an oversimplification of the basic unit of a social action theory: the actor-in-situation (Berger et al. 1989).

Bringing the actor back in (to paraphrase Homans 1964) means giving more attention to the important characteristics of actors, characteristics that indicate—as Therborn (1991) rightly states—that actors are not a given and therefore can not be treated in sociology as if they are.[6] On the other hand Therborn makes clear that the situations in which actors act are often variable, too. They are, moreover, not of their own choosing (Marx [1869] 1968). Berger et al.'s phrase "actor-in-situation" depicts quite well the fact that the actor and the situation are not separate entities. They are both aspects of one reality of action that, however, have to be separated analytically in a fruitful and useful sociology of action [cf. Archer's analytical dualism (1988)].

There are four features of actors that are important: needs, past experiences, agency, and the relation of an actor to its environment. The first feature, the actor's needs, points to exigencies that have a material or an ideal foundation (see above). When collective actors are taken as the unit of analysis,[7] these needs are better described as interests. Needs and interests refer to discrepancies of whatever kind between the wanted situation and the actual situation and they function as "activators" of action.

The second feature of the actor-concept concerns the fact that each actor has a history. Actors-in-situations are not tabulae rasae, but are enscribed by past experiences. On the individual level this feature points to the aspect of internalization—in terms of Mead ([1934] 1962) to

Me—and on the collective level to the aspect of institutionalization of ideas and procedures relevant to the internal management of a collectivity. In general terms, we have here the factors described before under the heading of action-structure, which are internalized or internally institutionalized. We will call this part of the action-structure the *internal structure*.

The third feature of the actor has to do with *agency*, which Berger et al. (1989) see as a fundamental property of any actor, both individual and collective. They describe agency as follows: "Actors make choices, decisions, evaluations; they "orient" themselves to situations and process information about them; they anticipate, expect, have policies" (p. 23). Put more systematically, as Dietz and Burns (1992) do, there is agency when actors (1) possess the ability or power to make a difference, (2) act intentionally, (3) are free to choose, and (4) have the ability to be reflexive about the consequences of their actions. The degree of agency may vary, however, from situation to situation. It is a continuous property of actors; in Sewell's words: "agency differs enormously in both kind and extent" (1992:20). This variation makes Thompson (1989) in his critique on Giddens skeptical about the assumption that actors need options in order to be agents.

Although we acknowledge that there are many situations in which the pressure on people to conform both in thinking and in acting is enormous, we still adhere to the assumption that the human action-situation always implies some degree of agency. Ego[8] is never completely determined by alter, nor by force, nor by manipulation, or in Giddens's words. "the individual could . . . have acted differently" (1984:9). Agency means a degree of freedom for every actor in coordinating and mediating the relation between his needs and interests on the one hand and the internal elements of the action-structure on the other. Through this coordination and mediation it becomes possible for an actor to act, i.e., to relate to the social environment in which one lives. Acting also means mediating and coordinating the demands and enticements coming from the agent's social environment.

This social environment—the fourth feature—makes the acting actor (ego) complete because his actions are directed to alter *and* because the actions of other actors have consequences for ego's actions. A social environment consists of two elements: on the one hand, the relations between ego and alter (and the relations of the other actors between each other) and, on the other hand, the symbols, meanings, values, norms, rules, etc., actors have in common. In other words, the social environment is both systemic and cultural and comprises all facilities and constraints of the action-structure that are not included in the aforementioned internal part of the action-structure and are thus external to the acting actor. This part of the action-structure therefore will hereafter be referred to as the *external structure.*

The Action Scheme. In the conceptualization of action we are developing in this section the action-structure remains a unity in which two aspects—the external and the internal structure—are analytically distinguished. Both aspects are dialectically related to the needs/interests of the acting actor and through the mediating aspect of the actor, i.e., agency, to his action. The basic outlines of this conceptualization are depicted schematically in Figure 2.3.

The dialectical relations between action-structure and action mean that this structure facilitates and constrains action and that action (re)produces structure. As Archer (1988) makes clear, the relationship between structure and action is best seen as a cyclical process in which time has a central place. It is an endless cycle of structural/cultural conditioning of action → social/cultural action → structural/cultural elaboration → conditioning, etc. Actions are ordered in a temporal sequence in which actions may change the facilities and constraints for future action (Therborn 1991). When we give time an explicit place in our action model, we get the following sequence: there is an effect of the external and internal structure upon action at t_1 that has a feedback effect on the same structures at t_2. This sets the stage for a new action at t_3, etc.

This feedback effect does not always lead to an unchanged reproduction of the action-structure. Transformation of the structure, i.e., social and cultural change, is a possibility (Archer 1988; Sewell 1992). Three types of these endogenous change processes can be distinguished: (1)

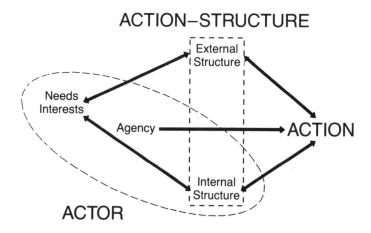

ACTION–STRUCTURE

Figure 2.3. Basic outlines of an action theory.

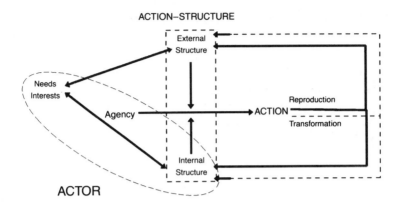

Figure 2.4. Action theory completed.

There is the possibility of imperceptible step-by-step changes. The effect (leading to change) goes unrecognized and is unintended. (2) The effect of transposing rules and schemas on other cases, which may mean changing—most of the time unintended as well—the rules and schemas used in the action. (3) Conscious actions intended to change the rules, schemas, belief systems, social relations, etc.

The breakdown of the dialectical relation between structure and action and the acknowledgment of the possibility of endogenous change through the feedback of action to structure leads to the adjustment of the foregoing action scheme shown in Figure 2.4.

We will end this section by developing an example[9] that highlights in a concrete way the important aspects of the action theory that we developed above in a more abstract manner.

> Our example starts with a young male, in his early twenties, who lives in the Netherlands at the end of the fifties. Let's call him Jan, and as many men of his age he is interested in girls. In the fifties, one of the typical ways to make contact with girls for young men like Jan was to go to dances, invite girls to dance, and try to escort them home. The last part of this is particularly important because it is the way to more intimate contacts and possibly lasting relationships.
>
> This short sketch points to several elements depicted in Figure 2.4. First of all, there is a need, contact with the opposite sex. Next, the environment offers external facilities, the dance evening and the custom of escorting girls home. Actually, there are external constraints in it as well. Dutch society was a pillarized society in those days and most events, dances included, were organized by

churches, like the Reformed or the Roman Catholic church, or by other "ideologically oriented" organizations. In Jan's case, the dances he went to were organized by the Roman Catholic parish of the neighborhood in which he lived. He was therefore likely to meet only Roman Catholic girls who would most probably come from the same status group. The pillarization together with the ways neighborhoods were socially stratified thus circumscribed the choice of girls for Jan.

The actor is important as well. The internal aspects of the action-structure contributed to Jan's endeavors to reach his goal. He needed, for example, to know how to dance and the proper ways to court girls. Both can be seen as internal resources. Then there is the agency aspect. Jan could have chosen to go to a club, bar, or dance hall instead, but this would not have helped him very much because in those days nice girls did not frequent those places.

In our example, one of these dance evenings led Jan into a lasting relationship, and again the external aspects of his action-structure guided his way. His relationship went through the conventional stages of courtship, engagement, and marriage. The wedding took place, needless to say, in the parish church and the party was held in the hall adjacent to the church where he had met his wife on one of the parish dance evenings. Jan (and all the others in comparable situations) reproduced through his actions the institutions that were there to facilitate the fulfillment of his needs and interests and restricted him at the same time.

At the end of the sixties, the situation concerning coming into contact with the opposite sex, courtship, engagement, and marriage changed drastically. First of all, the pillarized structure of Dutch society fell apart. New opportunities arose for boys and girls to meet and become involved. The dance as the socially segregated meeting place disappeared. There were other changes as well. For our example, one of the most important changes pertained to the institution of marriage. It was attacked as one of the symbols of repressive society. Instead of marrying, people chose cohabitation without a marriage certificate as the way to live as husband and wife. Cohabitation already existed as a format—called *hokken* in Dutch and common-law marriage in English—that until that time had been rather negatively valuated. This last aspect made it particularly attractive for the "revolutionaries" of the sixties.

By choosing this format they transformed the institutional structure with regard to living as husband and wife and added a new facility to the action-structure of young people in the Netherlands.

Later generations followed their example and reproduced cohabitation as an institutionalized format. For some it became the alternative for marriage, for others it meant the replacement of
engagement in the trio courtship–engagement–marriage. Other
actors in society, especially government agencies, reacted as well
and integrated cohabitation step by step into the social structure of
laws and regulations in the Netherlands. By now, cohabitation has
become an institutional feature alongside marriage. It is regulated
as much as a marriage is, gives about the same rights, and has a
similar status.

2.3 SOCIAL CHANGE CONCEPTUALIZED

In this section we will go into the general characteristics of the process
of social change in which social movements are involved. As we will see
in the next chapter, social movements primarily concern organized and
coordinated activities that people utilize when trying to reach some goal
in a nonroutine contentious way. The concept "social movement" thus
refers to specific forms of collective action, conflictual and organized.
Organization means that the actors we are dealing with are more often
than not collective actors and that, therefore, individuals will occupy
only a secondary place in the following. This also means that action will
be restricted to collective action in our conceptualization of social
change. Finally, looking at action in terms of social change means that
the action scheme of Figure 2.4 has to be converted into a social change
model.

From an Action Scheme to a Change Model. Social change means the
transformation of the action-structures of ego and/or alter. In the foregoing section we saw that actors do not act alone but that they do so in a
social environment: they live and act in a society. This society can be
seen as a system consisting of all sorts of networks in which individual
members of society and collective actors are related to each other. In this
system of relations every action may have consequences for the action-
structure of every other actor. When we look from the point of view of
ego, we see not only that his actions may reproduce or transform his
own (ego's) action-structure but that his actions may reproduce/
transform the action-structures of other actors as well. Likewise, the
actions of others (alter) may reproduce or transform ego's action-
structure.

Living in a society, then, means being related to each other through
reciprocal actions, such as exchange, love, and power, the outcomes of

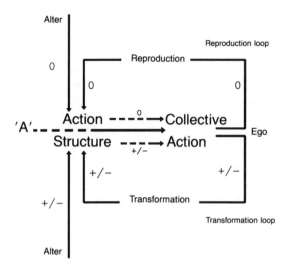

0   unchanged reproduction
+/- transformation

Figure 2.5. Basic model of collective action and social change.

which (alter's as well as ego's actions) may reproduce or transform any ego's action-structure. Reproduction or transformation (i.e., change) are thus the two possible consequences of ego's and/or alter's actions. This vision on social change resulting from the conversion of the action scheme into a social change model is schematically represented in Figure 2.5.[10] In this model we have simplified the action-structure by setting aside the analytical separation. We have also put together interests and agency under the letter "A" and left out the dialectical relations between interests and action-structure.

Collective action takes a central place in the social change model because this action functions as a kind of switch in "determining" whether the outcome of an action will be reproduction or change. The functioning of this switch is contingent on both the potentialities inherent in the action-structure (in a social change model this means whether this structure facilitates or constrains action directed at change) and the interests and agency (A) of the actor. As Berger et al. point out, change is difficult to explain "if one adopts the view that there is no pregiven structure" (1989:14). Action also depends on the decisions and choices of actors, which need not be made fully consciously or be rational. Change thus means the realization of the potential of the action-structure through agential action.

Moreover, if collective action leads to changing its "own" action-structure, this will either facilitate or constrain further collective actions, which then may further change its action-structure, and so on. Social change is thus not only contingent on the action-structure and the interests and decisions of the collective (action) actors at a given point in time but may be contingent on itself. The effect of this second type of contingency may be

a. setting in motion an ongoing change process, i.e., facilitating (enabling and/or enticing) further changes;
b. circumscribing change or preventing it altogether, i.e., constraining (guiding and/or limiting) further changes.

The basic dynamics of social change and collective action are depicted above in a rather abstract way but may be better comprehended if we go back to the example of the foregoing section. We stated there that cohabitation was accepted by government agencies and integrated in existing laws and regulations. This was no automatic response, however. The step-by-step adaptation of laws and regulations to this new institutional format was the effect of collective actions of people who for reasons of principle chose cohabitation. This dynamic is further clarified below with a more extended example. For this example, we use a study by Law and Walsh (1983) into the way a challenging group succeeded in bringing about desired change.

In 1981, a young contender died during a so-called Toughman Contest, a form of boxing with hardly any rules. This led to a campaign to ban these contests from Pennsylvania, the state in which this particular match was held. The organization that directed this campaign (JUST) originated in the extended network of the relatives and friends of the victim. The existence of such a network may be seen as a facilitating element of the action-structure within which JUST operated. This organization succeeded in involving the media—radio, newspapers, and TV—in the issue of the danger and immorality of these irregular prize fighting contests and through the media attention was able to get the cooperation of third parties, such as the national boxing elites, the state athletic commission, the state legislature, and the court system, to ban the contests. Both the media and these parties are existing facilities waiting, as it were, to be used in a campaign like JUST initiated.

JUST was not only able to muster these facilitating resources; it successfully avoided existing constraints in the action-structure as well. The organization refrained, for instance, from the mobilization of individuals and organizations on a larger-scale because the aversion against "meddling with an individual's freedom of choice" as well as the popularity of these contests, especially among workers, was expected to impede this kind of mobilization and thus the possibility of larger-scale popular actions. JUST also presented its case in such a way as not to threaten the professional and amateur boxing organizations, as resistance from these established organizations is very difficult to overcome for any challenging group. "Meddling" and counteractions of other actors would most probably have had negative effects on the action-structure of JUST—the ego in this example—and would thus have constrained the JUST campaign.

JUST succeeded in ending these contests by putting the organization behind these fights out of business. It also succeeded in getting the ban of these contests onto Pennsylvania's legislative agenda, and at the end of 1982 (the time Law and Walsh wrote their paper) JUST was close to legislative success. The collective action by JUST therefore changed the action-structure of the promoters of prize fights and therewith brought about some social change.

Some Analytical Refinements. As we have already seen, the action-structure is at the same time a producer and a product of social action. For every actor, however, the action-structure is for the most part pre-given. It may be seen as a Durkheimian social fact that is defined outside the acting person and that has a "compelling" influence on him (Durkheim [1895] 1967). This structure is institutionalized in both the culture and the social system of the society to which actors belong and in which they are located (Therborn 1991). As such, the action-structure forms part of the institutions of society.

These societal institutions (the action-structure included) confront each actor as a whole. As Archer (1988) rightly observes, this does not mean that society has to be dealt with as a whole in sociological research. Analytical distinctions are often needed for useful and fruitful studies[11] and we will also use these kinds of distinctions here. Three types of distinctions are necessary in order to grasp the dynamics of cultural change and the role social movement actors play in this respect.

In the first distinction we discriminate between the *manifest and the latent part of the action-structure.* Not all facilities and constraints at the level of action and interaction are relevant for any given action. An actor is affected in his actions only by a part of the action-structure, i.e., the manifest part, while the rest of this structure remains latent.

As we saw above, cohabitation was a long-standing, existing format for living like husband and wife. As a facility, however, it was not relevant for people like Jan because it was very negatively valued in the fifties and seen as something for marginal people. Decent people did not do such things. For them this format was a latent element in their action-structure that they could but would not use; they would not even think about it.

The choice of actors between alternative action scripts (DiMaggio 1991) and their recognition of existing boundaries and constraints is regulated by a logic of appropriateness or relevance (March and Olsen 1989). The relevance of elements of the action-structure for a particular action depends on the needs and interests, the stimuli and events in the environment, and the role and position of the actors.

Again we return to the example of Section 2.2. Today, the "marriage" format has become a viable option for the "cohabiting people of the sixties" and their heirs. It is, among other things, one of the simplest ways to settle the complicated legal matters concerning children. For the cohabitants, marriage was not relevant for years and was thus a latent part of their action-structure. Now it has again become a manifest facility, especially in cases where the cohabiting pairs are expecting a child.

The example makes clear that people make choices as each case arises, but that these choices are often institutionalized in status role complexes and in bundles of action strategies. This means that responses themselves and the relation between cue and response are often patterned and standardized. Action—in substance and form—depends in those cases on the connections made by these role status complexes, which act as Weber's switchmen invoking the appropriate line of response (DiMaggio 1991; March and Olsen 1989).

The fact that the latent part of the action-structure is always available for actors who may draw upon the facilities it offers or who may invoke its constraints to limit the actions of others may lead to unexpected dynamics in social life. Law is illustrative in this respect because: "[existing] legal symbols and discourses provide relatively malleable resources that are routinely reconstructed as citizens consciously seek to advance their interests and designs in everyday life" (McCann 1991:228). An action-structure at any one time is thus not a given that is passive and cannot be changed. What is available for action depends on the actor as well as on the existing facilities and resources. This dynamic relationship makes changes dependent on the ingenuity and drive of actors in exploring the possibilities an action-structure gives them and therefore makes change so difficult to predict.

The second distinction is a vertical distinction between *the level of the action-structure and that of society* that is mainly a distinction in the level of abstraction. The first, relatively concrete level is that of the action-structure. This structure comprises the concrete facilities and constraints that directly govern action: The "things" actors draw upon and that limit their actions, such as the rules, schemas, resources, and constraints that are relevant for specific actions. Analytically, the action-structure may best be characterized as a readily available tool kit (cf. Swidler 1986), a set of opportunities, and a prestructured action field.

The other level we distinguish is the more abstract level of society, i.e., the societal-structure. As Thompson describes, the potential of the action-structure is affected by features of institutions and organizations in society that are not "rules or resources" themselves but that "are better conceptualized . . . as a series of elements and their interrelations that together *limit* the kind of rules which are possible and which thereby *delimit* the scope for institutional variation" (1989:66). We have here the institutional and systemic elements that influence action indirectly. They form the foundation on which the action-structure functions in giving some actors opportunities and chances and restricting those of others.

> The pillarization with its extreme organizational segregation along religious and ideological lines concerns structures at the level of society. For example, the Roman Catholic pillar had its own youth organizations, schools, unions, organizations of employers, sports clubs, leisure organizations, etc. This structural segregation confronted Roman Catholics in every activity they undertook as an action-structure of facilities and constraints. It structured their lives and limited their choices. For a Roman Catholic like Jan, for example, it largely determined who could become his friends or his wife.

Below we present several examples to elucidate more completely the distinction we have in mind.

> The first example comes from Weber's work on religion. Weber makes a sharp distinction in this work between the ethical theory in theological books—the societal level—and the ethic of daily life that provides practical stimuli for action—the level of action. The former affects the latter, but only the latter directly influences action through positive and/or negative sanctions. (See, for example, Weber [1920] 1986:238 or [1920] 1976:97–98.) As Weber shows in his *Protestant Ethic*, it was not the Calvinist doctrine that was important

in guiding daily conduct but the way in which this doctrine was translated in the practice of pastoral work. Only the latter turned predestination into rules of self-control and methodical conduct and made them elements of the action-structure of the Puritan protestants at that time; it brought the monastic way of life into everyday living.

The same distinction can be made between the general principle concerning the equality of men—the Enlightenment heritage—and the corresponding article(s) in the declaration of human rights on the one hand, and the specific national laws forbidding discrimination on the other. These principles and laws belong to the societal structure. If sanctions based on these laws are actually applied, the abstract ideas are transformed into actual constraints. Only then will the constraints on discriminatory practices become part of the action-structures of people, and thus equality may—in some measure—be realized.

This distinction between the level of action and the level of society is useful because it opens up the possibility for showing how both levels affect each other. First, cultural elements and systemic relations (the societal level) affect the action potential of actors because they comprise the facilities and constraints for collective action and through this potential shape collective actions. Social transformations and historical events on the level of society are especially important in this respect. They may enlarge the possibilities of collective action by changing the action-structure of the actors involved or they may circumscribe these possibilities. Two examples may make this clear.

The explosion of protest against new nuclear weapons in the Netherlands in the 1980s is a fine illustration of how earlier developments may enlarge the possibilities for action. The famous *Hollanditis* that facilitated these actions was made possible by several earlier political developments in this country. The rapid depillarization of Dutch society in the sixties particularly cleared the way for ideas and collective actions that could easily be marginalized before. At this point, the growing popularity of anticapitalism and antimilitarism was striking and both profoundly affected public thinking about nuclear arms (Van Praag 1992).

An example of the restriction of action possibilities can be seen in the recent demise of the social democratic political parties in most West European countries. The economic transformations of the eighties resulted—grossly simplified—in bifurcating the (lower) middle and lower classes. A considerable part of these classes experienced a rise in income during those years and the rest (especially those with few intellectual, educational, and physical endowments) were marginalized. Both developments eroded the traditional support base of the social democratic parties and thus severely circumscribed their political possibilities.

Second, all kinds of practices, action strategies, and scripts—the level of the action-structure—may influence values, beliefs, power relations, etc.—the societal level. Collective actors, for instance, may affect public opinion and common beliefs through the way they frame issues, shape beliefs, and build collective identities within a social movement or interest group and therewith enlarge their own action potential and/or limit the potential of other actors (see the next example).

As Useem and Zald (1982) show, the antinuclear movement—partly aided by the accident at the Three Mile Island nuclear site—succeeded in (1) changing public opinion on nuclear energy (see also Gamson and Modigliani 1989), (2) negatively affecting governmental policies on nuclear energy, and (3) limiting the routine access of the nuclear industry to the decision-making circles. Thus, the action potential of the nuclear industry was severely curtailed.

The third distinction concerns horizontal distinctions at the level of society that can analytically be made between different *institutional orders*. We here follow the lead of Schluchter (1981), who has elaborated Weber's famous switchmen metaphor (see the beginning of this chapter). In Schluchter's view the notion of worldviews in Weber's statement represents the institutional order that mediates between the dynamic coming from interests and the influence of ideas. This order contains the socially relevant solutions for man's material and spiritual wants (his interests). It describes and prescribes what to eat and what not to eat when you are hungry; what to believe or not to believe when you search for meaning; and which means are available to attain these culturally formulated ends.[12]

The institutional order—typified in this way—comprises both the level of the action-structure and that of the societal structure. The way Schluchter elaborates this order, however, shows that he reserves the concept "institutional order" for the level of society. Following Weber he distinguishes four of these (partial) institutional orders: "the 'natural' order, which is tied to natural reproduction, especially family and kinship, and which is at the core of a much larger order, the *educational order*; the *economic order*, which meets the recurrent, normal wants of everyday life; the *cultural order*, of which religion is the most important element; the *political order*, which protects social life on a territorial basis internally and externally" (p. 28, emphasis added). We will follow Schluchter's elaboration: The term *institutional order* refers to the societal level and this order can be seen as consisting of several partial orders.[13]

Each of these partial orders can—analytically—be seen as an entity that is *relatively autonomous*. It has its own set of symbols, meanings, values, schemas, etc., i.e., a culture, and its own organization and set of relations, i.e., a social system. Art, a part of the cultural order, for example, differs in many respects from industry, which belongs to the economic order. Art for art's sake is difficult to compare with producing commodities for the market. Culturally, they are defined quite differently and are differently valued as well. The organization of industrial production also differs greatly from the way the "production" of art is organized; ideal-typically: large organizations vs. artists working on their own in their studios.

The relative autonomy means, moreover, that each order has a *dynamic of its own* (*Eigengesetzlichkeit*). A central notion in Weber's work. Actors who hold positions in one of the partial orders may therefore act to maintain the status quo because this is advantageous for them, or they may try to transform the order in order to make it more concurrent with their interests. To these ends, they employ the ideal and systemic tools at their disposal. In the main, there are two different types of dynamics to be distinguished.

First, there is the dynamic following from the activities of the functionaries of an order, such as priests or bureaucrats, whose normal task it is to "run" the order. In doing so, they may elaborate ideas and beliefs, improve rites, devise more effective rules, reconstruct organizations, etc., the (perverse) effect of which may be changes, mostly in a latent form, to the very order they are serving. The present-day deadlock most countries are experiencing as a result of their drug policies can be seen as an example of such a perverse effect.[14]

> Nowadays, it is hardly possible to imagine that "[i]n the late nineteenth and early twentieth centuries, narcotics were widely available: through doctors who indiscriminately prescribed morphine and later heroin as pain killers, through druggists who sold them openly, or through a wide variety of patent medicines" (Dickson 1968:148). The public viewed drug addiction as a habit that "was not approved, but neither was it regarded as criminal or monstrous. It was usually looked upon as a vice or personal misfortune, or much as alcoholism is viewed today" (Lindesmith in 1947, cited by Dickson 1968:148). Illustrative in this respect is the way A. Conan Doyle treats the drug use of his hero, Sherlock Holmes, and the reaction of his friend, Watson, to it.

That this situation changed was not the result of deliberate attempts to wage a war on drugs, but of a sequence of steps, each with its own restricted goals. Two types of steps proved to be especially important.: (1) The actions of the bureaucratic organizations that, since the Hague Convention of 1912, have found themselves in "control of narcotics" as part of their task. These organizations, as Dickson shows in his study of the Bureau of Narcotics in the United States, strove to get more funding for their activities out of "the normal, well-documented bureaucratic tendency toward growth and expansion" (p. 149). He makes clear that they could accomplish this growth only by convincing the public, the political decision-makers, and mostly the courts that the use of drugs—and therewith the production of and the traffic in drugs—was dangerous and a threat to society. (2) The choice of politicians—while this did not occur until much later—to use the drug issue in the competition for votes and as an aid to winning an election.

The dynamics of stepping up the war on drugs was put into a higher gear though, when the bureaucrats' tendency toward growth and the politicians' search for votes—both executing their normal tasks—became interlocked. This brought about the current situation with all kinds of constraints for the drug user and an enormous set of opportunities for those who illegally produce and supply drugs. It is a situation nobody seems to have wanted, but from which nobody seems capable of finding a way out. How fixed the situation is can be seen in the hostile reactions to the modest attempts in the Netherlands to effect a more sensible approach to the drug problem.

Second, in almost every situation there are people—individuals and groups—for whom the situation is not or not fully adequate. Inadequate institutions and organizations may induce actors to reform these (mostly piecemeal) in order to bring them more in line with their interests, or they may set off the dynamic of challengers versus power holders directed at more fundamental changes.[15] An example of the reform dynamic can be found in the actions of settled interest groups, mostly the representatives of the dominant in society, who deliberate with government officials over regulating competition, supporting business, subsidizing development and research, etc.

A recent example of this dynamic is the attack of the large companies in the retail business on the laws that regulate shopping hours in the Netherlands. For years, these companies pressed for permission to keep their shops open longer but were not very successful.

They recently renewed their attack, making use of both the fashionable argument of freer markets and fewer rules, and the formation of a new government without the party that traditionally defended the interests of small shop owners. At the moment, the prospects of the large companies are bright and their pressure seems to be resulting in some change.

An example of the more fundamental dynamic can be seen in the activities of social movement organizations and pressure groups that use extrainstitutional means, such as demonstrations, sit-ins, and strikes, to put pressure on authorities.[16] The British abolition movement is an example of this dynamic. As this movement is extensively treated in Part II, we refrain from elaborating it as an example here.

The autonomy of the partial orders is relative for it is circumscribed by interests, earlier institutionalization, existing power relations, and dominant ideas. It is also relative because developments in one order may influence the development in one or more of the other orders. Weber uses the concept "elective affinity" (*Wahlverwandtschaft*) to depict the relations between the different orders. Change processes in the partial orders are, in principle, independent of each other and are not strictly causally related. At one time or another, however, processes in different institutional orders may get in tune and thus amplify each other. An example of this affinity is the relationship between Western capitalism and the formal rationalization of Western law.

> The first impetus to the rationalization of law in Europe came from the reception of the relatively formalized body of Roman law in the early Middle Ages. The existence of formal law was one of the many conditions for the coming into being of Western capitalism (Collins 1980). The rise of capitalism, the acts of early capitalists, meant a further impetus for elaborating more formal legal rules and systems, because these capitalists hired legal specialists to invoke favorable court decisions and/or to induce authorities to make rules better suited to them. This development in turn promoted the growth of the capitalist economic system, which influenced the formal rationalization of law, and so on.

The inherent dynamics within the partial orders and the elective affinities between them condition and shape the action-structure which, as we have seen, is of key importance for collective action. They facilitate or constrain action through this structure and in this way increase the likelihood of one type of action—in substance as well as in form—relative to other lines of action.

2.4   COLLECTIVE ACTION AND SOCIAL CHANGE:
A CONCLUSION

In the foregoing section, we have expounded the notion that collective action may function as one of the decisive moments in the process of social (and thus of cultural) change; as a switch in the "choice" between reproducing or transforming the extant cultural and social system. As we have stated before, this turning of the switch depends on the potentialities of the structure within which actors act *and* on their interest-motivated decisions to act. The action-structure in relation to these decisions increases or decreases the likelihood of change, directs its course, and shapes the form as well as the substance of the changes in society. Both the action-structure and the interest-motivated decisions are the product of foregoing actions, events, developments, and transformation processes in society (in terms of our model, of ego as well as alter change). In this, collective action connects history with the future, and within it choice and determination are inextricably fused.

More is involved in the change process, however. The action-structure does not remain the same in this process. First, the actors involved in collective action will try to influence the conditions for their actions. They actively look for latent possibilities and for chances to improve the action situation, to enlarge its facilities, and to diminish its constraints. Thus, collective action may have a feedback effect on the action-structure. Second, actions of others, especially their reactions to the initial collective action, may affect the conditions for collective actions. They influence the action-structure of the actors who strive toward change through collective actions. The actions of adversaries offer the "change" actors more (or fewer) facilities for their activities *or* put more (or less) constraints on them. Thus, the ongoing activities in society and in its institutional orders may affect collective action through the action-structure.

Together, the dialectical interrelation of the dynamics on the societal level with those on the level of the action-structure, the relatively autonomous dynamics of the institutional orders in society and their interrelatedness, *and* the possibility that actors may tap latent potentialities inherent in their action-structures in order to reach their goals or to thwart those of others give the process of collective action and social change its contingent character. This continuing contingency of action upon action leads to paths of change that often exhibit the unexpected turns so familiar to those who look back into history.

This means that a collective action does not act as a one-time switch but that it triggers a process of action and reaction from which social

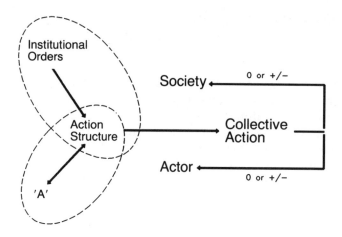

Figure 2.6. Contingent social change and collective action.

change results. Both aspects of this process of contingent social change with collective action as a key element are depicted—in a very simplified manner—in Figure 2.6. In this schematic illustration we have included the societal level, under the name of institutional orders, as a separate element. The feedback arrows represent the eventual transformation of society as well as the intermediate changes in the action-structure. In order to keep this figure clearly structured, we have combined the interests and agency under A and we have left the analytical refinements out.

NOTES

1. See, for example, Chapters 12 and 13 on human motivation in Hilgard, Atkinson, and Atkinson ([1953] 1971). Their Table 13-1 (p. 316) is especially illustrative in this respect.

2. We will follow Schluchter (1981) here in using the term *need* instead of *interest*.

3. This means that one's social environment and one's needs form a unity in which (a) the one cannot go without the other; they presuppose—or, better said, constitute—each other; (b) both elements affect—often contradictorily— each other simultaneously. For an example of the way the dialectical heritage of Hegel and Marx is employed in sociology, see Ritzer (1981).

4. It is, however, not always clear what Giddens means by structure. See, for example, the description of structure in *The Constitution of Society* (1984:17), in which it is difficult to recognize our conceptualization of action-structure. The discrepancy between both structure concepts seems to be much smaller, though, where Giddens describes structure in terms of rules and resources. It is from these

descriptions that we conclude that the correspondence to which we have alluded does exist. See also, among others, Abrams (1982), Lloyd (1986), and Sztompka (1994), who emphasize the dynamic of structuring and agency and the dual dependency of actors and society as fundamental building blocks for theories of social change.

5.   With his critique of Giddens, Thompson introduces de facto two concepts of structure: (1) structure as action-structure, and (2) structure as social structure (or social system). It is the Parsonian distinction between the 1937 structure of social action and the 1951 social system. In order to avoid misunderstandings in the following we will use the terms *system* and *systemic* as much as possible when referring to social structure.

6.   Therborn's paper makes implicitly clear that Homans, with his pioneering paper, did not bring *man* back in, but instead an amputated, mechanical dope who cannot but react to the rewards and punishments his environment offers him.

7.   We agree with Berger et al. that in interactor theories, i.e., theories that are directed at "the mechanisms or processes by which actors act in relation to other actors in situations of action," actors can be individual or collective actors (collective in the sense of corporate, which means that there are "means by which collective decisions are made and actions as collective are taken" (1989:21, 23).

8.   In this chapter the term *ego* points to the acting actor and *alter* to the other actor(s) to which ego's actions are oriented.

9.   Here and in the following section, we will use examples to clarify the rather abstract elaboration of the action and the change models. These will be presented in indented text in order to separate the abstract elaboration from the concrete examples.

10.   In this figure the effects of collective action on alter and the nonsocial changes (e.g., climatic changes) are kept outside the model in order to avoid further complication of the model.

11.   DiMaggio, for instance, shows that institutions work on two levels: "upon the availability and legitimacy of particular orientations and scripts and upon roles as switching systems invoking particular scripts and orientations" (1991:86). Thompson (1989) implicitly makes an analogous distinction between action-structure and social structure.

12.   These solutions are the product of men's needs and interests, of the existing symbolic universum, *and* of the functioning of the institutional order itself. The question of whether pigs are edible cannot be decided solely by the "edibility" of pig's meat itself or the need for food, but as much by the existing religious ideas about "clean" and "unclean" and the interest-driven struggle in the institutional order between priests, farmers, butchers, meat producers, etc.

13.   Following Weber, as Schluchter does, it is possible to make one more distinction, viz., between the level of the institutional orders and the level of ideas. The latter may be depicted as the highly abstract, symbolic, and central notions that are abstract enough to overarch the partial orders. This level of ideas is comparable to Durkheim's description of the collective conscience in modern organic society in his *Division of Labor* ([1893] 1964:Part II, Chapter 3). An

example of such an abstract idea is the notion of "freedom," which takes on different and more specific forms in the different institutional orders, e.g., the free market or the right of assembly. We will not make this analytical distinction here because we do not need it for our analysis.

14.   These policies are directed at ending the production, traffic, and use of drugs such as heroin, cocaine, marihuana, and amphetamines. These are goals that prove to be out of the reach of these policies. At the same time, antidrug policies produce all kinds of unwanted, negative effects such as boosting organized crime; spreading diseases like AIDS and hepatitis; causing deaths as the result of the drug use itself, the pollution of drugs, or gang wars; promoting theft and prostitution; and even the destabilization of whole countries by drug mafias.

15.   Especially the refusal of the authorities to improve the existing situation or the threat of worsening this situation coming from activities directed at change may act as powerful incentives for collective (counter-) actions.

16.   An important effect of the "elaboration" of the institutional order—as part of "normal" day-to-day activities within an order or as a consequence of deliberate attempts to change that order—may be the coming into existence of contradictions within and between the partial orders. These contradictions may again—as Marx rightly recognized—act as powerful incentives for collective efforts to dissolve them.

3

Social Movements and Cultural Change:
The Conceptual Model

3.1 INTRODUCTION

Social movements are important in bringing forth societal change. They turn—as Klandermans, Kriesi, and Tarrow (1988) tersely state—structure into action and possibly into social change. In the preceding chapter we developed a model of social change in which the interaction between societal structures and collective action occupies a central place. In this chapter we will specify this model by adjusting it to collective activities of social movements and then turn it into a conceptual model suitable for analyzing the role of specific social movements in processes of cultural change.

The first step in building this conceptual model will be the clarification of our position in the ongoing debate in scholarly literature regarding the conceptualization of social movements.[1] As we see it, there is an important kernel of commonality in this literature despite the diversity in theoretical viewpoints. This commonality will be used to arrive at a concept of social movements that is suitable for our conceptual model. This conceptual work is done in Section 3.2. The next step will be the transformation of the general change model of Chapter 2 into a model in which the activities of social movements occupy the central place. Here we follow Marwell and Oliver (1984) and take movement campaigns, and not the social movement as a whole, as the centerpiece of our conceptualization. This transformation is subject of the first part of Section 3.3. The rest of this section will be devoted to sketching the main contours of the conceptual model concerning social movements and cultural change. As the model we developed in Section 3.3 is still too general for use in actual research, we will elaborate the essential variable properties of the conceptual model in Section 3.4 in order to obtain an instrument for analyzing concrete movement campaigns. Finally, we close the chapter with a section in which the conceptual model is restated.

3.2   THE SOCIAL MOVEMENT CONCEPT

At its core, this concept refers to those times when people go off the institutionally beaten track and deviate from the routines of daily life. Instead of doing their daily chores, going to the movies, the theater, or a ball game, visiting friends or relatives, or staying at home reading or watching TV, people go out on the streets to demonstrate, come together in smoky meeting rooms, gather to chant rhymes, sit down at the feet of a guru, set fire to buildings, march with arms raised or fists clenched, etc. In short, from time to time people think, feel, talk, and act differently than one would expect, knowing the rules of and what is going on in a particular society. Moreover, these people do not act on their own, but do so collectively. Broadly defined, the notion of social movement refers to nonroutine concerted actions in and through which people try to change[2] their lives and to create situations within which they may—ideally and/or materially—live in comfort.

Tilly brings the notion of social movement a step further by defining it as "a sustained series of interactions between powerholders [authorities] and persons successfully claiming to speak on behalf of a constituency lacking formal representation [challengers]" (1982:26, 1984). Harding (1984) enlarges Tilly's definition somewhat further by including hegemonic worldviews in the notion of authorities, because authorities ultimately decide which of the contested worldviews will become or remain hegemonic.

This brings us to a first delimitation of the concept of "social movement." At its core, a social movement is the *challenge* of *dominant* and often self-evident cultural and systemic arrangements in society (and thereby of the authorities who are in charge of these arrangements) by or on behalf of groups and individuals who do not have a voice (who are outside the decision-making circles). Thus, a social movement concerns the dynamic of challengers vs. authorities.

This dynamic consists of interactions between these contenders and so the concept of "social movement" refers primarily to *action* and not to the actors involved (Tilly 1982). This action is, moreover, *collective*, which means that it is characterized by "bonds of positive solidarity" (Traugott 1978) and by—at least some degree of—organization and coordination (McCarthy and Zald 1977). Social movement actions are in part motivated by the fact that existing institutional arrangements fail (or are perceived to fail) to cater to the needs and interests of the excluded groups and categories in society. They are directed at changing these arrangements; movements are *anti-institutional in orientation* (Traugott 1978). Finally the fact that the challengers do not have access to decision-making processes and/or the fact that the causes for which they are contending are not acknowledged as legitimate objects of decision-making leaves the challengers no other choice than to "fight" their way in. They have to use *extrainstitutional strategies and tactics* in order to get the needed attention (Traugott 1978; Molotch 1979).[3]

One of the important aspects of the sustained collective actions we call a social movement is that it "involves a symbolic struggle" (Gamson 1988:219). Gamson's assessment that social movements *always* imply challenges at the cultural as well as the systemic level is central to the study of social movements in meaning construction processes.[4] This is obviously the case when movement actors act to change cultural definitions, which COYOTE did when trying to redefine prostitution as legitimate work (Jenness 1990). It also implies, however, a symbolic struggle when other changes are at stake. Whatever the collective actions are about and whichever kinds of changes are demanded, social movement actions always involve a struggle in which social meanings are constructed and reconstructed and within which movement actors function as signifying agents (Gamson 1988; Snow and Benford 1988).

A social movement is a meaning construction process because in every movement its initiators and leaders have to provide a rationale for action that tells people what is wrong and what they have to do to redress this wrong. This rationale—embodied in the ideology of the movement—mobilizes people into action, which means at the same time challenging the authorities and the society the authorities stand for. In building these kinds of ideologies, framing processes play a central role (Snow et al. 1986; Snow and Benford 1988; Gamson 1988; Gamson and Modigliani 1989). It is a form of cognitive praxis in which new ideas and frameworks are produced (Eyerman and Jamison 1991). In this process of challenging and mobilizing, the ideology of a social movement occupies a central place and is "a crucial component of social movements" (Marx and Wood 1975:382).

The ideology of a social movement is the—not always homogeneous—complex of ideas, theories, doctrines, and strategic and tactical principles movement actors use in their activities (Heberle 1951). It embodies the self-consciousness and the identity of the movement—its *collective* identity and consciousness—as well as cultural elements that are more specific to the instrumental aspects of these activities.[5] As we stated above, the ideology performs two functions in the activities of a social movement: (1) it is used as an instrument in the mobilization of resources; and (2) it embodies the challenges of authorities.[6]

The first function, consensus and action mobilization (Klandermans 1988), is mostly executed by those who carry the sustained collective action, i.e., social movement organization(s), (moral) entrepreneurs, or sponsors.[7] These actors draw upon the movement's ideology to "frame, or assign meaning to and interpret, relevant events and conditions in ways that are intended to mobilize potential adherents and constituents, to garner bystander support, and to demobilize antagonists" (Snow and Benford 1988:198). With the help of, among other things, these frames and, more generally, the movement's ideology the actors build a *network* of leaders and participants within which the members of a movement *communicate* with each other, the movement's action potential, and a *network of relations* with supporters outside the movement, the movement's support base in society (Tarrow 1988).

The second function, challenging authorities, is more important for understanding the cultural effect of social movements because this may lead to intended as well as unintended changes in society. Here the ideology functions as a tool kit (cf. Swidler 1986) for the movement entrepreneurs, who devise the more specific interpretive packages that are used in concrete discourses on concrete issues (Gamson and Modigliani 1989). The ideology is thus the source for these packages that are in a way ideologies on a smaller scale centered on specific issues. In these packages the entrepreneurs state what is going on, what is wrong and why, and what has to be done about it and why. A package is organized around a central idea, or frame, and condensed in symbols such as metaphors and catchphrases that express the issue in shorthand (ibid.). As Tarrow rightly emphasizes, these ideas and symbols are, moreover, selectively chosen from the available tool kit and creatively converted by these entrepreneurs into specific collective action frames (1994:119).

The role and functions of the ideology of a social movement are depicted in Figure 3.1.

Before going on to the conceptual model an important problem must be tackled, viz., the heterogeneity of social movements. As Oliver remarks: "Social movements are exceedingly complex phenomena" (1989:1). They encompass a great variety of issues, actions, events, and actors and they change—sometimes drastically—in form over time. This heterogeneity makes it difficult to conceptualize social movement activities and it may even turn this undertaking into a "theoretical nightmare" (Marwell and Oliver 1984). Two aspects of social movements are especially important in this respect: (1) the multiformity of collective action forms; and (2) the variety in the configurations of actors involved in a movement.

The first aspect, the multiformity of collective action, strikes the eye when looking at the action repertoire of social movements. Important examples of actions in this repertoire are demonstrations; marches; petitions; sit-ins; meetings; distributing pamphlets; posting signs, symbols, and slogans and wearing those on T-shirts and buttons. These demon-

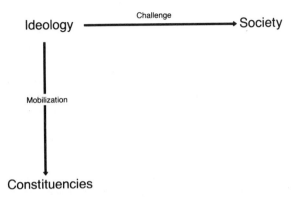

Figure 3.1. The role of the ideology of a social movement.

strate, as Tilly (1995) rightly states, the numbers, commitment, unity, and worthiness of those who support the challenge that a movement embodies. The actions are meant to put pressure on the power holders to change social arrangements in the direction that movement organizers claim. At the same time, they are often used to mobilize more supporters and to turn neutral publics toward a positive stand. The way the Abolition Committee, the social movement organization of the abolition movement in Great Britain, used the petition is a clear example of this dual use. On the one hand, petitions were used to put pressure on Parliament while, on the other, the signatures were assembled and petitions were publicized in a way that helped to mobilize public support (see also Chapter 7).

Although the same activity may function as a challenging and as a mobilizing device, an analytical distinction can be made between actions that are oriented at affecting society, especially the authorities, and actions that are internally oriented. The externally oriented movement actions can be broken down into phases of activities that we, following Marwell and Oliver (1984), will call collective campaigns. Each of these phases consists of a coherent and continuous set of distinct collective actions directed at specific goals. In the course of time, the character of these campaigns changes and campaigns oscillate between protest and disruptive action on the one hand—the extrainstitutional phase of a campaign—and regular contacts with authorities on the other, who are still challenged but in ways that are accepted. A social movement must also deal with its internal functioning, especially with the problem of mobilizing resources. Here the continuum of activities runs from action mobilization via the building of a collective identity to keeping the movement alive in adverse societal circumstances. Moreover, these changes in the character of the internal and external collective actions are connected to changes in society, especially to changes in the circumstances and conditions for protest. Protest and mobilization for protest come in waves or cycles (Tarrow 1988, 1994).

The second aspect of social movements concerns the actors involved in the activities of a movement (the *social movement actors*) and the relations between them or, in the words of Diani, "the intermediate structures of collective action, i.e., the networks that link individuals, groups and SMOs active in the same, or related, conflicts" (1992:18). A social movement implies a configuration of actors with potentially three poles. The first pole is formed by the organizations that carry the social movement, the SMOs. These consist of leaders and the rank and file membership, both of which are involved on a continual basis in working for the cause of the movement. They (partly) lead the movement, take care of the consensus and action mobilization, and direct and execute most of its actions.[8] The second pole concerns the participants in one or more of the collective actions such as the one-time demonstrators. The third pole refers to the support base of a social movement in society. Important here are the indirectly active—mostly financial—supporters and the sympathetic publics in society. Every movement differs in time and mostly from each other concerning the amount of people activated and the relative importance of each of these poles. The movement networks are dynamic and constantly changing.

The SMO is the most visible actor in a social movement and gives it its continuity. A SMO continually changes alongside the changes in the character of the collective actions. At the highest peak of the spiral of mobilization (Klandermans 1988) and during disruptive protest actions they more or less embody the challenge of authorities, although they are sometimes carried forward by the mobilized constituencies rather than leading them. In more quiet times they act primarily as representatives of a cause, figure as such in the media, and even consult with and advise the authorities. They begin then to resemble an interest group. In even more quiet times they just bring the message. At the low tide of movement activities they function as abeyance structures (Taylor 1989) and take care of keeping the cause of the movement alive. The Interkerkelijk Vredesberaad–IKV that was formed in 1966 as a peace organization by the Roman Catholic and Protestant churches in the Netherlands became the SMO of the Dutch peace movement. The history of this organization shows that it fulfilled all the above-mentioned functions in the course of its existence. It became, for instance, one of the central actors in organizing the protest against nuclear weapons, took care of the grass roots organization of peace activists, and functioned as a spokesperson on war and peace issues (Van Praag 1992).

3.3 CONCEPTUAL MODEL: THE MAIN LINES

Conceptualizing the role social movements play in processes of cultural change is not an easy task to undertake because both social movements and cultural change are complex phenomena. To ease this task we will break up the building of the model into five consecutive steps: (1) We will begin by taking the change model from the preceding chapter and transforming it to suit our purpose. (2) Next, we will elaborate the kernel or the rationale of the conceptual model. (3) The following step will be giving a sketch of the basic notions of our model. (4) After that we will introduce the time dimension inherent to processes of change and (5) will conclude by putting the pieces together into the main lines of our conceptual model.

Transformation of the Social Change Model. The diversity in movement activities and the heterogeneity in actor configurations can be grasped conceptually only if we limit the complexity of the field we are studying. The first limitation concerns the aspect of change that is taken into account. Thus far, we have spoken about social change in a very general manner. This remains so throughout the book; social change encompasses all kinds of changes in society. Within this general concept two analytical distinctions are made. The changes may primarily concern changes in relations between actors. We will refer to this type of change as *systemic change*. The changes may, on the other hand, relate primarily to changes in the symbolic realm such as changes in definitions, views, beliefs, and values. We will call these *cultural change* and our conceptual model is, above all, about these kinds of changes.

The second limitation has to do with the unit of analysis. We have chosen to give the concept of collective campaign a central place in our conceptual model and thus limit the span of attention quite considerably. A campaign is an episode of collective actions that form a series of sustained challenges to power holders and that is marked by a beginning and an end. Collective campaigns differ from both collective actions and social movements. Collective actions are the component parts of a campaign and do not have its sustained character. A movement, on the other hand, encompasses a far longer period of time, is more diffuse in terms of its beginning and ending, and consists mostly of more than one campaign. For an example of this differentiation, see the peace movement in the Netherlands, which became visible from time to time in its campaigns and its collective actions. The protest against the deployment of cruise missiles by NATO that took place between 1979 and 1986 is one of the collective campaigns of this movement. The campaign itself consisted of a series of collective actions, such as grass roots orga-

nization, two large peace demonstrations, and massive petitioning, that
formed—in a sense—a unity (Van Praag 1992). This decision to take the
collective campaign as the unit of analysis instead of the movement as a
whole also means taking a distinct period of time when studying a social
movement or dividing the period studied into several consecutive time
periods each corresponding to a specific campaign.

The collective campaign concept in this model occupies the same
place as the collective action concept did in the change model in Chapter
2. In processes of cultural change in which social movements are involved, collective campaigns act as the switches that may put society on
the track of transformation and change. They then convert the extant
possibilities for change into actual changes. In other words: collective
campaigns realize the cultural change potential in society.

The foregoing is represented in schematic form in Figure 3.2. This
figure is an adaption of Figure 2.6 in which we have replaced *collective
action* by *collective campaign*. We have adjusted the schematic representation on two other points as well. First, the term *actor* is replaced by *social
movement actors (SMAs)*. This concept refers to the network of actors
involved in the movement. Second, the feedback loops are given specific
names indicating the function they have in movement processes. The
upper feedback loop concerns the challenging aspects of the campaign
and the lower the mobilization activities.

The Rationale of the Conceptual Model.   The rationale (Willer 1967) of
the conceptual model we develop here lies in the relationship between

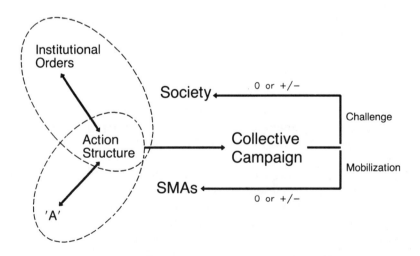

Figure 3.2.   Social movements as collective campaigns.

the cultural aspect of a social movement involved in a collective campaign, its ideology, and the cultural realm of society (in shorthand, the collective definitions). In this, the ideology of a social movement is seen as the set of resources for every new collective campaign or, in the words of Swidler, "In . . . periods [of social transformation] ideologies . . . *establish* new styles or strategies of action" (1986:278). Movement ideologies—it cannot be emphasized enough—are not static but are continually in the making within a movement. Movement actors have to adjust their ideas and symbols to the demands that their challenges pose. As Eyerman and Jamison (1991) point out, these idea-producing activities are the core of the functioning of a movement because they are essential both for mobilizing and challenging purposes. In their words, "It is precisely in the creation, articulation, formulation of new thoughts and ideas—new knowledge—that a social movement defines itself in society" (p. 55).[9]

A collective movement campaign implies the challenge of extant collective definitions. It does so because the actors involved put forward visions and causes in the form of specific issues that have not gained access to the systemic or societal agenda: the set of issues, topics, proposals, etc., that are at that moment under discussion in society (Cobb and Elder 1972). In other words, the claims of a movement and the way they are formulated fall outside the dominant cultural realm. The issues are framed as interpretive packages that give people the possibility of making sense of what is happening around them and to them, to tell them what is wrong and what ought to be done about it (Gamson and Modigliani 1989; see also Hirsch 1986, on the functions of linguistic frames).

A fine example of how a vision was brought to the fore in the form of an issue is found in Gamson (1988). He shows how anti–nuclear power groups brought the safety of nuclear energy into the debate in the seventies. One of the packages that was promoted—the soft-path package—framed the choice for nuclear energy as one that followed from the choice for a wrong way of life. People would not need this kind of energy in a society that was not based on waste and technology or, as this package stated, "We should change our way of life to conserve energy as much as possible and to develop sources of energy that are ecologically safe, renewable and that lend themselves to decentralized production—for example, sun, wind, and water. Small is beautiful" (p. 233). This way of presenting a case clearly demonstrates how bringing a not yet accepted issue forward implies bringing forward a non-hegemonic definition of a social situation.

Reaching the societal agenda means creating a public discourse on these issues or taking part in an existing one (Gamson and Modigliani

1989). This means that social movement actors put forward their claims and interpretations framed as issues and therewith involve other actors, who either go along with them or who resist the movement actors by putting forward their own interpretations and counterclaims. In every issue discourse, thus, two elements can be distinguished analytically: the framing or cultural side of the discourse, the issue culture; and the relational side, the issue arena.

   1. *The Issue Culture.* This concept refers to the substance of the discourse, i.e., to the ideas that clash. It is the set of ideas, metaphors, arguments, texts, symbols, etc., organized as competing interpretive packages in which challenges of extant arrangements and their defense are framed (Gamson 1988; Gamson and Modigliani 1989).

   2. *The Issue Arena.*[10] This concept concerns the actors who are involved in the discourse. Creating or entering a discourse implies that the set of relations inherent in a social movement is extended. There also arise relations with supporters and adversaries, with sympathetic and antipathetic publics, and with the (mostly political) actors needed for reaching the ends of the movement. The issue arena comprises, according to Hilgartner and Bosk (1988), who put forward this concept under the name of "public arena," among other things, branches of government, media, political organizations, and interest and professional organizations. The social movement actors are naturally also part of this arena as the initiators of the cooperation and conflict inherent in public discourses. Klandermans (1992) proposes another concept, the multiorganizational field, which encompasses the same set of relations. We prefer the term *arena* because of its association with *struggle*.

   A discourse may be viewed in light of its static characteristics, i.e., which actors are involved and how the issues are framed. It can also be seen as a dynamic process in which its substance and the network of actors involved continually change as a consequence of the actions of movement actors and the (re)actions of others. The extent to which the first succeed—*nolens* or *volens*—in involving other actors in their cause is essential for the course and outcome of a discourse, because the contribution of each actor may affect the way issues will be framed. Especially important in this respect is the often occurring dynamic of movement and countermovement campaigns.

   Seen as a dynamic process, a discourse is a competition between actors and the interpretive packages they bring into the competition. This competition may lead to changes in collective definitions through two related but analytically different processes: (1) *diffusion* (unobtrusive changes in collective definitions), and (2) *specific action, directly* (by changing existing beliefs and values) or *indirectly* (by changing [legal] norms or other arrangements in society, which later results in changes in values or beliefs). As a concept, collective definitions refer to the way people view social reality and the events around them. Definitions comprise descriptions and interpretations of social reality as well as beliefs about the way things are or ought to be. Collective definitions are present in all kinds of statements about society and its functioning.

The rationale of the conceptual model is depicted in Figure 3.3. It is basically the upper feedback loop of the model in Figure 3.2, but only as far as it concerns the feedback in the cultural realm. This loop is now portrayed as a sequence of independent, intermediate, and dependent variables. In this, the ideology of a movement is seen as the source of the cultural changes that are brought about by the dynamic of the movement campaign and the ensuing public discourse.

Basic Notions Underlying the Conceptual Model. Collective campaigns are seen here as possible realizations of extant cultural change potentials in society because actors involved in those campaigns use these potentials in challenging dominant cultural and systemic arrangements in society. Whether a particular campaign actually "succeeds" in this respect depends on three interrelated sets of factors: (1) the existence of a cause for initiating a campaign; (2) the decisions of the SMAs to act for that cause; and (3) the possibilities the action-structure offers for executing the campaign. We will see below that the core of the rather abstract conceptualization in Chapter 2, agency, action-structure, and the analytical separation of different aspects of the action-structure, will also occupy a pivotal position in the specific model that is developed in this chapter.

The first set of factors concerns the cause or issue for which a collective campaign is undertaken. Campaigns are about "things" that are

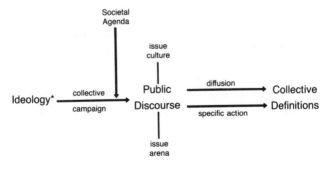

Figure 3.3. The effect of the movement ideology.

seen as being wrong and therefore grievances need a place in theories of social movements. Or as Buechler rightly states in his clarifying review of the current situation regarding social movement theory, "grievances cannot be assumed to be a constant background factor in the study of social movements" (1993:222). A cause is in itself a social construction and as such the product of (a) agency, in this case the "constructive" activities of the movement actors, (b) objective circumstances, i.e., structural exigencies, strain, and interests, and (c) the possibilities the action-structure offers for constructing these circumstances into an issue that attracts support and that forces authorities to respond. This means that the construction of issues basically involves the framing of interpretive packages.

The second set of determinants concerns the agency aspect involved in movement activities. It refers to the commitment of movement actors to dedicate the assembled resources to the cause of the collective campaign, to their resolve to use the opportunities that are at hand for waging the campaign, and to the determination to overcome resistance in society. Agency, however, does not mean that movement actors make such decisions wholly on their own. As we have seen in Chapter 2, these decisions are related to the characteristics of the action-structure (see for instance, the dialectical relation between A and action-structure in Figure 3.2) without being fully determined by this structure.

The third set of factors refers on the one hand to the cultural and systemic resources the movement actors have assembled, the internal side of the action-structure, and on the other hand to the facilities and constraints these actors meet, the external side of the action-structure. We will call the internal side of the action-structure *power structure* and the external side *opportunity structure*. The power concept we use here has its base in Weber's *Wirtschaft und Gesellschaft* and refers to the capacity of ego to determine the actions of others (alter) even against their will ([1921] 1976). This determination may be direct, e.g., by force, or indirect by shaping the cultural and systemic aspects of the situation in which alter acts (see in this respect Bachrach and Baratz 1962; Lukes 1974). Opportunity structure is a concept whose roots are to be found in Merton's structural functionalism (Sztompka 1986b), in exchange theory (Tallman and Ihinger-Tallman 1979; Stolte 1983), and in the political science tradition (among others see Eisinger 1973; Tilly 1978; Tarrow 1988). In naming this part of the action-structure, we follow convention, while at the same time acknowledging that the external part of the action-structure—as Sztompka (see Section 2.2) shows—comprises more than opportunities.

The power structure has—analytically seen—two dimensions. First, there is power on the *cultural* plane, which is embodied in the ideology of a social movement and expressed in the interpretive packages, frames, and symbols used in mobilization practices and in the struggle for the movement's cause. These cultural "instruments" differ in the amount of support they may mobilize and in their cogency for the dominant in society. Second, the movement actors have power on the *systemic* level. This refers to the number of people mobilized and the extent of support organized in society.

In the opportunity structure of a movement, two analytically different aspects can be discerned. First, the elements of the structure that facilitate collective actions: important in this respect are existing action strategies and repertoires, laws and rights, and access to the media. Second, the elements of the action-structure that constrain collective actions: important characteristics in this respect are the reactions of authorities and the resistance of others in society, such as countermovements and negative publics. Together, facilities and constraints determine the conduciveness of the opportunity structure. A conduciveness that is represented on the *structural* or *systemic* level (Smelser 1962) and on the *cultural* level (Gamson 1988).

Time. So far we have sketched a relatively clear picture of the process in which structure is transformed into action and cultural change. As Joppke (1992) points out, time plays an important role in these transformation processes. In Chapter 2 we followed the lead of Archer (1988) and Therborn (1991) and introduced time as an element in our conceptualization of social action. Further elaboration, however, is needed and this will complicate the conceptualization of cultural change and social movements quite considerably.

First, the situation in which a collective campaign emerges is the product of cultural and systemic processes, historical events, and other conjunctures antedating the campaign. History, as we will call the chain of events and actions leading up to the movement campaign, shapes the action-structure of the social movement actors at the beginning of that campaign and with that influences its outcome. Historical studies of antislavery make abundantly clear the importance of "history" in explaining the abolition and emancipation campaigns (see, among others, Anstey 1975; Davis 1966, 1975; Drescher 1986).

Second, a collective campaign always involves a process stretched in time during which the campaign may affect the conditions of that campaign. The dynamics of a collective campaign, which is essentially a process of action and reaction, recursively shapes and transforms the context, i.e., the action-structure in which the campaign occurs (Joppke 1992). The activities of the provos in Amsterdam in the sixties give an illustrative example in this respect. Their initial—relatively modest and playful—actions led to overreactions from the authorities, which then enlarged the support for subsequent actions of the provos (Koopmans 1992).

Third, society "carries on" during a campaign. The ongoing processes and events (see above) may influence the action-structure of the movement actors involved in the campaign and thus enlarge or circumscribe the action-potentialities. An example of such an "outside" influence is the energy crisis of the 1970s, which operated as a turning point in the career of the German and American antinuclear movements (Joppke 1992). Another example of such an outside influence is the radical turn in the French Revolution in the early 1790s. This turn negatively affected the movement for parliamentary reform in Great Britain at that time (Cannon 1973).

The introduction of the time dimension in the process of cultural change by social movements thus means two things. First, it points to the necessity of analyzing this process in two phases, the phase of history and the phase of the collective campaign itself. Second, it means that as far as the collective campaign is concerned, attention must be paid not only to the effects of the properties of the action-structure (agency and cause included) but to the effects of the campaign on itself as well as the outside influences upon it. We see here the double contingency mentioned in Chapter 2. But other elements of social action that we described there are implied in these two points as well. Both the campaigning actors and others in society will look for manifest and latent possibilities in their action-structures in order to further their own activities and to constrain those of others. At the same time, campaigns are in the course of time affected by cultural and structural factors and developments in society. These are, moreover, often interrelated as well. More insight into this tangle of factors and developments, however, will be given in Part II, when we descend to the level of concrete events in the abolition campaign.

The Conceptual Model: The Main Lines. As we stated before, social movements are too complex to study in one piece. Instead, we propose to divide the movement process into discernible parts and to study these parts separately, i.e., to study the collective campaigns that movement actors wage in order to reach the goal(s) of the movement. As every movement campaign takes off in a situation that is shaped and conditioned by foregoing developments and events—by history—this means studying this history as well.

The period before the onset of a campaign involves (1) the formation of consensus on the cause and the necessity of the campaign (Klandermans 1988)[11] and (2) the shaping of the conditions and opportunities for that campaign, which means the formation of the action-structure for the movement actors. To study the history of a movement campaign, we do not need a conceptual model, as we are not interested in an explanation of this history but in a description of it and in its results. The latter form a part of the explanation of the ensuing campaign.

The conceptual model concerns the campaign itself, which transforms the potentialities inherent in society into collective actions, which may have led to the changes we seek to explain. In the model, we focus on the campaign as the challenge of authorities, and thus on its external aspects. We will consider the internal aspects of a campaign, such as identity formation and mobilization, only if needed.

The challenge of authorities involves transforming the cause of the campaign into issues, which means framing it in one or more interpretive packages. The campaigning actors seek to get these issues on the societal agenda. This means that they create a public discourse on these issues or enter an existing one with them. Putting forward issues by social movement actors challenges by definition the authorities, who will most likely react. Others may react as well, either by countering or by supporting the issues brought forward. An issue discourse is thus a dynamic process with a continuously changing arena of contestants and a culture specific to the issues at stake, which changes in this discourse as well.

A collective campaign implies a clash of ideas that may become part of the culture of a society. It may change the existing collective definitions both by diffusion and by actions that are the content of that campaign. Whether these cultural changes will occur depends—as we have seen before—on (1) the existence of a cause to campaign for, (2) the decision of the movement actors to wage a campaign for that cause, and (3) the properties of the action-structure in which the campaign takes place. The first two elements are necessary conditions for bringing about cultural changes by social movements because they determine whether there will be a campaign that will give a voice to nonrepresented demands. The third element refers on the one hand to the degree to which social movement actors can determine the action of other actors in society, their power, and on the other to the degree society makes their actions possible, its conduciveness. Causally stated, *if* there is a cause and movement actors decide to act on it *and* their assets prevail over those of others, *then* the actions of these movement actors will result in changes of which the cultural ones are a part.

The conceptual model is portrayed in Figure 3.4, which is, at its core, an adaptation of the basic conceptualization of contingent social change and collective action at the end of Chapter 2 (Figure 2.6). In Figure 3.4, the feedback loops of the campaign to its own conditions are left out and

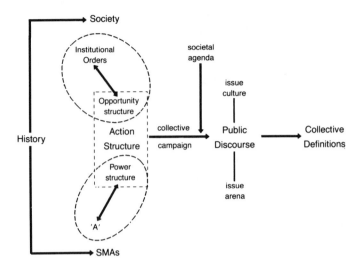

Figure 3.4. The conceptual model.

agency and the cause of the campaign are taken together under the letter
A. The influence of critical events is to be found in the dialectical relation
between the institutional orders on the societal level and the action-
structure. It is not mentioned as a separate element in the conceptual
model. Moreover, the conceptual model is presented in this schema as a
causal model in which the cultural realm—the collective definitions—is
the dependent variable.

3.4   THE CONCEPTUAL MODEL: A FURTHER ELABORATION

Cultural change as an effect of social movement campaigns depends—as we concluded above—on three sets of factors. In our conceptual model, the first and second set are to be seen as *binary* factors, i.e.,
movement actors decide to act on a cause or they do not; there is a cause
or issue constructed or there is not. As the overviews of theory and
research on social movements, especially the critiques of the resource
mobilization theorists, have made clear, both these sets of factors are
necessary but not sufficient conditions for bringing about changes in the
collective definitions. The latter also depends on the circumstances within which the movement actors act that facilitate or constrain their actions. In other words, the changes depend on the properties of the

action-structure within which the campaigning actors (the SMAs) operate: properties as they are at the beginning of a campaign and as they
change during that campaign. This makes those properties the central
part of our conceptual model and they determine the outcome within
the first-mentioned sets of conditions.

In the above, we have briefly typified the variable properties of the
action-structure. This is not as specified as it should be for an analysis of
the dynamics of a specific movement campaign and of its impact. A
further elaboration of these properties is needed and is the subject of
this section. In our model, we distinguish four types of properties of the
action-structure. The first and the second type refer to the internal aspects of this structure, the action-structure as power structure; the third
and the fourth refer to its external aspects, the action-structure as opportunity structure. In both cases cultural and systemic elements are to be
discerned.

1. *The Framing of the Interpretive Packages.*[12]   The way the packages
that are used in collective campaigns are framed represent the *cultural
power* of the campaigning actors. These packages are important weapons
in the ideological struggle that public discourses always are and their
effectiveness in this struggle depends largely on the ways these packages are framed. In the words of Snow and Benford, it depends on the
way in which a frame—in their terminology, a collective action frame—
"simplifies and condenses the 'world out there,'" singles out what is
wrong, attributes a cause to this wrong and states what must be done
about it, and enables "activists to articulate and align a vast array of
events and experiences so that they hang together in a relatively unified
and meaningful fashion" (1992:137–38). The framing of packages is important because it may enhance the mobilization capacity of a movement
and therewith its systemic power (see below). The framing is, however,
even more important in respect to its cogency, i.e., its capacity to change
the way people in society think and perceive. At this point we again
emphasize that both aspects of interpretive packages, the mobilization
and cogency aspect, are always present in every package because a
package always functions as a mobilization device *and* as a means for
challenging authorities (see in this respect Figure 3.1).

In the conceptualization we are devising here, the second aspect occupies the central place and we are predominantly interested in the
question of which properties or characteristics of an interpretive package
convince people that the stated definition or vision is the correct one. In
this respect, different authors name different characteristics as important
to the success of a particular package (see, for example, Best 1987; Gam-

son 1988; Snow and Benford 1988; Gamson and Modigliani 1989; Schudson 1989).[13] In spite of these differences it seems possible to summarize these varying characteristics under four headings.

a. Cultural resonance.   Resonance means that a package appears as natural and familiar because it responds to themes, values, or beliefs in the larger cultural system (Gamson and Modigliani 1989). This characteristic corresponds with Snow and Benford's notion of "narrative fidelity," which points to "the degree to which proffered framings resonate with cultural narrations, that is, with the stories, myths, and folktales that are part and parcel of one's cultural heritage and that thus function to inform events and experiences in the immediate present" (1988:210). It also includes three of the five dimensions of potency of a cultural object that Schudson (1989) discerns: the retrievability or availability of such an object; its resonance with the life of an audience; and the degree to which an object is part of an extant institution—institutional retention.

b. Empirical credibility.   This characteristic refers to the fit between the way a package is framed and the events in the world (Snow and Benford 1988). More specifically, it raises the question of whether there are "events or occurrences that can be pointed to as evidence substantiating the . . . claims of the movement" (p. 208).[14] The extent to which actors succeed in making events part of a pattern in which they are causally explained especially enhances the credibility of a package (Stallings 1990). The proffered frame proves as it were that the campaigning actors are right.

c. Rhetorical force.   A package is powerful to the degree to which its phrases, symbols, frames, and metaphors attract and hold attention and, above all, justify conclusions drawn from the package (Best 1987; Schudson 1989).

d. Resolution.   Packages that are clear about what is wrong and what has to change have an advantage over packages with a more diffuse content (Schudson 1989).

The more these characteristics are present in a package the more—culturally—powerful that package is (Schudson 1989), especially in convincing those in power that the message of the movement is correct. We therefore predict that interpretive packages that are more culturally resonant, empirically credible, rhetorically forceful, and that have a high resolution have a greater chance of effecting the collective definitions than packages that are less culturally resonant, empirically credible, rhetorically forceful, and with a lower resolution.

2. The Amount of Support for the Issues That Are at Stake in the Movement Campaign.[15]   This property refers to the amount of *systemic power* that movements have assembled at the beginning of—or will assemble during—the campaign. It is this set of factors that has been the focus of resource mobilization theory. As these factors have only a secondary place in our conceptual model, we will treat them here much less extensively. Issue support means giving some of the movement actors the capability or power to act as the sponsor of the interpretive package in which the issue is framed. This way, systemic power enables movement actors to function as signifying agents who produce and change meaning (Gamson and Modigliani 1989; Snow and Benford 1988). Moreover, power increases the chance that a movement will attain victories in realms other than the cultural that will affect the collective definitions at a later date (see the indirect path of influence dealt with above).

The amount of systemic power depends on:

a.   The amount of people mobilized into action and the energy they are ready to put into those actions; together, the amount of pressure the campaigning movement actors are able to exert on society and its decision-makers. We have here the product of consensus and action mobilization processes (Klandermans 1988).

b.   The amount of support the movement actors have organized. Two sources of support are important in this respect: first, the (often financial) support of individuals and organizations who are otherwise not actively involved in the movement campaign; second, the support of those who are interested in the ideas and proposals put forward and take a positive stand, the positive public.[16]

Concerning this second set of factors we predict that the more widespread this support is the greater the chances are of gaining access to the societal agenda and eventually changing collective definitions.[17]

3. The Cultural Conduciveness of the Opportunity Structure.   This property represents the degree to which the existing cultural arrangements in society facilitate or constrain a collective campaign. The structure of facilities and constraints within which a collective campaign is conducted is, culturally seen, more or less congenial to the interpretive packages put forward in that campaign. This will effect the outcome of the campaign. Culturally, the opportunity structure functions somewhere between a tool kit with readily available idea elements usable in a particular movement campaign and a straitjacket that makes different conceptualizations nearly impossible [cf. the notion of mobilization of bias in Bachrach and Baratz (1962) or the third dimension of Lukes's power concept (1974)]. Which ideas, metaphors, or symbols are influential depends on the sphere in which movement actors are campaigning, e.g., daily life, politics, or economics. In general, four types of cultural elements are important in enlarging (or diminishing) the cultural impact of a campaign.

First, every society has its basic assumptions and rules, *basic cultural rules*, that define who the legitimate participants are, which issues are permissible, and which kinds of relations are accepted in society (cf. Joppke 1992). Connotations related to the sponsors of a package or to the frames that are used are important here. An example is the persistent relating of prostitution to immorality and sin, which considerably constrained COYOTE's campaign attempting to define prostitution as work (Jenness 1990). These assumptions may also embody the ways, when, and how to resist and oppose the powers that be, the *basic oppositional political rules* (Tarrow 1992). The latter are especially important for those who challenge the status quo.

Second, there are elements that movements may use as *cultural tools* (cf. Swidler 1986). In every campaign movement actors draw upon the existing meaning systems for talking, writing, and thinking about the objects of the campaign (Gamson 1988). The more these systems contain ideas that may be used in challenging authorities the more a campaign is helped in reaching its ends. Snow and Marshall (1984) give an interesting example in this respect, when they show how religion, in their case Islam, contributes to social movements and their impact. Its religious ideas help to build the movement's ideology and its rituals and networks furnish the mobilization potential.

Third, in every culture *dominant themes* and their negation, *counterthemes*, are present. According to Gamson (1988, 1992a), a cultural theme is a relatively general framework guiding the perceptions of and the attitudes toward everything that is going on—themes like equality or individual responsibility. Interesting in this respect is Gamson's idea that every theme carries with it its denial or countertheme, which shares with the dominant theme its "taken-for-granted-ness." A countertheme, however, challenges "some specific aspect of the mainstream culture; [it is] adversarial, contentious, oppositional" (1988:221). These themes thus guide perceptions of and attitudes toward the issues of a campaign and make issue packages more or less acceptable, and in this way function as constraints or facilities for movement campaigns.

Fourth, every society is characterized by its own general *cultural climate* (Gamson 1988) or Zeitgeist (Brand 1990), which changes in time.[18] Brand typifies this climate as "the particular configuration of worldviews, thoughts and emotions, fears and hopes, beliefs and utopias, feelings of crisis or security, of pessimism or optimism, which prevail in a specific period" (p. 10). A cultural climate functions "as a cyclically changing filter or amplifier for the different elements of the available national pool of symbols, themes and counter-themes" (p. 12). In this way the cultural climate, as it is at a certain point in time, promotes the rise and impact of challenging packages (and the mobilization of resources and support) or discourages this.

Concerning the cultural aspect of the opportunity structure, we predict that the more cultural elements enable and entice challenging actions and the less these actions are guided and limited by these elements, the more chance there is that these actions lead to changes of the collective definitions.

4. The Structural or Systemic Conduciveness of the Opportunity Structure. We have here the systemic component of the opportunity structure. Systemic conduciveness points to the organizational arrangements in society that may either facilitate or constrain movement campaigns and therewith help to determine their impact. We distinguish the following systemic arrangements.

a. The societal agenda. Attaining agenda status is the first important barrier for movement actors to cross, and several aspects of the way such an agenda functions are important for the "height" of this barrier. First, there is the way the agenda-setting process is organized. This process functions very differently in pluralistic societies than in societies that are dominated by one elite or ethnic group. Second, it is important to know who the gatekeepers are (e.g., media or political functionaries or others) and which principles of selection they employ (e.g., novelty, dramatic aspects, or selling capacity). Third, the space in society for discourse is limited and thus the number of issues an agenda can accommodate, or its carrying capacity, is finite (cf. Hilgartner and Bosk 1988); moreover, there is less room on the agenda in societies where discourses around "old" issues such as class, religion, and ethnic antagonisms are still raging than in societies where these questions have been pacified (Duyvendak and Koopmans 1992). Finally, triggering devices (see below) or a turnover of political power, may create the possibility of getting new issues on the agenda, Kingdon's window-openings (1984).

b. The media.[19] In movement campaigns the mobilization of people and their resources, the organization of support, and the symbolic struggle itself are, to an important degree, carried out in and through media. Face-to-face contact is limited in most campaigns and people generally learn what a campaign is about indirectly through newspapers, radio, television, books, pamphlets, posters, etc. In terms of Molotch and Lester (1974), a movement campaign is news and it involves "accounts of the unobserved" that are brought by the media to those who were not present. The way news is produced is elaborated further in Appendix A. In this appendix more attention is also given to the characteristics of news production that presumably have impact on the outcome of a collective campaign, like the centrality of media in social life, the media routines, the status of media, and the control of/over media.

c.   The political system.   The way a society is politically organized and structured conditions collective campaigns because this offers facilities and constraints that encourage or discourage these campaigns and influence their content (Tarrow 1988; Joppke 1992). The main characteristics[20] of political systems that affect campaigns are its degree of openness and its stability. The former concerns the openness or closure of the political system for political protests and collective campaigns. When a political system is fully open, a social movement is not necessary as every cause will have a voice, while in a fully closed system a movement will not be possible at all. This means that a relatively open/closed system is most conducive to collective campaigns (see also Tarrow 1983). The latter refers to the stability or instability of political alignments.[21] The more a political system is unstable and the more political elites are divided on central policy questions, the more the system offers opportunities for challenging authorities. Stable systems and united elites, on the other hand, may rather easily fend off those challenges.

d.   The existence of a movement potential.   A social movement is only possible when there are actors available who are able to initiate collective action, to mobilize constituencies, and to organize a support base in society *and* when there are individuals in society who may be mobilized for the cause of a social movement or may be won over for its support. This potential refers to the existence of people who are convinced that their collective activities may make a difference (Gamson 1992a). Important in this respect are the preexisting networks in which people live and interact. These provide for the "leaders" of a movement, the SMOs, and facilitate mobilization and organization. For instance, religious groups and organizations, unions, neighborhoods, and peasant communities are traditional providers for these kinds of networks (Snow and Marshall 1984; Klandermans and Tarrow 1988; Kriesi 1988; McCarthy 1987; Zald and McCarthy 1987). Another support potential is to be found in the existence of "indigenous organizations that might sustain a challenge" (Amenta and Zylan 1991).

e.   The resistance in society.   A movement campaign may not only challenge authorities but may also threaten the interests of others in society. The changes that movement actors propagate may endanger those who benefit from the existing situation or may threaten the values, norms, and life-styles that people cherish. It is also possible that the object of a movement campaign is a goal which other organizations claim as their rightful object of activities [cf. Gusfield's owners of social problems (1989)]. A collective campaign may thus lead to the dynamics of resistance that may take different forms. It may come forward (1) as a countermovement that will try to wipe out the campaign altogether; (2) as competing organizations that will try to block the entrance to and to limit the space in the public discourse on an issue; and (3) as negative publics that dismiss the call for support of and participation in the movement campaign.

Concerning this fourth set of factors, we predict that the more systemically conducive the action-structure is, i.e., the more facilitating and less constraining, the more chance there is that collective campaigns will lead to changing the extant collective definitions.

These four properties of the action-structure—each with its own dimensions (see Table 3.1)—are the product of historical processes and events, but they are not static. First, these properties may change as a consequence of the campaign itself. It will, for example, be easier for a frame that is resonant with larger cultural themes to win the ear of the media, whose attention then enlarges the mobilizing capacity of a movement and thus adds to the support of the issue at stake (Gamson 1988).

Table 3.1 Properties of the action-structure

1. Framing of the interpretive packages
   a. cultural resonance
   b. empirical credibility
   c. rhetorical force
   d. resolution
2. Issue support
   a. mobilized resources
   b. organized support
3. Cultural conduciveness
   a. basic cultural rules
   b. cultural tools
   c. cultural (counter)themes
   d. cultural climate
4. Systemic conduciveness
   a. societal agenda
   b. media
   c. political system
   d. movement potential
   e. resistance

Second, they may change because of some critical event that occurs during the campaign. A specific type of such an event is the triggering device (Cobb and Elder 1972) or event. Triggering events may play a role in setting off a collective campaign or they may change its course.

Triggering events are dramatic and/or dramatized events that by their dramatic character catch the attention of people and make them realize that something is wrong and has to be changed. Examples of these events are disasters such as floods or earthquakes; accidents such as airline crashes or the stranding of an oil tanker; or actions of authorities such as the killing of people in riots or demonstrations. The 1953 flood in the Netherlands, for instance, triggered a large program of building dikes; the Schoharie Creek Bridge collapse set off a discourse on the unsafety of bridges due to failing public policies (Stallings 1990); and the Finkbein thalidomide case started the discussion on abortion in the United States (Tatalovich and Daynes 1981).

In collective campaigns, movement actors and others will often look for occurrences that may be used as material for constructing triggering events (cf. Molotch and Lester 1974; Stallings 1990). Batiot (1982), for instance, shows how this was done in the struggle on abortion in France, which started in 1969 with a series of legislative proposals presented by an organization mainly consisting of GPs. Here in 1971, 343 women—celebrities and noncelebrities—declared in a manifesto that they had undergone an abortion and in that manifesto pressed for free abortion on demand. In 1972 an abortion trial was turned into a public event through testimony for the defense by well-known actresses, celebrities, and politicians. These eye-catching events definitively put abortion as an issue on the societal and political agenda and forced all political organizations to take a position on it. In words of Batiot: "From then on, events concerning abortion rolled on" (1982:138).

3.5 RESTATING THE CONCEPTUAL MODEL

Social movements may play an important role in processes of cultural change because they imply the challenge of dominant arrangements in society by or on behalf of outsiders. This means that movement actors always attempt to break through ongoing reproduction processes in society. An essential part of the struggle movement actors wage concerns telling people why they should act to change things. This is done in the ideology movement actors build, which contains the answers to the questions of what, who, why, and how. Social movements thus invariably involve contests in the symbolic realm around causes and issues that are outside the normal ways of thinking and acting. This means that a movement implies the construction of new meanings and the reconstruction of existing ones. Herewith, social movements may change existing definitions of the situation.

The conceptualization of social movements acting as signifying agents in changing cultural aspects of society rests on two choices we have made. First, we have decided not to take the social movement as a whole, but to focus instead on collective campaigns. This choice reduces the complexity of the phenomenon studied considerably and it brings the social movement down to a series of discernible campaigns each directed at specific goals and each possibly leading to intended and unintended changes. Second, we have chosen to regard the symbolic part of a movement campaign as a discourse, i.e., as a dynamic contest between competing interpretive packages on specific issues. Each package is organized around a central idea or frame and just like the ideology of a movement—in which the package originates—it tells people what is going on, what is wrong and why, and what has to be done about it and why. The clash of ideas, which either challenge or defend the status quo, and of the actors involved may directly or indirectly lead to changes in the cultural realm.

Whether these changes occur depends on three sets of interrelated factors:

1. the existence of a cause to campaign for;
2. agency of the movement actors, i.e., the decisions taken by the movement actors;
3. the properties of the action-structure within which the social movement actors operate that are shaped by history, the dynamics of the campaign itself, and by critical events during that campaign.

The first and second set of factors are necessary but not sufficient conditions for cultural changes; they "produce" the campaign. Whether such a campaign will have effect and how depends on the third set of factors, the variable properties of the action-structure. These properties are the framing of the interpretive packages; the support for the issues at stake; and the cultural and systemic conduciveness of the action-structure. On the basis of these properties we predict that there is a greater chance for changes in the extant collective definitions if:

1. the framing of the interpretive packages is culturally resonant, empirically credible, rhetorically forceful, and has a high resolution;
2. the number of people mobilized into action and the number of people ready to support the cause is large;
3. the opportunity structure contains more cultural elements that

enable and entice movement actions and fewer elements that guide and limit these actions; and

4. the opportunity structure contains systemic arrangements that facilitate movement actions more and constrain them less.

This set of properties thus forms the central part of our explanation of cultural change as these properties determine the success or failure of collective movement campaigns. Although causal determination is implied in the model presented above, the model as a whole is underdetermined because of the presence of voluntary elements in agency. In every movement, people have to decide whether they will initiate a campaign and whether they will join or support it. These decisions partially depend on "contingent givens" in one's action-structure. These givens, however, do not fully determine the choices people make. This freedom of choice gives movement processes their familiar indeterminate character.

NOTES

1. We will not try to give an accurate review of the social movement literature here but will only use those notions and concepts we deem most useful for conceptualizing the problem this book is dealing with, viz., cultural change and the role social movements play in this. Important books and papers on social movements are Blumer (1939), Smelser (1962), Gusfield (1970), Turner and Killian (1972), Tilly (1978), Jenkins (1983), Zald and McCarthy (1987), Klandermans, Kriesi, and Tarrow (1988), Morris and McClurg Mueller (1992), Tarrow (1994).

2. As the literature mentioned in note 7 of Chapter 1 makes clear, movement scholars agree that social movements are directed at changing the social order or at preventing that.

3. Not every challenge of authorities that steps out of the boundaries of institutional behavior may, however, be designated as a social movement. As Marwell and Oliver rightly state, "social movements are most usefully understood as complex *aggregates* of collective actions or events, aggregates which meet certain criteria of scope and size" (1984:6). Moreover, they involve actions that will endure a longer time period. In other words, a social movement is more than a whim, a fad, or a single protest.

4. The symbolic side of social movements has a central place in our conceptualization because the cultural side of the movement process is the topic of this book. This does not, however, imply that we downplay the importance of the structural or systemic dimensions of the movement process or that we see this cultural side as the central aspect of social movements as Eyerman and Jamison (1991) do with their conceptualization of movements as "cognitive praxis." As Oliver (1989) states, social movements are as sets of collective events too complicated to be grasped by one theory or to be studied as a whole in one research

project. Every theory and every research project necessarily highlights some key features while ignoring others.

5. The conceptualization of social movements as challenges implies a strategic focus on the activities of movements. This does not, however, exclude—as Gamson (1992a) rightly contends—the identity aspect from a strategically oriented theory on social movements, especially not in a theoretical model focused on cultural challenges. In such a model, the construction of a collective identity is a strategic step in achieving cultural changes. The formation of a collective identity influences the ideology of a movement and, through that, will have an effect on the culture of a society.

6. The ideological beliefs of a social movement must—in order to successfully execute both functions—(1) give an *interpretation* and *diagnosis* of what is going on in society, why that is wrong and unjust, and what caused this wrong; (2) propose a solution to the diagnosed problem, i.e., the *goals* of the movement; (3) *mobilize* people into *action;* and (4) *legitimate* what the movement is doing and *delegitimate* what others, especially the authorities, are doing, i.e., delegitimate the existing social order the movement attacks (Blumer 1939; Smelser 1962; Turner and Killian 1972; Marx and Wood 1975; Lang and Lang 1978; Snow and Benford 1988; Klandermans 1988).

7. These are different terms for the same type of actor. The first term was coined by McCarthy and Zald (1977), the second by Becker (1970), and the third by Gamson and Modigliani (1989). In all these cases, this concerns a central function in collective action that all kinds of actors, mostly organizations, may—as their main task or as a "part-time job"—fulfill. Köbben (1983) uses in this respect a rather appropriate name, viz. "caretaker." This points to an important aspect of many social movements, i.e., to act on behalf of powerless others (see also Tilly 1982).

8. As Marwell and Oliver (1984) state, SMOs do not cover all activities and events within a social movement and must not mistakenly be confused with the totality of a social movement.

9. Problematic in their conceptualization is their assumption of a deeper meaning inherent in social movements brought to the surface by "movement intellectuals." Such deeper meanings are difficult to reconcile with the contingency approach in this book in which the construction of meaning is an open-ended process circumscribed by the historically produced context in which movements operate. A concept like "deeper meaning" with its suggestion of an internal developmental logic may bring with it the same problems as concepts like "progress" or the "inevitable laws of history" have done in the past (see, for example, Sztompka 1993:181–90).

10. This concept is proposed by Gamson (1988), who uses it, however, in a somewhat different fashion than we do.

11. Consensus formation is, as Ferree (1992) rightly states, not limited to the history phase, but often also occurs during the campaign as a consequence of action mobilization.

12. As the properties of these packages cannot simply be assessed we have developed a scheme for analyzing these interpretive packages in appendix B.

13. We haven chosen to employ only those characteristics that we expect to be important in having cultural effects. At this point, the analytical distinction

between the mobilization and the cogency aspect of interpretive packages and the collective action frames must be kept in mind. We have therefore refrained from using the set of components of collective action frames that Gamson puts forward in his *Talking Politics* (1992b). These components are (1) injustice, i.e., something is morally wrong and unjust; (2) agency, i.e., something must *and* can be done about this wrong; and (3) identity, i.e., *we* are the ones who have to do this and have to "fight" against the ones—*them*—who will not let us. The components are crucial in shaping people's political consciousnesses and in motivating them into collective actions. As such, they will, however, not convince the—not active—publics and/or the authorities. The aspects Gamson mentions appear, moreover, in a different way in the conceptual model we propose in this book.

14.   As Gamson (1992a) shows, it is not clear whether Snow and Benford mean an objective correspondence between frame and reality or a subjective correspondence, i.e., as perceived by the audience; in the first case "empirical validity" would be a better term and in the second "empirical plausibility." We agree with Gamson that clear concepts are essential but as clarity at this point is also related to the discussion about constructionism in Section 1.2, it seems to be more appropriate to maintain the Snow and Benford concept for the moment in order to see how this concept fares in the analysis and to return to this point in Chapter 8.

15.   In support we analytically distinguish between support potential and actualized support. The former we consider a facility and we deal with it accordingly. Here we will take only the resources that are actually at the disposal of the movement actors.

16.   Publics may be differentiated according to the level of involvement with the issues at stake in a campaign and their attitude toward these. Publics range from positive to negative (and everything in between). (See, among others, Blumer 1939; Turner and Killian 1972; Cobb and Elder 1972, 1983).

17.   Support includes the legitimation that some supporters can give to the causes of a campaign. The position of the actors who propagate or support the proposals of a social movement is especially important in the diffusion process. A movement that succeeds in enlisting actors with legitimate authority in society stands a greater chance of having elements of its ideology diffuse into the stock of collective definitions than movements that lack this kind of support. (For similar processes see the diffusion of fads, fashions, or innovations).

18.   Zeitgeist is about the same as the concept of general social movements of Blumer (1939) and Smelser (1962).

19.   We will treat the media briefly here, viz., only in relationship to the impact of collective campaigns. We know communication through media involves a far more complicated process than is portrayed here and it has therefore become the subject of a separate subdiscipline, the sociology of mass communication. For reviews of this field see, for example, Holz and Wright (1979) and McQuail (1985).

20.   For the authors on which Tarrow bases his account of the importance of the political opportunity structure, see Tarrow (1988:429). Relatively recent examples of studies into the effect of political opportunities on recent social move-

ments are to be found in Duyvendak, Van Der Heijden, Koopmans, and Wijmans (1992).

21.   A relatively specific example of this variable is Kitschelt's "capacity of
political systems to implement policies" (1986). State apparatuses that are cen-
tralized, effectively control market participants, and are relatively independent
of the judiciary deal more easily with challenges than weaker ones.

II

The Case Study
The Anti–Slave Trade Movement in Great Britain

PREFACE TO THE CASE STUDY[1]

The change in opinion regarding the justice and expediency of slavery and the accompanying trade in slaves that took place in the eighteenth century was not only great but probably unprecedented in history (Klingberg 1926; Davis 1984). In the case of Britain, Klingberg observed that the *asiento*—the privilege to import black slaves into the Spanish colonies of America—was regarded as one of the great triumphs of the Utrecht peace treaty of 1713, while in 1815 the articles denouncing the African slave trade in the Vienna peace treaty were seen as the noblest of that treaty (1926:22). Klingberg put the diametrical character of this change even more sharply with his statement: "The elder Pitt was still a champion of the slave trade; the younger Pitt struggled to have it abolished" (ibid.).

The general question underlying the case study of the abolition[2] of the slave trade in Great Britain concerns the explanation of this diametrical change in public thought. The obvious answer to this question would seem to lie in the endeavors of the abolition movement that arose in the late 1780s. This movement succeeded in arousing public opinion and ultimately abolishing the British slave trade.

This straightforward answer is, however, deceiving in its simplicity. The notion of movement or social movement is, as we have already pointed out (see Section 3.2), not at all clear as it refers to phenomena that are heterogeneous and complex. This is also the case with the British abolition movement. This movement consisted of a series of consecutive collective and political campaigns that differed considerably from each other. In the unfolding of the movement, each campaign partially set the stage for the ensuing one. The abolition movement is best seen as the set of abolitionist activities encompassing two decades that, as a continuing process, was contingent on preceding as well as ongoing historical processes and events.

Understanding the abolition movement therefore demands knowledge of the activities undertaken by the movement and its actors *and* an insight into its historical and episodic context. We have already made clear that studying social movements—almost necessarily—implies limiting the field of study to discrete campaigns. In this case study, this means concentrating on the campaign that proved to be decisive in bringing about the indicated change in public thinking. This campaign occurred between 1787 and 1792.

The year 1787 marks the beginning of the abolition movement, because in that year the Abolition Committee was founded. This committee acted as the central social movement organization and launched the first public nationwide campaign directed at the prohibition of the slave trade by Britons. Before this year the opinion on slavery and the slave trade had been far from clear-cut. The importance of the Afro-Caribbean slave system for Great Britain was widely acknowledged, although by the 1770s educated men in Britain were likely to regard slavery as morally and philosophically condemned. Antislavery and abolition of the slave trade were not issues on the public or the political agenda in the 1780s. In fact, the slave trade was seen as a practice that was deeply rooted. Howse cites a London publicist who "expressed no solitary opinion when he wrote in 1764: 'The impossibility of doing without slaves will always prevent this traffic being dropped. The necessity, the absolute necessity, then, of carrying it on, must, since there is no other, be its excuse'" (1952:30).

The year 1792 is taken as the ending point because the opinion on the issue of slavery and slave trade had by that time been completely reversed. The abolitionists succeeded in changing the framework of political discourse so completely that antislavery could no longer be treated as a fad or fashion. In books on international trade, in literature, and in politics, the view of slavery as an inevitable evil steadily disappeared. An openly proslavery point of view was nearly impossible at that time in Britain and the opposition to the abolitionist proposals rested mainly on arguments of expediency. Moreover, those who opposed abolition preferred a low-key approach directed at civil servants and cabinet ministers: the balance of expressed opinion usually weighed heavily against them. The year 1792 also meant the end of the first collective campaign of the abolition movement, since in that period the political climate changed drastically. The Jacobin turn in the French Revolution and the related slave revolt in French Saint Domingue (now Haiti), both with their terrors, made all political movements and all political changes suspect. With Burke the nation turned conservative.

In this part of the book we will therefore look for an answer to the question of the diametrical change in public thought on slavery and slave trade in Great Britain and we will seek the answer in the public and collective abolition campaign that took place between 1787 and 1792. There is, however, one major problem in taking this approach: the economic explanation of abolition, the so-called Williams thesis. This thesis explains the abolition as the effect of actions of the rising capitalists. As Williams succinctly states, "The capitalists had first encouraged West Indian slavery and then helped to destroy it" ([1944] 1972:169). If the abolition was indeed largely the effect of decisions made by the economic elite of Great Britain (a form of capitalist euthanasia, Drescher 1986:4), it would be pointless to look very deeply into the kind-hearted but rather superfluous actions of the abolitionists and our narrative could more or less end here.

We think, however, that this is not necessary. First, our goal is to explain the diametrical change in public thought on slavery and the slave trade that took place in Great Britain between 1787 and 1792.[3] More specifically, who (i.e., which actors) brought about this change? When studying the historical record on British antislavery activities in this period, as well as much later, no trace of Williams's capitalists can be found. We, therefore, must look elsewhere. Second, as Drescher (1977a, 1986), among others, shows, there were no economic reasons at the end of the eighteenth and the first part of the nineteenth century to end the slave trade (or slavery); or, in any case, as Solow and Engerman assess, "the West Indian slave system [was not, as Williams contended,] an obstacle to British growth" (1987:15). As we will show below, reasons abound to look at the abolition movement as the main actor in this change in public thought and to leave the Williams thesis aside. As Drescher states:

> At every major juncture in the history of abolition British policy was undertaken in the teeth of a world economic context which placed a premium on the expansion of slavery. (1986:4)
>
> From 1788 until 1806 the abolitionists seemed to be men hammering away at a rising system, who struck hardest when its prospects were brightest and where it was vigorous. This was an appropriate strategic for embattled militants, not for capitalists and MPs acting according to the norms of political economy. (1977a:174)

We will thus continue with the analysis of the historical studies as intended. As we have stated above, this campaign cannot be understood unless the historical and episodic context is taken into account. The question is, however, What is this context?

This is first the question of context in a geographical sense, i.e., Great Britain as a nation evolving into an empire and into the leading power in the world system. The emphasis will be placed on the metropolitan part of Great Britain. It was there that the struggle took place and the political decisions were eventually taken. Developments and events in other parts of the empire or in other countries will only be taken into account in as much as they influenced the struggle on the public mind in the metropolis.

Second, we must take into account context in a historical sense, i.e., that of the time period. This will be the eighteenth century up to the onset of the abolition movement in 1787. The beginning of this century—the reign of Queen Anne—differed, according to Ashley, "markedly from that of the reigns of King Charles II and King James II" (1973:246). The Glorious Revolution and the ensuing war against France had brought England definitively out of the Middle Ages and onto the threshold of the modern era (ibid.). The first meant a new system of government, a constitutional monarchy in embryonic form; the second, a deeper involvement of the nation in slavery and the slave trade as empire in the making and holder of the *asiento*. The century also witnessed new cultural developments in the areas of science, philosophy, and religion; the Enlightenment and related developments in the religious sphere proved especially crucial for the fate of slavery.

Third, the question of context also regards the realms of British societal life that must be taken into account. Obviously, these are the realms in which developments occurred that positively or negatively related to antislavery. This, however, does not easily lead to a systematic approach. We have therefore chosen to look at eighteenth-century British society from two angles. First, we will look into the relevant cultural developments affecting the change of the public mind on slavery, i.e., the way slavery and related phenomena were collectively defined. These developments may be seen as processes with their own dynamics (Weber's *Eigengesetzlichkeit* of cultural developments, [1920] 1986:252). Second, we will look into the actions of actors involved in the cultural dynamics, i.e., into systemic developments. Cultural developments are processes produced by people. As Weber also shows in his work, cultural *Eigengesetzlichkeit* does not take place outside the social world but in it.[4]

Summarized, the case study concerning the campaign directed at the abolition of the slave trade in Great Britain between 1787 and 1792 involves the following questions:

1. Which actors and factors determined the onset of the abolition movement in general and this campaign in particular and shaped its content?
2. What were the effects of the campaign on public thought on slavery and the slave trade and which (f)actors determined these effects?

These questions will be dealt with as follows. First, the more long-term developments in British society preceding the abolition movement will be elaborated: the cultural developments in Chapter 4, the structural ones in Chapter 5. Second, the episodic context of the movement will be brought to the fore in Chapter 6. In that chapter, three events crucial to the rise of the movement will be treated. In the closing section we will, moreover, look into the way these developments and events shaped the action-structure of the abolition movement on the eve of the first campaign. Finally, the organizational context, the actual campaign between 1787 and 1792, will be described in Chapter 7, where we will above all show what the abolitionists did and what the effects of their actions were.

NOTES

1. This case study consists of a secondary analysis of a number of studies concerning the abolition of the slave trade in Great Britain: Anstey (1975); Anstey and Hair (1976); Blackburn (1988); Bruns (1977); Craton (1974); Craton, Walvin, and Wright (1976); Davis (1966, 1975); Drescher (1986); Eltis and Walvin (1981); Fladeland (1972); Porter (1970); Rice (1975); Walvin (1982). Of these studies, four are the basis on which the analysis rests in particular: Anstey (1975), Davis (1966, 1975), Drescher (1986). The other studies are used as a complement to these four. In the text, these studies are not referred to unless specific elements or citations of an author are used.

2. In this text we will follow the tradition of the British historians who, with the terms *abolition* and *abolitionists*, usually refer to the abolition of the slave trade and to those who were active for this cause (Davis 1975:21).

3. As Holt (1990) shows in his penetrating review of Drescher's *Capitalism and Antislavery*, the subject of abolition (and eventually emancipation) involves three different questions: (1) how and why slavery came to be seen as an unmitigated, intolerable evil; (2) the process of the mobilization as a social movement; and (3) the explanation of how and why the government came to legally restrict slavery and the slave trade. The first is the main question of this study and the third that of Williams, while in his book Drescher focuses on the second.

4. Culture is a product of social actors, acting in their interests. At the same time, however, it shapes people's lives (see, for example, Weber's famous remark about the "iron cage" in which modern people are forced to live; [1920] 1976:181). Therefore, culture and structure may be separated in the analysis but in sociological explanations both are needed to complement each other (see Weber's closing remarks in the *Protestant Ethic* 1920 1976:183, esp. notes 118 and 119).

4

Cultural Trends in Great Britain
in the Eighteenth Century

4.1 INTRODUCTION

Roger Anstey, the great historian of British antislavery, makes it clear, in a posthumously published paper summarizing the findings of a lifetime, that the process leading to the abolition of the slave trade in Great Britain and to the later emancipation began with "the preparation of the ground by changes in philosophical and theological ideas" (1980:36). In eighteenth-century philosophical and religious thought, there was "much common ground . . . in what pertained to antislavery" (p. 20).

The eighteenth century is often referred to as the Age of Reason and the dominant strand of philosophical thinking of that period is appropriately called the Enlightenment. The Enlightenment can be seen as the intellectual elaboration of ideas that fermented in the turmoil of the seventeenth century (Ashley 1973). Its main ideas are, on the one hand, rooted in the revolution in scientific thinking; on the other, they contain the reaction to the intolerance of the period as well as to the authoritarian leadership of the seventeenth and eighteenth centuries. Human reason, in this view, does not only shed its light onto the mysteries of the physical world but onto those of the social world as well. It also promises to guide man out of the realm of ignorance and superstition into the "paradise" of a reasonable and happy life.

The eighteenth century was also the age of profound change in religious and theological thinking. The violent sectarian quarrels of the preceding century, with their accompanying excesses, gave rise to a natural longing for rest and a more peaceful life (Ashley 1973). Religion also had to come to terms with the new scientific and philosophical developments and to find anew a place in the age of science and reason. This meant that as far as ritual and worship were concerned, "Christians became content with things as they were . . . a pattern of reasonable Christianity"; as far as the normative side of daily life was concerned, however, the emphasis shifted to the importance of moral precepts, i.e., "the virtues of decent and charitable conduct and the 'reformation of manners'" (pp. 239–40). These developments also affected the realm of theological thinking and led to the elaboration of the idea of benevolence and the doctrine of Providence (Anstey 1980). Both strengthened, moreover, the importance of the aforementioned moral precepts.

The developments in both strands of thought are clearly related and they influence each other without one being the cause of the other; they form a relationship that Weber ([1920] 1976) refers to as "elective affinity" (see also Chapter 2 on this point). The work of John Locke is exemplary in this respect. He was the inspiration for the spirit of (religious) toleration that made the eighteenth century so different from the seventeenth. He can also be seen as one of the founders of the theory of natural and inalienable rights and of the government as the trustee of the people in charge of the protection of "life, liberty, and property" (Ashley 1973:243).

The above-mentioned trends in philosophical and religious thought not only affected antislavery thinking directly, but indirectly as well. The philosophy of the Enlightenment profoundly influenced the realms of political and economic theory and both the Enlightenment and religious ideas found expression in the literature of the eighteenth century. In all these cases, the reception of the new intellectual ideas and concepts affected the way Africa, Africans, the related slave trade, and slavery were seen, and thus the conduciveness of the cultural climate to antislavery actions.

In the next sections we will trace the cultural developments of the eighteenth century connected with the subject of slavery and the slave trade. In Sections 4.2 and 4.3, we will look into the realms of philosophy and religious thinking. In Sections 4.4–4.6, the world of printed matter, of political thought, and of economic theory will be dealt with. In the closing section of this chapter, we will turn to the cultural climate that developed during the eighteenth century, in particular those ideas, beliefs, and attitudes that made the acceptance or rejection of slavery more or less probable.

4.2   THE ENLIGHTENMENT PHILOSOPHY

John Locke can be seen as the most important precursor of the secular theories of the Enlightenment, given his quest "to free the individual from authority based on revelation, precedent, or sheer might" (Davis

1966:119). It therefore does not come as a surprise that his opinion of slavery was negative. As Craton, Walvin, and Wright contend, Locke was "temperamentally opposed to slavery" (1976:196) as can be seen in his statement, "Slavery is so vile and miserable Estate of Man" that nobody should plead for it (cited in Davis 1966:118). He was, however, also against this institution on rational grounds, as it was contrary to his conception of liberty. According to Locke, "The natural liberty of man is to be free from any superior power on earth, and not to be under the will or legislative authority of man, but to have only the law of Nature for his rule. The liberty of man in society is to be under no other legislative power but that established by consent in the commonwealth, nor under the dominion of any will, or restraint of any law, but what that legislative shall enact according to the trust put in it." Slavery, in his view, is not even possible with the consent of the slave himself. Yet he accepted this loathsome institution and justified it by putting slavery outside the realm of freedom and natural rights, i.e., outside the social contract. This is the case if someone has "by his fault forfeited his own life by some act that deserves death, he to whom he has forfeited it may [legitimately enslave him]. This is the perfect condition of slavery, which is nothing else but the state of war continued between lawful conqueror and a captive" (from Locke's *Two Treatises,* cited in Craton et al. 1976:203–4).

The Enlightenment, when seen as the general social movement reflecting the endeavors of the philosophes[1] "to open people's eyes, change their minds, and encourage them to think" (Porter 1990a:11), is a very complex and diverse phenomenon. As the papers in the volume on the Enlightenment edited by Porter and Teich (1981) show, there are important differences between countries. For example, the Enlightenment in England differed greatly from the Enlightenment in France, due to the vastly different social and political circumstances in both countries. The differences in time are important as well. As Porter contends, "[T]he baby Enlightenment's first words were spoken in an English nursery" (p. 7). The French *philosophes,* in particular Montesquieu, soon became the torchbearers of the movement, and their work became the foundation of much of the later Enlightenment writings in England and Scotland. Scotland, in particular, became an internationally renowned center of learning and letters with the work of Adam Smith, John Millar, and Adam Ferguson in the 1760s. This Scottish Enlightenment in turn affected "the salons and classrooms of England, France, Germany, Italy and America" (Phillipson 1981:19).[2]

In this section we will not deal with the Enlightenment at length. For our purposes, it suffices to show the main elements of this movement and its influence on the opinion of slavery. We do this by first presenting the main characteristics of the Enlightenment. These are further elaborated with the help of the work of Montesquieu and Hutcheson. We chose these writers because, as Anstey contends, their work was "seminal and inspired in varying measure a number of the others" (1975:97). Both, moreover, dealt with the question of slavery, and their work, especially that of Montesquieu, is extensively used by the antislavery writers.

The following three characteristics of the Enlightenment are important for the development of antislavery thought: faith in reason, the philosophy of natural rights, and the concept of the self-governing individual. They are dealt with consecutively.

1. Faith in reason.   Human reasoning, if indeed combined with experience and experiment (Porter 1990a), was seen as the only way to make things clearer or in Hamilton's words "'the light of reason,' shining brightly into all dark recesses of ignorance and superstition" (1992:26). This faith in reason had its roots in the scientific revolution of the seventeenth century in which human reason had triumphed (Ashley 1973; Hamilton 1992). Within this faith in reason, two aspects are especially important.

> a. Human reason as an instrument of critique, i.e., as a way to look critically at all that is with the intention to unmask "all the frauds and errors of the past" (Davis 1966:418). This critique is the necessary step toward understanding and knowledge of the laws of nature, those of human nature included. The Enlightenment is primarily the true "Science of Man" (Porter 1990a).
>
> b. Human reason as the means to find the right way to create a just, expedient, and therefore more humane, happy society. The *philosophes* "were men . . . seeking not just to understand the world but to change it" (Porter 1990a:3). In the Enlightenment, utility and happiness often went hand in hand.

The almost unreserved faith in reason led, on the one hand, to an unfettered belief in progress; in the words of Hamilton, "[T]he application of reason to the affairs of men would encourage a general advance of civilization" (1992:29). On the other hand, it encouraged a critical attitude toward all that is, including traditions, standard teachings of churches, and religious and worldly authority (Porter 1990a).

2. Philosophy of natural rights.   This philosophy is based on "nature" as the standard for societal life. In particular, the philosophy concerns all that man by nature possesses without being corrupted by social

institutions; it is founded on the notion that uncorrupted human nature is a universal standard of truth and virtue. Man's innate capacity for the latter makes him capable of infinite perfection (Davis 1966:400; Porter 1981). This strand of philosophical thought is rooted in a tradition going back to classical antiquity (see Davis for a thorough analysis of this tradition in relation to slavery). It also comes from the above-mentioned revolution in science, in which nature was no longer only the object of study but became the ultimate proof of truth as well. At the end of the seventeenth and the beginning of the eighteenth century, Nature came to the fore in all kinds of realms, such as religion, theology, law, and philosophy. In Enlightenment thinking it became the universal basis for social harmony and order (Porter 1981).

Two aspects of this natural rights philosophy are especially important with regard to the rise of antislavery thought.

> a. Man by nature possesses inalienable rights. Of these rights, "individual and civil liberty, together with liberty of conscience, speech, publication, of commerce and of industry" are the most important (Anstey 1975:119). Of these, the liberty of commerce and industry, the rights of property, are fundamental as they are seen as the foundation of liberty.
>
> b. Natural law is seen as the touchstone of existing societal arrangements and rules. Positive law is the result of the will and the decisions of the sovereign, who is (or at least should be) guided by social utility and public welfare. This law *needs* a higher, universal standard to prevent deviations of nature based on pragmatic considerations.

The notion of a universal law of nature leads to the notion of a sphere of rights within which each individual is (relatively) free from interference, by both the authorities and his fellowmen. It also leads to the higher-law doctrine, which distinguishes between the absolute *ius naturale* and the relative rules of positive law, which may be put to the test by the former.

3. The concept of the self-governing individual. In this concept, man is considered a discrete entity: a being with his own rights, choices, and responsibility. Especially the idea that man's status and rights were no longer dependent on his membership of a group or estate is probably the most important break with the ideas of the past. As Davis shows, we have here the heritage of Locke, the "belief that society is composed of discrete, self-governing individuals whose true humanity lies in their proprietorship of their own persons [and whose] moral freedom [lies] in a lack of dependence upon the will of others, in the natural exercise of

the human faculties, and in the unfettered pursuit of enlightened self-interest" (1966:412) and in "the power to say 'je veux' or 'je ne veux pas'" (pp. 418–19).

These characteristics can already be found in the work of Locke, who provided a blueprint, as it were, for an enlightened society.

The work of Montesquieu is, as that of most Enlightenment writers, inherently a challenge to authority, albeit predominantly a cautious and moderate one. Montesquieu is a pivotal figure of the Enlightenment: not only because of his interest in civil and political liberty or his belief in the natural equality of all men, but essentially because of his stance that answers to the questions of how to order society and how to come to solutions for social and political problems can only be found by studying the "nature of things."

His main work, *L'Esprit des Lois* is primarily a scientific undertaking.[3] In this study Montesquieu compares different social and political systems in order to find the causes of these different arrangements and to ascertain which conditions make for "a good society."[4] One of his most important findings is the concept of the separation—or better said, "balance"—of powers, which he derives from the work of Locke on the English constitution. This balance is in Montesquieu's view the essential condition for liberty.

Montesquieu's feeling for liberty and equality[5] also led him to the subject of slavery. On principle, Montesquieu was passionately against the institution of slavery as is shown by his refutation of the justifications of slavery in Roman law. In his *Pensées* he "asserted that 'L'esclavage est contre le Droit naturel, par lequel tous les hommes naissent libre & indépendant'; and eloquently concluded: 'En vain, les lois civiles forment des chaines; la Loi naturelle les rompra toujours'" (cited in Davis 1966:406).

Yet, Montesquieu's moderateness and caution exposes itself in his treatment of slavery as well. First, his empirical approach forced him to acknowledge that slavery existed in some countries, mainly due to the influence of climate, and was thus, in those cases, founded on natural reason. Still, as we have seen before, he maintained that moral considerations had primacy and that this institution should be molded by moral ideas. Second, he clothed much of his critique on slavery in satire and irony, often so subtle that he was easily misunderstood. His satirical remarks in conjunction with his "acceptance" of geographical justifications were even used by proslavery writers to defend the institution.

The importance of Montesquieu to the development of antislavery thought in the eighteenth century lay in the fact that he was an accepted philosophical authority. His authority was, moreover, aided by the scien-

tific method he used. His critical treatment was not the product of normative, wishful (armchair) thinking but had an empirical foundation.
Another reason for his importance was the abundance of easily accessible material that later writers could use in their treatment of slavery. In
this they often went further than Montesquieu's work justified.

Hutcheson's work is of importance because it emphasizes another
central component of Enlightenment thought: happiness. Hutcheson's
main aim was to motivate people to take "that course of action which
tends most effectually to promote their greatest happiness and perfection" (cited in Anstey 1975:98). Particularly important in this respect is
Hutcheson's conclusion that men have "two grand determinations . . .
one towards our own great happiness, the other towards the greatest
general good" (p. 99). Both determinations are innate and natural. The
latter concerns the moral sense to benevolence and social utility which—
in conflict with the former—has precedence over man's self-interest.
This makes Hutcheson's benevolence an active and dynamic one.

Hutcheson's ideas concerning benevolence combined with his view of
liberty and equality as natural rights[6] brought him quite naturally to a
qualified denunciation of slavery. Sypher ([1942] 1969) even sees
Hutcheson's work as the turning point in the way slavery was justified
until the early part of the eighteenth century. The new humanitarian
ethics propagated by Hutcheson[7] enervated the classical Christian theory of slavery that accepted slavery either as a consequence of natural
inferiority or of conquest in war. Although, as Davis (1966) contends,
the Christian justification of slavery had been narrowed down, mainly
through the writings of Hobbes and Locke, it was Hutcheson and Montesquieu who first authoritatively condemned this institution. Moreover,
Hutcheson's call to active benevolence contained, however implicit, a
threat to the existence of slavery itself.

The development of Enlightenment ideas gave rise to a set of views
that could easily come into conflict with the flourishing institution of
slavery in the American colonies of the West European countries.[8] Davis
puts it even stronger: "When brought together, these approaches
[Hutcheson's and Montesquieu's] would provide a theoretical basis for
effective antislavery action" (p. 406). Slavery was, in many respects, the
denial of much of what the Enlightenment stood for and it is almost
logical to witness that the negative views—on the intellectual level—
grew in importance in the first half of the eighteenth century.

This growth can be seen in the fact that slavery became a topic for
essays and debating contests at several universities in the 1760s and
1770s.[9] Another indication of intellectual change was the statement that
Marmontel, a writer of a melodramatic play in the 1770s, put in the
mouth of Las Casas (who in 1514 was one of the first to come out against

the enslavement of Indians by his fellow Spaniards): "Mon frère, tu es mon esclave, est une absurdité dans la bouche d'un homme, un parjure et un blasphème dans la bouche d'un chrétien" (Davis 1966:410). Finally, the meaning of words such as *slavery, enslave,* and *bondage* changed from the 1750s onwards. They became synonymous with all threats of freedom as well as with all forms of nonlegitimate use of power (pp. 438–43). Gradually the slavery concept changed into a threat to civil and political liberties in general, acquiring a definitive negative connotation in the Enlightenment legacy. In Anstey's words, "What cannot be in dispute is the striking unanimity in the condemnation of slavery by philosophers of great diversity; what cannot be gainsaid is that none of any rank defended the institution" (1975:124).

4.3   THE REALM OF RELIGIOUS THINKING

Religion in Great Britain at the beginning of the eighteenth century was dominated by the reactions to and the consequences of the religious, social, and political conflicts of the seventeenth century. Especially important in this respect were (1) the struggle to keep protestant England "safe from Rome"- related to such conflicts as those around the Stuart monarchy, the position of Ireland, and world dominance;[10] and (2) the internal Protestant strife—in which the establishment of a fundamentalist puritan society, Cromwell's Holy Commonwealth, was at stake. In the aftermath of the turmoil of the seventeenth century, three effects are notable in characterizing the religious climate at the beginning of the eighteenth century.

The first concerns the tendency to turn away from the "fanatical" toward the "reasonable." In religious matters, there was a marked trend toward moderation and a preference for a "decent life" over disputes concerning "the sacraments and ritual" (Ashley 1973:238). In relation to this, the desire for (religious) toleration was growing: in spirit (see, in particular, Locke's writings) as well as in practice. Although acts against Roman Catholics and nonconformists were still passed, "restrictions on freedom and worship were often ignored or avoided [and in the case of conflicts] passions over religious questions were not nearly so strong as [before]" (pp. 238–39).

This drift away from the "fanatical" toward moderation and tolerance was legitimated by a religious doctrine that elevated reason above the unassailable authority of biblical revelation as interpreted by the "elect and the virtuous." In the words of Locke, "revelation must be judged by reason" (cited in Ashley 1973:238), because, in the vision of the proponents of this doctrine, "Intolerance and radicalism [are] inevitable when religion [rejects] reason in favor of unbridled revelation" (p. 173). In this doctrine, usually referred to as *natural religion* or *deism*, the central tenet is that of nature being governed by eternal and unalterable laws.[11] Nature is created by God and is therefore, as such, good and just. According to deism, Christianity is as old as creation itself and has (its truths included) been known to men always and everywhere. This makes revelation superfluous. Deism leads to the view that the natural is reasonable and that everything in the world that has always existed ought to be there. In the words of Zaret, "natural religion taught that we are reasonable creatures who live in the best of all possible worlds" (p. 174).

The second outcome of seventeenth-century turmoil was the fact that much of what the Puritans stood for became a self-evident part of the precepts of daily life. Puritanism was internalized, as it were, and its leading ideas regarding daily life—"the virtues of decent and charitable conduct and the reformation of manners"—became standards of conduct in the Court of Queen Anne, and following that example became the messages of contemporary popular writers and teachers (Ashley 1973:240). In our case the emphasis on philanthropy is important. As Davis shows, private philanthropy had a relatively long tradition and was, as such, a response to social problems emanating from enclosure and "the disintegration of medieval patterns of social responsibility" (1966:334). It became part of the emergent capitalist ethic, and likewise placed an emphasis on individual effort and responsibility for the giver and the recipient alike. In line with this ethic, philanthropy had to remain within the boundaries of the existing social order. In this way philanthropy became primarily a private affair and a limited moral response, and less a program for social reform.

Protestant dissent did not disappear in the eighteenth century but— and this is the third outcome—became the undercurrent in the realm of religion. "Old Dissent lost its spur to zeal and minded its own business" (Porter 1990b:179) but its associations remained intact and functioned as abeyance structures (Taylor 1989) in which the heritage of dissent was kept alive (Porter 1990b:179). Godwyn's crusade against the West Indian planters and their leaning toward materialism, greed, luxury, and licentiousness is an example of an eruption of this constant dissent-inspired spiritual undercurrent. As the dissent was not incorporated in the political structure, with its corrupting spoils of offices and sinecures, it remained flexible and ready to adapt to the more promising circumstances of the 1760s and 1770s (Porter 1990b).

The reactions to the turmoil of the seventeenth century described above produced several effects in the course of the eighteenth century. Concerning the coming-into-being of an antislavery cast of thought, Anstey points to two related theological developments, viz., the concept of benevolence and the doctrine of Providence, which—partly parallel to and partly in combination with the unfolding of the Enlightenment philosophy—"played a part in producing a cast of mind prepared to contemplate reform" (1975:126). In the late seventeenth and first half of the eighteenth century there were also signs of growing discomfort with slavery. An antislavery argument arose especially in dissenting circles, above all, among the Quakers, which proved to have important effects on the abolition struggle at the end of the eighteenth century.

The emergence of a philosophy and ethic of benevolence was rooted in the philanthropic tradition already mentioned. It was also a reaction "to the Calvinist and Hobbesian views of man's incapacity for virtue" (Davis 1975:45–46). In this, the notion of benevolence owed much to the Enlightenment's emphasis on nature, which encompassed man's natural sense of virtue as well. The theological elaboration of these ideas takes the line that man has a nature created by God, part of which is an affection for his fellowmen and a sensibility for their sufferings. This makes philanthropy, good works, and a dedication to worthy causes not only natural, but a self-evident pleasure as well. The elaboration of the subjective side of benevolence is, however, not the whole story. In the concept of benevolence, "the moral sensibility was [also] inseparable from social duty" (Davis 1966:356). Benevolence thus was both a normal and natural tendency, and a religious and ethical duty. This made the eighteenth century not only the age of reason, but one of compassion as well.

The doctrine of Providence was developed in the theology of the first half of the eighteenth century. Although the idea of a providential God already had a long and respectable history in theology, "it was a particular tenet of Deism which led to the development of [this specific doctrine viz.] the deistic assertion that 'any religion necessary for salvation must be one that has always and everywhere been known to men'" (Anstey 1975:130). The conclusion following from this tenet—that evils, both past and present, were to be accepted as belonging to the natural order of things—led to the elaboration of the idea of progressive revelation. In this vision, God is portrayed as a wise and benevolent ruler who accepts temporary exceptions to the rules of his divine morality. He gave and gives dispensations because man, at particular points in time, was not up to those rules because his moral sense was still in an undeveloped state. In this view God's truth is eternal, but he times his revelations to fit man's cultural stages (Davis 1975:530). God has a divine plan in which these evils are progressively eliminated and he gradually reveals to mankind the knowledge of this plan, the truth about divine morality, and his intentions with man and society. In short, we have here the notion of Providence as moral progress running parallel to the

Enlightenment's faith in progress. This made the ideas of the Enlightenment *philosophes* more acceptable and accessible for religious people and vice versa.

The elaboration of the doctrine of Providence did not, however, stop here. The idea of a divine providential plan became (mainly through the works of Berkeley and Butler) the foundation of practical morals. By reflection and study, man could discover God's plans and intentions, enabling him to work actively in the world to realize God's design. In this way God directs, rules, and governs the world: Providence as God's moral government realized through the active involvement of mankind. Joseph Butler stated this vision on Providence as follows: "And, since the certain natural Course of Things is the Conduct of Providence or the Government of God, though carried on by the Instrumentality of Men, Mankind find themselves placed by Him in such Circumstances as that they are unavoidably accountable for their Behavior, in the view of their being mischevious, or eminently beneficial to Society" (cited in Anstey 1975:136). This belief in Providence as the moral government of the universe became quite general. Both strands of theological thought, i.e., natural benevolence and the notion of historical progress, moreover, merged—as Davis (1966) states—in the works of the Anglican divines in the 1740s and 1760s.

The Anglican church—at the practical level of catering to the daily spiritual needs—accepted slavery as a fact of life, and as Sypher states, "Many of the recognized leaders of the century . . . are silent on slavery" ([1942] 1969:64). The church only concerned itself with the harsh treatment of slaves and their Christianization. Churchmen were even involved in slavery.[12] This was not very different in the sectarian tradition, the submerged Protestant dissent of the seventeenth century; as Davis states, "For most sectarians . . . slavery presented no problem" (1966:303). Still there were differences, not in the least because among dissenters there was a stronger emphasis on the brotherhood of men in which all men are equal. There were instances of disapproval of slavery and the slave trade, e.g., the well-known dissenting preacher Richard Baxter depicted the slave trade as a "heinous sin" and "one of the worst kinds of thievery" (cited, respectively, in Davis 1966:338; Sypher [1942] 1969:66).[13] Another example was James Foster, a famous dissenting preacher and a propagator of many of Hutcheson's ideas, who called the African slave trade an "outrageous violation of natural rights" (Davis 1966:379). These protests, however, remained private and one-shot affairs.

Within the sectarian tradition, the Quakers were an exception. Among them antislavery was, time and again, brought forward and grew in strength as an issue. The Quakers formed a religious community—the Society of Friends—on both sides of the Atlantic. It originated as a sect in the religious turmoil of seventeenth-century Britain. It put an emphasis on a life characterized by an "innerworldly" strife for religious purity and perfection. Through constant soul-searching the Quakers had to discover for themselves what was right or wrong: "God's precepts are in every man and they must be discovered by every individual so that he may live by them" (Hurwitz 1973:24). The norms for daily life were therefore not imposed on the Quakers by ecclesiastical authorities, but the precepts "found" by individual Quakers were discussed and eventually established in the so-called "Meetings of Friends."

As Davis (1966) states, the Quakers were the only sect of the seventeenth century that succeeded in finding a practical solution to the dilemma posed by the demands originating in its religious ideals and the necessity to come to terms with the surrounding nonsectarian society. Their pragmatic accommodation consisted of adhering to the sectarian impulse for perfection. They did this, however, in such a way that the impulse was directed at concrete objectives such as antislavery at a later date, and not to changing the whole social order as the other sects of the seventeenth century had tried to do. In Davis's words, "It was the Quaker genius, then, to achieve a dynamic balance between an impulse to perfection and a way of life tending to crystallize the impulse in forms that could meet the demands of reality" (p. 302).

This pragmatic solution, however, brought about its own problems, because as Davis remarks, "the necessity of maintaining an equilibrium between moral principles and daily life [led to] constant tension and soulsearching" (ibid.). This resulted, among other things, in every Quaker in the Society of Friends being able to put forward new rules and norms of behavior, or revisions of existing ones; these were then discussed in the Meetings and eventually established as binding. In this the Quakers were "[u]nhampered by dogmatic theology, guided by the continuing revelations of the Inner Light, . . . partly immune from rationalizations which identified ancient custom with natural law [in short a] frame of mind that enabled [them] to judge slavery" (pp. 306–7).

It was no more than logical that slavery would eventually become a topic among the Friends. The innerworldly activities of the Quakers, among them trading and banking, involved them heavily in slavery and the slave trade. This produced tensions within the Quaker community since slavery was obviously opposed to Quaker ideals. As early as 1657, George Fox, the founder of the Society of Friends, although accepting Negro slavery as an institution, put forward the "conception of the brotherhood under God of all men, including slaves" (Craton et al. 1976:202). For the Quakers, the fact that "Christ died for all men, . . . postulat[ed] a fundamental equality between them" and they, therefore, accepted "the call to love all men" (Anstey 1975:203). This ideal of limitless equality obviously did not agree very well with the inherent extreme inequality of slavery. Moreover, the luxury and idleness that usually accompanied slavery were clearly at odds with the Quaker ideal of a quiet and humble life.

For some Quakers, the involvement in slavery and slave trade became quite naturally a problem, especially in North America. In 1676, William Edmundson sent out a general letter critical of slavery to Quakers in slaveholding colonies, and in 1688, the Quakers of Germantown signed a petition against slavery directed at one of their Meetings. Both protests remained without effect but were relevant because such actions "forced a response from the highest official bodies of the Society of Friends [who] could not [just] defend their position by citing noted theologians and classical authorities" (Davis 1966:309). This implied an argumentative discussion because these bodies had to justify their position on slavery.

Several other antislavery protests and actions followed at the end of the seventeenth and the beginning of the eighteenth century and "a number of Quaker meetings in America were stirred by antislavery agitation" (p. 312). Still, slavery—though under somewhat restricted conditions—remained accepted; nonetheless, the Friends were cautioned against involving themselves in any way with the trade in slaves. In 1715, John Hepburn published a tract, *The American Defence of the Christian Golden Rule*, to which he had added two antislavery articles written by others:

> Taken together, these remarkable essays answered virtually every proslavery argument that would appear during the next century and a half. By 1713 it had already been said that the slave trade encouraged wars and crimes in Africa, that enslavement was not the necessary consequence of sparing a captive's life, that it was unlawful to punish without a reason or to profit from labor without recompense, that bondage defaced the image of God, that it compelled men to act in ways that brought cruel punishment, that it led to the separation of families, to adultery, and to the violation of all the Commandments. [The writer] took special pains to discredit the significantly secular argument that Negroes were far *happier* as American slaves than as African savages. (p. 317)

In the second quarter of the eighteenth century, the disciplinarian climate within the Society of Friends changed in reaction to the economic success resulting from hard work and sober living. The acquired wealth threatened, at least in the eyes of the Quaker leaders, the religious purity of the Friends and led to actions directed at tightening internal discipline. In this changing climate, Elihu Coleman resumed the attack on slavery in 1733; his antislavery tract was the first to receive official approval from a Quaker Meeting. His tract was quite similar to that of Hepburn, and both writings "had assimilated, to some degree, the ideas and mood of the Early Enlightenment [the] taste for irony and satire [included]" (pp. 316–18). Important in the tracts of both Hepburn and Coleman was the notion that the Quaker community had somehow been corrupted by wealth and compromise with the surrounding society, and that the enslavement of blacks was a symbol of the Quakers' spiritual situation, being bonded to the vices and temptations of worldly society, which blocked their way to redemption.

In the same period, these themes were radicalized in the life and works of two Quaker perfectionists, Ralph Sandiford and Benjamin Lay. They "made abolitionism the core of their religion and the center of their existence [for which they] were ready to be ostracized or even to die [and for them] slavery had come to symbolize not only sin and death but every violation of the Christian ideal of love and brotherhood" (pp. 320–26). For both, slavery was the ultimate sin and the cause of all kinds of other evils; therefore, a crusade against slavery was needed both to purify the Society of Friends in a moral sense and to free it from sin. Sandiford and Lay were, however, marginal figures in the Quaker community; Lay especially was considered very eccentric and this restricted the effectiveness of their actions.

From 1676 onwards, antislavery was a recurrent topic within the Society of Friends. The result was that antislavery arguments took shape and could get a central place in Quaker religious life. In the first half of the eighteenth century, the conviction gained ground that slavery is a sin and an evil from which Quakers should refrain. The early antislavery actions, moreover, led to certain measures being taken against the slave trade as well as to exhortations directed at Quaker masters to treat their slaves well (Davis 1975). The antislavery issue, nonetheless, remained relatively marginal in the life of most Quakers, who did not massively withdraw from slavery and trades tinged by it (see Davis 1975:213–14, especially note 1). In the words of Rice, "these first voices against slavery cried in the wilderness" (1975:154).

Mainstream Protestantism in Great Britain in the first three-quarters of the eighteenth century accepted slavery as a fact of life. As far as slavery was concerned, the focus was on acting upon the moral conscience of the slave owners, and that of the colonial authorities, to treat the slaves in a more humane way and to allow their Christianization. In this regard, the Anglican church (as well as several other dissenting sects) became active in missionary work in the American colonies. In general, the church acted in line with the prevailing mood of benevolence and the need to reform manners.

As far as the changes within mainstream theology are concerned, they did not directly affect thought about slavery but contributed to the more general feeling that society needed reform. This reform proved to be important to the abolition struggle later on, especially among those who "transformed the quest for salvation from a sinful world into a mission to cleanse the world of sin" (Davis 1975:46). In the same period (and some time before as well) an articulated antislavery argument arose within the Quaker community, especially in North America. Around 1715, all the elements later used in the antislavery and abolition discourse were already in place.

The theological developments concerning the concept of benevolence and the doctrine of Providence were related to the development of Enlightenment philosophy. As Anstey (1975) contends, the notion of progressive revelation probably contributed as much to the general idea of progress as the work of the *philosophes* did. It was also the case that reciprocal influences existed with regard to the development of the idea of benevolence. At this point, however, theology is more important than philosophy and is bound to have more effect on the attitudes of people, because theological thinking is interwoven with daily religious practices in a religious society such as Great Britain. This is far less the case with the more remote philosophical ideas. On the other hand, the Enlightenment affected religious thinking as well as the elaboration of the antislavery argument. Taken together, this crisscross pattern of lines of influence is a fine example of Weber's concept of elective affinity, i.e., a set of relationships between cultural processes whose dynamics are otherwise independent of each other.

4.4 THE WORLD OF PRINT

Between 1600 and 1800, especially early in the seventeenth century, literacy in Great Britain grew rapidly, and in the eighteenth century "the daily habits of a modern, print-centered culture were well on their way to being established" (Hunter 1990:65). This growth took place, above all, in the rising urban middle classes, which constituted an important part of the new reading public, and was accompanied by a fixation on contemporaneity (Altick [1957] 1983; Oldfield 1989; Hunter 1990). As Hunter shows, this expressed itself among other things in intellectual curiosity, interest in novelty (see, for example, the increasing number of scientific clubs and societies and the spate of travel accounts), and an enlightened desire to be au courant, which was satisfied by a proliferation of newspapers, periodicals, and pamphlets.

From the late seventeenth century onwards, print became an important way of mediating culture. As Ashley (1973) contends, the newspaper and the periodical originated during the reign of Queen Anne. The press grew—in London as well as in the provinces—at a fast pace, and journalism became a new and important profession. Another print-based medium, the pamphlet, flourished too; according to Plumb, "Every political and religious development produced a plethora of pamphlets" ([1950] 1968:30), and in the words of Barry, in the 1750s and 1760s "the use of print was standard in [political] disputes" (1991:57). In this period, there was also a great increase in literature. Especially literature other than theology and travel was growing,[14] reaching an audience other than the traditional "gentle" reader (Plumb [1950] 1968; Speck 1983). Important to spreading the habit of reading were the production of cheaper editions and chapbooks, the opportunity to read newspapers and periodicals in coffeehouses, and the rapid proliferation of circulating libraries after 1725 (Altick [1957] 1983; Speck 1983).

In the eighteenth century, writing was primarily seen as a means rather than an end in itself. This utilitarian view is quite in line with the spirit of the times, as are the following four main characteristics of what appeared in print. Printed matter[15] was generally:

1. Religious in content.   As Hunter contends, "moral treatises and theological discourses continued to be by far the most frequently printed materials until the end of the eighteenth century" (1990:234).

2. Moralistic in tone.   Much literature—the new children's literature included—was directed at inculcating moral values and rules. It contained above all moral messages that were ideological in nature: under the guise of the invocation of the public good, they defended the interests of either the landed gentry (mostly Tory), the dominating Whig magnates, or the rising commercial middle classes.

3. Didactic in intent.   Didactism (see, for example, the continuing attempts to reform manners) is one of the main characteristics of the eighteenth century. It is above all based on the Enlightenment notion that argument can affect behavior. This characteristic links up nicely with the growing demand for practical knowledge, information, and guidance in practical affairs.[16]

4. Realistic in presentation.   As the popularity of travel accounts shows, there was a leaning toward factual knowledge of the larger world. This is reflected in the literature, especially in the early novel, in which fiction is represented as fact (for example, Defoe's *Robinson Crusoe*). It can also be seen in the growing output of tracts about all kinds of things worth knowing, in the rising interest in periodicals such as the *Tatler* or the *Spectator*, and in the changing content of the newspapers.

These four characteristics made print a perfect vehicle for later antislavery writing and propaganda. The antislavery movement originated mainly in religious circles, attacked the institution of slavery above all as a case of (im)morality, employed print as a means to educate people, and used all kinds of empirical data in a great many tracts and pamphlets.

This suitability of print for the antislavery cause was, moreover, enhanced by the effect of the Enlightenment on literature. The turn to nature and the natural by the *philosophes*[17] infused the literature of the late seventeenth and the eighteenth century with the myth of the noble savage uncorrupted by civilization, as well as with the notion of benevolence as a trait natural to human beings. This myth embodied a strain toward primitivism containing at the same time an awe-inspiring image of beastlike brutality and the tantalizing bliss of paradise as being naturally free, virtuous, and happy; the mix with benevolism led at it best to humanitarianism and at its worst to sentimentalism (Sypher [1942] 1969). This mix produced in any case a heightened sensibility to "the misfortunes of the innocent" (Davis 1966:356). This sensibility was directed especially at the dismal fate of the conquered and often enslaved primitive peoples.

The myth of the noble savage—in the literature transformed into a cult of the noble savage—rested more on unproven assumptions regarding man's essential virtue in his primitive state than on what was known about the so-called primitive societies. As Sypher states, "There was, in truth, an incorrigible will to believe in the noble savage" [(1942] 1969:107). Originally, the image of the noble savage pertained to all primitive peoples, South Sea Islanders, American Indians, and black Africans alike. During the eighteenth century it became more and more restricted to the image of the noble Negro; an image that was at the same time at odds with the less than positive views on Africa and the Africans. In the words of Davis:

> In eighteenth-century literature, a feeling of shock and indignation at the physical cruelties of Negro slavery increasingly became a test of sensibility, just as the cruelties themselves became a symbol of man's inhumanity to man. (1966:411–12)

The literary tradition of the noble Negro is rooted in two legends, viz., that of Oroonoko and that of Inkle and Yarico.[18] The first was written by Aphra Benn—according to Sypher "the originator of the Oroonoko legend, or perhaps even the originator of the noble Negro" ([1942] 1969:108)—who portrayed Oroonoko as an African prince who was far too noble to be a slave and thus revolts. Oroonoko is especially noble in his love for Imoinda, in his killing of Imoinda to preserve her honor, and in his stoic endurance of the pains of torture.[19] The second legend is based on Jean Mocquet's *Voyages* (1616) in which the writer tells a story about an English pilot, Inkle, who betrayed an Indian girl, Yarico, who had saved him from a sure death after being shipwrecked. This story was idealized and transformed in a series of consecutive versions into a tale about an African (sometimes still an Indian) princess of extreme beauty who rescues the English pilot, falls in love with him, and is—in the end—sold by him as a slave.

Both legends[20] remained very popular throughout the eighteenth century, although they were not really antislavery in content. Moreover, the central image of the cult of the noble savage, that of the princely Negro, unfit for slavery and ready to rebel, is not very well suited for arousing pity, with the exception of his personal, undeserved—for ignoble—fate. The cult could nevertheless play such an important role in antislavery only in the eighteenth century because in "that century the *genre* interacted with a heightened awareness of liberty, humanity, and equality" (Anstey 1975:148). It was this combination of the cult with the predominant concerns of the age—benevolence, liberty, and happiness—that made it possible to see "the African as a man of feeling whose desire for liberty and capacity for a moral life could not be extinguished by the most oppressive environment" (Davis 1966:147). It made it possible for "[t]he noble Negro, begot of primitivism and fostered by sensibility" to become an important symbol of the later antislavery crusade (Sypher [1942] 1969:155).

As we stated above (and as is also demonstrated by Sypher in detail), this image is ill-suited for its main goal—arousing pity. The inherent tendency to rebel excites if anything "terror" and "fear." It is, therefore, no wonder that later antislavery writers also turned to the plight of the ordinary, downtrodden black slave whose fate was undeserved because it was mainly based on the color of his skin. It led to a different literary theme, that of the suffering slave, the natural human being who is corrupted by civilization and therefore merits one's compassion. As Davis shows, both figures, that of the noble Negro and that of the suffering slave

> played essential roles in conditioning antislavery opinion. If the Negro was a terrifying avenger, returning blow for blow, . . . he struck a response in white man's nature [as this was the way] the European should want to act if he were a slave. But if the Negro patiently accepted flagellation and torture . . . he struck an equally important response of pity and fascination. This was, after all, the way Christians were supposed to behave. In both postures the Negro was unmistakably a sensitive man and not a brute. In both postures he challenged the traditional ideal of Christian servitude [the traditional Christian justification of slavery] as a relationship of reciprocal love and obligation. (1966:480–81)

Together, the eighteenth century produced two distinct types of literature having consequences for the abolition struggle at the end of the century.

1. The general literature of the age in which slaves and slavery sometimes played a role. In this literature, the dominant notions from the realm of philosophy and theology—liberty, benevolence, and happiness—occupied a central place. Benevolence is especially omnipresent as literary theme (Anstey 1975).

2. Specific antislavery literature that used the themes of the general literature for its own specific ends. In this mostly fictional verse and prose, the fate of the slave and the objectional sides of slavery occupy a central place. This literature is treated by Sypher in his *Guinea's Captive Kings*. In this literature, the theme of the noble Negro often stood in an uneasy relationship with the antislavery goal of arousing pity. While it sometimes reflected authentic humanitarianism, it often also reflected false sentimentalism.

The literary products of the eighteenth century were, at the same time, the reflection of that which concerned the people of that age and the means with which the culture of that period was shaped.[21] This shaping aspect meant that the literature of this period—the general and the specific antislavery writings alike—did not remain without effect. In the words of Anstey:

> The expression in contemporary literature, poetry and drama of anti-slavery themes gave a heightened awareness of slavery for, by making it possible to imagine what it was like to be a slave, directness and intensity was lent to the propositions of reason, whilst a theme expressed in novels, in verse, and in theatre reached a wider public than when confined to philosophy. Thus philosophical, intellectual condemnation of slavery was accompanied by a relatively widely disseminated sensitivity to it and a generally hostile verdict upon it. (1975:150–51)

The world of print contributed to the cause of antislavery in two important ways. First, the way print developed in the eighteenth century made it a perfect vehicle for waging the abolition struggle at a later date, i.e., its format of being religious in content, moralistic in tone, didactic in intent, and realistic in presentation. Second, a literature emerged that proved to be important for antislavery in several respects. In literature, the compassion with the plight of the slave and the sensibility seen as an ethical imperative to do something about this were enlarged and this would not have proceeded as fast as it did without the work of novelists and poets (Davis 1966; Anstey 1975; Rice 1980). The literature of the age of feeling also functioned as a resource for the later antislavery campaigners who used verse and prose as an important weapon in the abolition struggle, and it helped in several ways—as Oldfield states with regard to children's books—"to create a climate conducive to reform" (1989:49).

4.5 EIGHTEENTH-CENTURY POLITICAL THOUGHT

Politically, British society in the eighteenth century was shaped by the Glorious Revolution. This revolution put, on the one hand, an end to the claim of the puritan "virtuosi" concerning the predominance of revelation over rational political decision-making and, on the other, limited the absolute power of the monarch. The Glorious Revolution did not, however, succeed in completely separating the realms of religion and politics or in establishing a full-fledged constitutional monarchy (Ashley 1973). Eighteenth-century Britain was a modern political society, albeit in rudimentary form.

This political renewal was influenced by new political ideas that were seen at the same time as a reflection of the renewal itself. The state of the new political ideology at the end of the seventeenth century is exemplified in the political writings of Locke, especially in his *Treatises on Government* (1690). In these writings, according to Ashley, "Locke refuted the accepted Tory view of an absolutist monarchy deriving from a patriarchal view of society. [He] denied that men were born into political subjection. . . . On the contrary, [men were] born free and equal" (1973:242).

Ashley continues: "Locke's political ideas spread like wildfire . . . to France [and] were embedded . . . in the . . . American Constitution. . . . His ideas endured as the characteristic political philosophy of the governing classes of Great Britain for about two hundred years" (pp. 243–44). This spread was not in the least the effect of the incorporation of Locke's work into the body of Enlightenment thought. In Great Britain, Locke's views affected—directly and indirectly through their Enlightenment elaborations—later political doctrines, especially those which arose from the discrepancies between the promises of the Glorious Revolution and the daily practice of corrupt aristocratic rule. This rule is rather sharply characterized by Corrigan and Sayer, who state, "For much of the century, 'the State' was, not to put too fine a point on it, a racket, run by particular groups largely for their own benefit" (1991:89). The tension between ideal and practical reality manifested itself, time and again, in ideas, proposals, and actions concerning political reform.

In the realm of political thought, it is possible to discern, rather crudely, two types of doctrines regarding the reform of British politics. The first type is that of careful reform, which stays in line with the exigencies of reality and with the "law of historical continuity" (Lewis 1978:57). It represents the conservative interpretation of Locke's and Montesquieu's heritage and is exemplified in the work of Burke. The second type is the more radical variant, in which liberty and natural rights are extended to far more people and far more realms of life. A free and just society promises, in this second view, more happiness to more people. This type is, in its most extreme form, found in the life and work of Thomas Paine and—less extremely—in the person of Fox (in many respects the opposite of Burke in British politics).

Burke's work is, originally, an extension of Montesquieu's ideas on liberty and happiness to British society (its colonies included). It also represents a turn toward a more conservative direction in the political philosophy of the Enlightenment.[22] His leaning toward conservative points of view originates, above all, in his acceptance of the inevitable dark sides of reality, his reverence for existing institutions as the products of experience and the wisdom of the past, and his aversion to sudden changes. He made "a careful case . . . for reform when political institutions permitted despotism to deny liberty, or when political and civil liberty required reinforcement" (Anstey 1975:109). Abuses, per se, were for Burke not enough to demand reform—as abuses exist and are often necessary in all governments. Only great abuses do this because they impede good government and therewith the happiness of the people.

For British politics, this meant that Burke advocated mitigated political reforms that boiled down to the limitation of the powers of the Crown and the ministers in Great Britain and to the conception of imperial trusteeship (Lewis 1978) for its colonies. As for slavery, Burke accepted it as a necessary institution,[23] on the one hand, but, on the other, he supported Wilberforce's motions for total abolition of the slave trade in 1789 and 1791. It is no surprise that Burke already in the 1780s had put forward a plan to ameliorate the slave trade and slavery and, in 1792, a plan for gradual abolition of the trade. In spite of his conservative attitude and his acceptance of the painful necessities of social life, Burke saw in the end no place for slavery in society.

The radical variant of political reform thinking originated in the circles of the Rational Dissenters, who were compelled to live in the margin of official society. As they were excluded from the universities, they founded their own academies that were not bound to the traditional curriculum and were freer to teach new subjects—economics, history, and natural sciences—and to espouse new ideas, such as liberty, right, and reason. In the dissenting academies, these ideas were elaborated on in penetrating intellectual studies, giving them depth and universality and resulting in a philosophical liberalism with the academies as the main resource for political radicalism. The Rational Dissenters advocated political democracy of which the extension of the suffrage and profound reform of Parliament were the cornerstones. In this, they sympathized with Wilkes's struggle (not with his morals) and led the agitation for parliamentary reform, i.e., the association movement of Wyvill (Plumb [1950] 1968).

However, radical thought was more a potential for reform than a doctrine that guided a movement toward this goal. It took an insurrection, the American War of Independence, and a revolution in France to crystallize this potential into its radical Painite or its less radical Foxite form. In the words of Porter, "'Rights of Man' radicalism, republican toasts, dark mutterings about peers and priests being strung up—all, of course, tapped a libertarian rage that had flowed largely underground since the collapse of the Puritan revolution" (1990b:348). The first radicalization drew on the middle-class foundations laid by Rational Dissent and on the potential formed by the working men's friendly societies.[24] It formed a left wing of working men with middle-class leaders (Plumb [1950] 1968). The second was composed of young Whigs "devoted to parliamentary reform and the person of Fox" (p. 156). In both cases there was a true and deep aversion to slavery and the slave trade. Paine, for example, wrote an essay entitled *African Slavery in America* (1775) in which he characterized slavery as theft of freedom (Davis 1975). For Fox, abolition was a cause that he had always prized and in which he later actively engaged (Plumb [1950] 1968; Anstey 1975, see especially his treatment of the parliamentary proceedings concerning the abolition).

One of the effects of the development of ideas about social and political reform was that "change" became a more popular topic in the second half of the eighteenth century.[25] The intellectual climate of that period, in particular, favored ideas and actions toward the reformation of existing institutions and situations. This is seen in the support for Wilkes in his quest to warrant civil liberties, in the support for the American struggle for independence, and in the sympathetic receipt of the French Revolution in its early stages. Yet, this supporting climate proved to be rather volatile when actual violence broke out (see, for example, the reactions to the Gordon riots or to the Jacobin phase of the French Revolution). The enlightened mind was in favor of change but only when tempered by reason and calm deliberation. Such a climate was conducive to antislavery as it no longer simply accepted the self-evidence of the status quo (the age-old institution of slavery included). Moreover, the drive toward political reform seemed quite naturally to go hand in hand with antislavery,[26] although political reformers were more often also sympathetic to abolition than the other way round.

4.6 ECONOMIC THEORY

Slavery is an institution that is predominantly economically motivated.[27] It is a way to induce people to labor *and* to reap the fruits of their labor. Great Britain became involved in slavery through the trade in slaves in the second half of the sixteenth century. At a later date the involvement went further, as Britain also began employing slaves in its colonies to produce commodities like sugar, tobacco, coffee, and cotton. Slavery and the trade in slaves were both part of a closed economic circuit, the triangular trade. In this system, British ships brought British manufactures to Africa to buy slaves. They transported the slaves to the Americas and sold them mostly in British, French, and Spanish colonies. Then the ships took the produce of the colonies back to Great Britain and from there to other European countries.

This triangular trade system was an important element of an economic system, mercantilism, in which the national wealth (and thus strength) was seen as the product of economic activities, predominantly trade, backed by military power (see section 5.2 on mercantilism). In this politicoeconomic system "England's colonies . . . and her colonial trade [were] a vital part of the national strength" (Semmel 1970:6). The economic theory at the end of the seventeenth and in the first half of the eighteenth century justified—as economic theories often do—the monopolies in and the protection of trade and industry at home and abroad. An important defender of mercantilist economics, Malachy Postlethwait, depicted the British Empire as "a magnificent structure of American commerce and naval power on a African foundation" (cited in Lewis 1978:27). Moreover, he wrote in 1746, "The *Negroe-Trade* and the natural Consequences resulting from it, may be justly esteemed an inexhaustible Fund of Wealth and Naval Power to this Nation" (cited in Davis 1966:150).

Mercantilist economic theory, especially the ideas regarding colonial monopoly, protection, and in their wake often—but not necessarily—slavery,[28] came under fire from the 1750s onwards. New ideas about how to organize economic life arose in an effort to make sense of the economic transformation British society was undergoing in the eighteenth century. A growing economy after 1740, the extension of the colonial empire, and the expansion of the overseas trade led, among other things, to higher real incomes, more opportunities for advancement and new enterprises, and a growing demand and supply of erstwhile luxury goods, above all from the colonies. These developments led in turn to a commercialization of all realms of life, to a new commercial civilization (Plumb [1950] 1968; Temperley 1981; Porter 1990b). The answers to this transformation came predominantly from the moral philosophers of the Enlightenment, especially from those of the Scottish Enlightenment, notably John Millar and Adam Smith (Davis 1966; Phillipson 1981).

The first attack on colonial monopoly and protection was launched from mercantilist quarters. Josiah Tucker, a mercantilist economist who wrote primarily on questions of trade, developed—in reaction to Hume's theoretical ideas on trade—a "law," which stated "[t]hat *operose, or complicated Manufactures* are cheapest in rich Countries;—and *raw Materials* in poor ones: And therefore in Proportion as any Commodity approaches to one, or other of these *Extremes*, in that Proportion it will be found to be cheaper, or dearer in a rich, or a poor Country" (cited in Semmel 1970:16). Manufacturing countries could grow richer, thereby strengthening their position, if their entrepreneurs and merchants were free to buy raw materials at their cheapest and to sell the products made thereof at their dearest. In this way free trade, and not monopoly and protection, was the surest way to reach mercantilist goals and was thus in the national interest. In Tucker's eyes, "colonies were absolutely useless to Great Britain, and . . . the various restrictions of the old colonial system, so long regarded as of great advantage, were positively injurious to British commerce" (p. 20).

In France, another vision of the fundaments of the economic health of a country came forward. Here a group of economic theorists, the physiocrats, advanced a new economic doctrine in which land became the basis of all wealth. These economists "championed agrarianism and free trade, rustic simplicity and economic progress, natural rights and social utility [and were] highly critical of the wastefulness of the old colonial system" (Davis 1966:429). According to Semmel, who emphasizes the critical aspects of the physiocratic doctrine more strongly, the physiocrats "disavowed the commercial system root and branch, found trade wholly unproductive and the profits of foreign trade procured by a species of thievery" (1970:24). It is thus not surprising that the physiocrats were also critical of slavery; on the one hand because this institution was immoral, and on the other because it was—in the long run—uneconomical.

In Great Britain, an economic theory, partly under the influence of physiocratic thinking, arose in which the freedom of men as economic agents became the centerpiece. Its founder was Adam Smith, who developed his economic insights in the *Wealth of Nations* (1776). Adam Smith contends that man's main economic motive is to "better one's condition." This leads to profit-seeking behavior and, when not interfered with, to competition in the market in which people try to further their interests by offering what other people are looking for. The market—when free—functions as an invisible hand steering the outcome of man's economic activities, i.e., desired products and services at the lowest possible price (Brown 1992). This outcome is in the interest of all and this individual self-interest could—in the right circumstances—advance the public good (Davis 1966).

Smith's *Wealth of Nations* was the first reasoned critique of the mercantilist system; the economic notions developed therein put Smith and his followers fundamentally against monopoly, protectionism, and, as result, the way the colonial empire of Britain was organized (Semmel 1970). In Smith's view, "At every point, the mercantile system sacrificed the interest of the consumer of goods to that of the producer and the merchant; indeed, 'the home-consumers have been burdened with the whole expense of maintaining' the empire" (p. 25). This plea of Adam Smith for free trade, however, was a mixture of two different notions:[29] each notion having different consequences for the valuation of slavery and the slave trade.

The first notion sees free trade as the natural thing to do and sees, therefore, all economic activities that depend on government regulations and force as uneconomic by definition. The second notion is based on the view of free trade as the most efficient way—in terms of cost efficiency—of operating in the economic realm.[30] A system based on force, such as slavery, is, according to the second notion, uneconomical only if it can be proved that it is not profitable or at least less profitable than other systems. In the case of slavery and the slave trade this would have been very difficult, as both were profitable, at least in the 1780s.[31] This second notion is thus, in principle, far less useful in attacking slavery than the first.[32]

As Temperley (1977) shows, Smith's authoritative condemnation of slavery and the slave trade was based more on his view of slavery as an unnatural economic practice than on a comparison of its costs and profits.[33] Slavery flew in the face of his basic law of human motivation, i.e., men labor in order to acquire property. Moreover, when they are allowed to do so in freedom it will make them and others prosperous. Adam Smith (and the classical economists after him) assumed—and this was, after all, the British experience—that "freedom and prosperity went hand in hand" (p. 108). By definition, a system of forced labor could therefore not lead to the latter—generally desired—state. The rejection of slavery by Adam Smith became, because of his authority, common ground in economic thinking at the end of the eighteenth century. Moreover, his influence went further than the realm of the economists. As Semmel (1970) makes clear, his views also affected quite a few contemporary British politicians, notably Shelburne and Pitt. In Semmel's words:

It was in the second half of this [the eighteenth] century that a first generation of free-trade economists were to see colonies, regarded as a necessity
by the mercantilists, as useless, and to see the advantages of a freer foreign
trade to Great Britain if she were to maintain and extend her position. It
was at that time, also, that these political economists made their first
conversions among British statesmen; by the 1780s the converts [especially
Shelburne and Pitt] were seeking to put the new principles into practical
effect. (p. 13)

The economic theorizing of the last quarter of the eighteenth century
along with the general acceptance of the work of Adam Smith helped
antislavery become a part of the reigning ideology of the 1780s. Notably,
it made the assumption that slavery was an economic anachronism to an
uncontested wisdom (Temperley 1981). Even the "brilliant tribe" of political economists between Adam Smith and John Stuart Mill bypassed this
whole issue and never put this assumption to the test (Drescher 1977b).
This ideology reflected, as Davis (1975) contends, the needs and values
of the emerging capitalist order. It was, according to Temperley, "the
economic and social assumptions it [the emerging order] had conjured
up [which] threatened the slave societies . . . and not [its] economic
interests" (1985:106).[34] The economic ideas and assumptions could do so
because they facilitated the antislavery cause in two ways:

• They helped to shape a cultural climate that was conducive to
antislavery arguments as these ideas contradicted what people "had
hitherto taken for granted, namely that slavery was an economic necessity" (p. 105).
• They formed one of the resources for the abolitionist protagonists
to use in the abolition struggle. These protagonists were, as Temperley
(1981) states, fond of citing Adam Smith and used economic arguments
alongside other ones [see, for example, Davis (1975:352–53, note 11)
regarding the way Clarkson presented the case on the unprofitability of
the slave trade in 1787].

Still, the stock of free trade arguments was not the reserve of the abolitionists. Defenders of slavery and the slave trade also used free trade
arguments on occasion (see, for an example, Drescher 1976: note 49,
p. 195).

4.7 EIGHTEENTH-CENTURY CULTURAL CLIMATE AND ANTISLAVERY THOUGHT

Culturally, eighteenth-century Britain changed enormously. Following
the lead of John Locke, philosophers, religious thinkers, writers, and

various social, political, and economic theorists developed the ideological contours of the coming modern society with its cornerstones of political rights, constitutional democracy, free-market system, and predominance of individual self-governance. They did not, however, see the emergence of a new society as something that would occur automatically, but as the result of man's endeavors. Progress and happiness, freedom and prosperity were within reach if men would use the powers of reason that they possessed by nature. The eighteenth century in Great Britain was, moreover, not only the Age of Reason but one of compassion as well.

In relation to slavery, four elements of the evolving cultural climate stood out:

1. Liberty. Freedom was depicted as a normative end and as an empirical fact, at least as far as Great Britain was concerned. The emphasis on liberty, however, also implied the often still implicit condemnation of slavery. In the words of Drescher, "Throughout the entire period when Britons were expanding New World slavery, British pamphleteers, jurists, newspaper editors and geographers presented England as an island of liberty in a world filled with slaves" (1986:16–17).

2. Happiness. Striving toward one's own happiness and that of others was seen as a natural thing to do. As Anstey states, "happiness becomes the great principle of utility, and slavery, thereby, can only be wanting" (1975:404–5). The "gospel" of happiness, moreover, also enhanced the coming into being of the new ethic of benevolence (see below).

3. Benevolence. Empathy and doing good are seen both as an innate tendency of man and as a social duty, which induce "a heightened response to the need of the poor and outcast" (Anstey 1975:405). Davis (1966) typifies this response as a "cult of moral sensibility."

4. Reform. The secularly founded faith in progress combined with the religious doctrine of Providence brought reform to the fore of much eighteenth-century thought.[35] Social reform was a sensible thing to do and "a part of the divine plan" (Anstey 1975:404).

Together, the developments in the cultural realms led, among other things, to "a growing disposition to effect change in the area of natural, civil, and political liberty" (Anstey 1980:20). Evils in society were no longer—at least not all of them—accepted as inevitable. Recognition grew in intellectual circles that there were things in society that *should* and more importantly *could* be changed. As far as slavery was concerned, this institution was no longer accepted as a fact of life, and what was more, "fundamental in the whole attack on slavery was the belief that it was removable" (Temperley 1981:28–29).

These changes shaped a cultural climate with specific sets of ideas, beliefs, attitudes, and perceptions that had important consequences for the continuance of the acceptance of slavery and thus—in the end—for the possibilities of antislavery action. First, there were the ideas and views about Africa and the Africans, and subsequent changes therein.[36] British knowledge of Africa and black Africans, at the beginning of the eighteenth century, was mainly based on early travel accounts, reports of slave traders, and experiences with black slaves on West Indian plantations. As knowledge, it was partly based on facts and partly on fiction and myths. It was, moreover, often biased by the self-interests of traders and planters, and by the behavior of blacks in captivity. What was more, Africa was everything Britain was not: the fierce climate, the exuberant nature, the mysteries of the largely unknown inland, the nonfamiliar rituals and customs, the blackness of its people, and their nakedness.[37]

This negation of "Britishness" was on the whole negatively valued as it was ethnocentrically seen as the negation of true and civilized humanity. All in all, the image of the African at the beginning of the eighteenth century was quite diverse, shifting between recognition of the African as a human being—wholly in accordance to the Christian belief in the common nature and origin of mankind—and the negative depiction of the African as being subhuman, inferior, and related to apes. This latter—still a minority—depiction was strengthened by the growth of the slave trade in which blacks were dehumanized and treated as commodities.

During the eighteenth century the image of the African was further shaped under the influence of four trends:

1. The arising scientific interest and curiosity regarding non-European territories. This led to an extension of factual knowledge about Africa although, as Davis states, "[even] the most informed pictures of Africa were usually blurred by mists of exotic fantasy" (1966:464).

2. The implications of the moral philosophy of the Enlightenment for non-European peoples. In general, the Enlightenment thinkers pushed in the direction of including the Africans in the "human family" and toward the idea of the indivisibility of the rights of all men, black and white. This vision of the black African as a human being represents not so much a change in thinking as a continuation of a Christian tradition—the unified ancestry of all mankind. There were, however, opposite opinions—mostly based on antireligion motives—in which blacks were depicted as being naturally inferior (see, for example, Hume and Voltaire).

3. The literary cultivation of the myth of the noble savage. This biased the image of the African in the direction of the unrealistic portrayal of Africans as natural and virtuous beings uncorrupted by civilization.

4. The debate between antislavery and proslavery proponents resulting in the abolition struggle at the end of the century in which those opposed to slavery tended to exaggerate the positive characteristics of the black Africans and those in favor diminished them.

Because of the biases in these trends the image of the black African remained diverse, yet the trends also resulted in a rough consensus on three main points. First, the overall image of Africa remained unfavorable: "[d]espite attitudes varying between the extreme of sympathy and hostility toward the Negro" (Barker 1978:196). Second, blacks were recognized as human beings, i.e., the continuation of a long-standing Christian tradition. As Barker states, "eighteenth century thought [on the whole, proved unsuitable] as a vehicle for the pseudo-intellectual racism of Edward Long" (p. 84), although—as Drescher (1992) contends—Long's opinions were accepted by quite a few people. Third, a deeply entrenched ethnocentrism regarding the cultural inferiority of African culture permeated most of the accounts of Africa and the Africans. Blacks were depicted as primitive and culturally backward but nonetheless in possession—as all human beings—of the potential to improve. In general, "the Negro was seen as a man, certainly, but as a wild, untutored cousin rather than a brother" (Barker 1978:200).

The second important set of ideas, beliefs, and attitudes regards the way slavery was seen and the changes in that view (and consequently in the view of the slave trade). As Davis (1966) and Anstey (1975) show, slavery was an—albeit unpleasant—accepted fact of life at the beginning of the eighteenth century: "a necessary evil . . . not unmixed with blessings" (Davis 1966:396). Drescher aptly typifies the cultural context of British overseas slavery: "On the one hand it was treated as a stain from which British-born subjects were forever free. . . . On the other hand it was an overriding historical social fact" (1986:17). Davis and Anstey, however, both conclude that the view of slavery, particularly among the intellectual elite, changed dramatically during the century:

By the early 1770's a large number of moralists, poets, intellectuals, and reformers had come to regard American slavery as an unmitigated evil. (Davis 1966:488)

The world of the late eighteenth century was quite different [in terms of values, beliefs and attitudes.] Nowhere is the change of view more marked than in attitudes towards slavery and the slave trade. The plain fact is that little serious intellectual defence of slavery was any longer being attempted . . . the content of received wisdom had so altered by the 1780s that educated men and the political nation, provided they had no direct interest in the slave system, would be likely to regard slavery and the slave

trade as morally condemned, as no longer philosophically defensible. (Anstey 1975:94–96)

The third set of cultural ideas concerned the image of the West Indian
planter. As the eighteenth century passed and the West Indian colonies
flourished, Britain was increasingly confronted with the phenomenon of
the successful planter returning "home" "to buy a country seat, marry
into the country aristocracy, and found a family" (Lewis 1978:24). With
his wealth he bought political influence, especially to defend the protected West Indian interests against the encroaching free trade policies,
invested his money in the metropolitan economy, and often led a life full
of luxuries and extravagances. Above all, his nouveau riche behavior
was out of tune with the staunch English society dominated by the
landed aristocracy and gentry. Moreover, it clashed with the puritanic
streak in this society, prominently present in the rising middling classes.

All in all, the West Indian was viewed rather negatively in British
society, as is clearly shown in the literature of the eighteenth century (see
Sypher [1942] 1969:86–90 on this). He was depicted as arrogant, coarse,
overbearing, spendthrift, devoid of taste, and licentious and was, according to Sypher, "an odious figure in the eyes of most" (p. 86). The negative
aspects of this image were further strengthened by the way whites be-
haved in the West Indies. On the one hand, their behavior was associated
with greed and avarice in its ruthless and brutal exploitation of slaves, and
on the other, with immorality due to excessive drinking, concubinage,
and other sexual depravities (Davis 1975; Drescher 1986). Somehow, the
unmitigated drive for wealth responsible for the slave trade and slavery
corrupted the image of the West Indian and therewith the slave system
"could symbolize all the forces that threatened to unravel the fabric of
traditional deference, patronage, and hereditary status" (Davis 1975:453–
54). This way it could corrupt all involved in slavery.

From the 1760s onwards it is clear that a cultural climate emerged that
represented "a cast of thought which [was] increasingly incompatible
with slavery and which [leaned] tentatively towards the possibility and
desirability of appropriate reforms" (Anstey 1975:96–97). There was,
however, an important exception to this trend. The Enlightenment produced a belief that impeded actions against slavery, i.e., the sanctity of
the right of property (see Porter 1990b:136–37 for illuminating illustra-
tions). This right was depicted—as we have seen before—as the very
foundation of liberty and it was as such (by definition) opposed to emancipation. The cause of antislavery (the abolition of the slave trade included) in the eighteenth century was continually adversely affected not
only because the political elites and the public believed in this sanctity
but because the abolitionists did (and very strongly) as well.

The developments in the cultural realms are important in that they:

1.   formed the resources on which sponsors and movement entre-preneurs might draw to forge the symbolical weapons for their abolition struggle;
2.   changed the way of thinking of the right-minded part of the nation that then could filter into the other strata of society;
3.   changed the conduciveness of the cultural climate. Most of the developments made the climate more conducive to antislavery actions, but one—the increasing emphasis on the right of property—made it less conducive because it acted as an important constraint on these actions.

Anstey characterizes the importance of eighteenth-century cultural changes at the end of his study of the abolition of the slave trade in Great Britain in the following manner:

> All in all changes in ideas have been shown to be both more and less important than is commonly supposed: more important, because the marked anti-slavery tendency of eighteenth-century thought, and the change in intellectual climate which resulted, have been demonstrated with some thoroughness; less important because a change in ideas has been shown to have been unable of itself to end the slave trade, let alone slavery. (1975:405)

NOTES

1.   The term *philosophe* does not fully correspond with the modern descrip-tion of a philosopher. *Philosophe* is "best translated as 'a man of letters who is also a freethinker'" (Hamilton 1992:24).
2.   In the case of British antislavery this route through time is clearly visible. The British antislavery writers leaned rather heavily on the work of the Ameri-can Quaker Anthony Benezet, who was in turn greatly indebted to Montesquieu and the Scottish Enlightenment writers.
3.   So much so that Aron (1965) considers Montesquieu one of the great sociological theorists.
4.   In this work, Montesquieu reconciles his empirical stance that nature is to be found in factual social arrangements and his normative preference for liberty and equality by stating the primacy of moral considerations. For instance, climatic factors may promote the institution of slavery but they do not determine its establishment. Authorities can always counteract these natural tendencies on moral grounds (Aron 1965). Wise sovereigns, in the view of Davis, "would shape and adjust institutions in conformity with natural law" (1966:405).
5.   As Aron states, "Montesquieu . . . was in no sense a doctrinaire of equality" (1965:59). He accepted inequality as an inevitable fact of social life but

here again he felt that existing inequalities could be moderated on moral grounds.

6.   The following citations taken from Anstey sufficiently illustrate Hutcheson's strong feelings in this respect: "All men have strong desires of liberty and property, have notions of right, and strong natural impulses to marriage, families, and offspring, and earnest desires of their safety . . . no endowments, natural or acquired, can give a perfect right to assume power over others, without their consent" (1975:100–1).

7.   As Davis (1966) shows, this new emphasis on benevolence did not originate with Hutcheson. It was as much a product of the seventeenth century, especially of the religious conflicts in that period.

8.   As Davis (1966) shows, Enlightenment ideas could be (and were) used almost as easily to justify slavery. Especially the fact that slavery was an age-old institution made it easy to contend that it was obviously in concordance with natural reason.

9.   Of these contests, the one at Cambridge University in 1785 has become the most well-known, not in the least through its resulting in the conversion of its indefatigable apostle Thomas Clarkson to the cause of antislavery.

10.   For Colley (1992), the combination of the religious and political conflicts, i.e., protestant vs. Roman Catholic and England vs. France, led to the "coming-into-being" of Great Britain as a nation and the accompanying specific British national identity, of which Protestantism became the cornerstone.

11.   This vision is in part a consequence of the scientific revolution, but one that is based on the conviction that religion is not incompatible with this new science. As Zaret (1989) contends, this conviction contributed to the rise of a different version of Protestantism in which nature—just as in empirical science—gives answers to all kinds of questions in the realm of religion.

12.   Missionaries employed slaves in their houses and the missionary organization of the church (the Society for the Propagation of the Gospel, SPG) even got involved in the exploitation of two plantations in Barbados. These were meant as models to show that a Christian, humane, and profitable exploitation of slave labor was possible. This experiment failed signally and the treatment of slaves at the S.P.G. plantations was as bad (if not worse) as at the other plantations.

13.   Nonetheless, Baxter accepted slavery under restricted conditions.

14.   Barry, for example, in his study of Bristol finds that in this city the "public demand for belles-lettres, science and similar topics" was growing in the 1740s and 1750s (1991:62). Oldfield (1989) points to the same tendency in another segment of literature, viz., literature for children, which grew rapidly after 1750.

15.   The characterization of printed matter in this period is based on Plumb ([1950] 1968), Altick ([1957] 1983), Speck (1983), Oldfield (1989), Hunter (1990), and Barry (1991).

16.   As Altick ([1957] 1983) shows, this demand originates in the fundamental transformation of British society in this age.

17.   This turn was strengthened in Great Britain by related developments in the realm of religion. See Section 4.3. Davis also gives a good example of these developments (see 1966:351–52).

18. The following part of this section is based mainly on Sypher ([1942] 1969), Davis (1966), and Anstey (1975).

19. The book was transformed into a play that remained very popular for many years.

20. There were other popular legends in the noble Negro tradition, but these were not pivotal. See Sypher ([1942] 1969:137–44) on these legends.

21. Important writers in this period were: (1) Daniel Defoe, who wrote *Robinson Crusoe*, in which slavery was an accepted fact of life, but who also wrote "the earliest unmistakably anti-slavery verse in the eighteenth century [in] his biting *Reformation of Manners* (1702)," (Sypher [1942] 1969:157); (2) Laurence Sterne, the writer of *Tristram Shandy* (1767), a book full of sentiment and the most important and widely read novel of the eighteenth century (Rice 1980); (3) *Thomas Day,* who wrote the immensely popular poem *The Dying Negro* (1773); and (4) Henry Mackenzie, with his *Man of Feeling,* a book whose title epitomizes the literature of that age.

22. According to Porter (1981), Burke abandoned the Enlightenment altogether. This occurred, however, only after the outbreak of the French Revolution, which "radicalized" Burke, and many others in Great Britain, in the opposite direction. See also Plumb, who depicts Burke after 1789 as an "erstwhile reformer" ([1950] 1968:156).

23. As Davis (1966) contends, Burke had stated already in 1757 that nothing could justify the slave trade (which included the murder of several thousand innocent men) but the necessity to people the colonies and the consideration that these slaves were already slaves in Africa.

24. Ironically, the new dissent of Wesley had done much to free the lower classes from their social lethargy: It "had loosened fiery tongues which easily switched from religious to political scores" (Porter 1990b:349), although Methodism itself was fiercely antirevolutionary.

25. As Colley states, the very legitimacy of the power elite was called into question in this period and "from the 1780s . . . this kind of criticism enter[ed] the main stream of political discourse in Britain" (1992:152). The popularity of *The Rights of Man* by Thomas Paine gives an indication of the extent of discontent with existing society: Volume 1 of this book sold some 50,000 copies in 1791 and volume 2 about 200,000 by 1793 (Tilly 1991:1).

26. As Blackburn (1988) contends, the 1760s and 1770s were a period of a profound social and imperial crisis in Britain in which conflicts were often conceived in terms of the opposition between freedom and tyranny, and liberty and slavery.

27. This is at least the case in the Americas in the seventeenth and eighteenth century when the exploration of the colonies was part of the economics of mercantilism. Yet, slavery is—as Davis (1966) contends—always more than an economic system. It is the ultimate debasement of humanity and it often functions as a forceful symbol of human depravity in other realms as well.

28. As Drescher rightly contends, the existing relationship of slavery with overseas colonies does not mean that slavery is a necessary element of mercantilism. Slavery and the slave trade could perfectly accommodate the conditions of free trade and free trade capitalism as they already partly did (see, in particular, 1977b:174–77; see also Davis 1975:358 on this point).

29.   Hilton discerns in this respect "two discrete, if sometimes overlapping, models of Free Trade in the first half of the nineteenth century" (1988:69). The first originated in the Scottish political economy and was later appropriated by evangelically inspired economists, both of which contributed to its moral undertone; the second is the now dominating economic model in the English political economy, with its leaning to utilitarianism and materialism.

30.   The first notion is on the one hand inspired by the ideas of the French *philosophes* and physiocrats and on the other owes much to emerging religious conception of Providence. As Anstey states, Smith's invisible hand "is an important part of Smith's ideas of Providence" (1975:118). The second notion fits in very well with the emerging dominance of utility in Enlightenment thinking in Great Britain.

31.   On the topic of profitability see Drescher's *Econocide* (1977a). As Davis (1966) shows, the fact that slavery was profitable posed problems for Adam Smith. See, for example, Drescher (1977a:434–35) about the way he tried to solve paradoxes and puzzles in his treatment of slavery.

32.   Nevertheless, "the main stream of Utilitarian thought, beginning with Bentham and William Paley, was profoundly antithetical to West Indian slavery" (Davis 1975:354, note 13). But Davis acknowledges at the same time, "Logically, the rapid growth of Utilitarianism should have been a boon to the defenders of colonial slave trade" and utilitarian arguments were actually used in defense of slavery (pp. 353–54).

33.   "If we look at the evidence [Adam Smith] cites one thing is immediately clear: it is not based on any sort of cost analysis. This is surprising because elsewhere in *The Wealth of Nations* he shows himself perfectly capable of reckoning profit and loss" (Temperley 1977:107).

34.   These assertions have provoked a prolonged debate regarding the question of the relationship between capitalism and antislavery, particularly regarding the question in what manner and to what degree antislavery functioned as an ideology validating and legitimating the emerging capitalist industrial order. This debate came forth from a restatement of the strong thesis by Williams; the "softer" version put the relationship in terms of ideology. See, among others, Drescher and Davis in Solow and Engerman (1987); Davis (1992), Haskell (1992), and Ashworth (1992) in *The Antislavery Debate;* and Drescher in a thorough review of that book (1993) and in a recent paper in the *American Historical Review* (1994b).

This debate extends far beyond the point made in this section, viz., showing the relationship between the work of Adam Smith and the abolition struggle. As this relationship only regards one element in the first abolition campaign, we will refrain from entering this debate. The extent of the contribution that Adam Smith's thinking made in this struggle will become clear in Chapter 7.

35.   Progress as a secular faith rested on the notion that a better society could be reached if one followed the guidelines of reason. The religious foundation of the idea of progress consisted of (1) the belief that God reveals to man bit by bit what his plans are, i.e., the notion of "revelation as progressive" and (2) "the necessary corollary that the Christian was called to new commitments, as he received new revelations" (Anstey 1980:20).

36.   Alongside the literature mentioned earlier (see preface), we have used

Walvin (1973) and Barker (1978) on the subject of the image of Africa and its inhabitants. We abstained, however, from going too deeply into the subtleties of the argument on black images, as this would lead to a study of its own (see, for example, the discussion between Barker and Walvin regarding the role black presence played in Britain).

37.   Especially the color of skin and absence of clothing were the opposite of British life. Black was already a color to which negative connotations had been attached for a long time. Its opposite, white, was, moreover, at its peak of positive valuation at the time of the first British-African contacts in the Elizabethan era. Nakedness was almost self-evidently—in the context of British puritanism and prudery—related to sexual depravity and loose morals.

5

From England to British Empire:
Structural Transformations in the Eighteenth Century

5.1 INTRODUCTION

The beginning of the eighteenth century was quite different from the preceding seventeenth century. The force of the Puritan rebellion and the reaction to it had by then subsided. The turmoils of the seventeenth century had ended with the Glorious Revolution, sanctified by the Christian rationalist John Locke; both this revolution and the ensuing war against France had brought England to the beginning of modernity. The country had become far more prosperous than it had been at the beginning of the seventeenth century; it was at last united with Scotland into one kingdom, Great Britain; and an overseas empire had come into being. Politically, the contours of a modern constitutional monarchy and democratic state became visible in which the power of the Crown was circumscribed, a cabinet with a prime minister emerged, the House of Commons rose—carefully but steadily—to a position of dominance, and political parties became important political actors (Ashley 1973).

The main trend with regard to the structural transformation of Great Britain in this century, along with the aforementioned reconstruction of society, was Britain's rise to world dominance. In the seventeenth century, Britain and France surpassed Holland as hegemonic world powers. The next century subsequently became the stage for a new struggle for world hegemony, this time between France and Great Britain (Wallerstein 1980). This contest was waged in three domains: First, there was the struggle on the military plane. There were French-Anglo wars in the beginning, in the middle, and in the last part of the eighteenth century of which the Seven Years War (1756–1763) proved to be decisive. Britain established its military superiority predominantly at sea and in the western hemisphere with a view, above all, to the contest in the second domain, the economic one. The economic contest was waged in the field of commerce, and trade was seen as the foundation of wealth and power

(Plumb [1950] 1968). At the heart of the British strategy was a mercantilist policy in which military power backed up the protection of commercial activities, i.e., agriculture, the overseas trade, and Britain's industry.
The third domain of struggle was on the ideological level. As Colley
(1992) shows, the British nation was forged in the wars with France.
These wars led to a specific British identity in which the emphasis was
placed on everything France (often allegedly) was not, specifically with
regard to the self-definition of a Briton as being Protestant and as a free
citizen with political rights.

The effects of the reconstruction after 1688 and the simultaneous rise
to world dominance were radical in terms of the structure of British
society. In the following, we will look consecutively into each of these
effects insofar as they bear on the question of the emergence of antislavery. The first effect is the extension of the British empire with the concomitant growing involvement in slavery (Section 5.2). The second effect
concerns the emergence of commercial capitalism as the dominant system in Britain and its transformation into a new form, industrial capitalism (Section 5.3). Thereafter, the focus will be placed on the (de facto)
political system and its consequences (Section 5.4) and on the related
organization of religion (Section 5.5) in Great Britain. Section 5.6 will be
devoted to one of the most typical outgrowths of commercialization, the
emerging media as link between public and polity. In the last section,
the effects of the systemic transformation of Britain will be summarized.

5.2 GREAT BRITAIN AS EMPIRE

The formation of the British Empire originated during the reign of
King James I at the beginning of the seventeenth century. It was not the
product of a conscious colonial policy, but the result of disparate initiatives: undertaken mostly by adventurers, merchants, and sectarian fugi-
tives, backed by the military power of the Crown. The military was
especially important and this empire (usually referred to as the first
empire) "like all empires, was acquired chiefly by the exercise of military
and naval strength" (Ashley 1973:215–16). The underlying motives were
mainly economic and arose from the quest for precious metals, the need
for naval supplies, and the demand for spices. During the seventeenth
and eighteenth centuries, the foreign colonies became above all the
"supplier of goods that were needed and could not be produced at home
or might be re-sold profitably abroad," which concerned goods such as
fish, lumber, sugar, and tobacco (p. 225; see also Craton 1974:xix).

The process of empire formation advanced gradually throughout the
seventeenth century and accelerated at the beginning of the eighteenth

century with the Treaty of Utrecht (1713), which "was a milestone on the road that led to the first British empire" (Ashley 1973:215). With the signing of the treaty, Britain acquired Hudson Bay, Novia Scotia, Newfoundland, and the West Indian island of St. Kitts from France. The empire was completed in 1763 after the Seven Years' War, when Great Britain became the sole colonial power in eastern North America. The most important parts of the colonial empire were the colonies in the West Indies, especially Jamaica, Barbados, and the Bahamas; those in North America, such as New England, Pennsylvania, Virginia, and Canada; and the trading posts in India and West Africa. The crux of this first empire was the Atlantic triangle formed by Britain itself, West Africa, and the North American and West Indian colonial possessions.

The British Empire, especially the first one, was organized around a specific economic system, i.e., mercantilism. The core mercantilist idea was that national wealth was represented by the amount of precious metals hoarded, metals that could only be acquired through trade.[1] The advantages of trade could in turn only be secured by military power—in this case naval power—the amount of which then depended on the successes in the realm of trade. The pivotal position of trade—which gave mercantilism its name—is succinctly typified by Plumb: "Trade was wealth and power" ([1950] 1968:112). British military might protected agriculture and industry within Great Britain, the trade executed by British ships, and the tropical product–producing plantations in the colonies from the competition from others, especially France and the Low Countries. In the British case, this meant, above all, protection of and monopolies for private entrepreneurs and traders, making for a curious mix of mercantilist policies and ruthless individual enterprise under the mantle of British mercantilism (Watson 1963).

Thus, the first British Empire was the politicoeconomic combination of naval power, commercial conquest, protection, and monopoly (Wallerstein 1980; Inikori and Engerman 1992). It is (with an emphasis on its colonial part) described by Semmel in the following manner:

> According to mercantilist canon, colonies were prized because their possession made more practicable the autarchic ideal of a self-sufficient empire, with colonies supplying needed imports rather than the competing foreigner, thereby bringing profits to one's own countrymen, helping to conserve the necessary hoard of the precious metals, and even, possibly, through re-export of staples, helping to increase that hoard. The colonial would serve as a customer of metropolitan manufactures—industries which might compete with those of the mother country were prohibited in the colonies—and as a supplier of tropical products, for the colonialism of the eighteenth century, resting upon sea-power, was based upon the trade in the staples, like tobacco, sugar, coffee, tea, spices, raised mostly by

slave labor in the New World or in East Asia. (1970:19; see also the depiction by Williams [1944] 1972:56)

In the mercantilist system of the British Empire, slavery was one of the important elements (Craton 1974). First, African slaves were a commodity in which British merchants traded from the end of the sixteenth century onwards. In particular, obtaining the *asiento*—the right to supply Spanish colonies with slaves—with the Peace of Utrecht in 1713 boosted the British slave trade, and in the eighteenth century Great Britain became the largest trader in slaves. This contributed greatly to the incorporation of West Africa, as a peripheral economy, into the world economy (Wallerstein 1989). Second, the plantation economies of the West Indies and partly of North America depended heavily on slave labor. The empire thus meant the creation of a new "division of labor across diverse regions of the world, all linked together by the Atlantic Ocean" (Inikori and Engerman 1992:9). Moreover, it meant creating a system of forced labor "beyond the line" that divided the metropolis from its overseas colonies (Drescher 1986).

Shortly after the conclusion of the Seven Years' War in 1763, difficulties arose between the metropolis and its colonies in North America. Due partly to the disappearance of the French threat to the American colonies, partly to the negative effects of mercantilism on the colonies, and partly to the awkward handling of these difficulties, a serious conflict arose, which led to the war of independence waged by the American colonists (1775–1783).[2] In 1783, Great Britain recognized American independence and the United States were born.

American independence meant the end of the first empire and—according to Williams ([1944] 1972)—destroyed the mercantile system. This, however, can better be termed the beginning of the end of this system. As Eric Stokes states in his foreword to Anstey's book on the abolition of the slave trade, "Britain retained down to the 1850s an essentially protectionist and in many ways mercantilist economy" (1975:xii). Drescher (1976) comes essentially to the same conclusion as he asserts that the swing to free trade principles does not occur earlier than the 1820s. As far as slavery is concerned, American independence meant that the potential for resisting the later antislavery attacks was severely curtailed; potential all-American Interest became West Indian Interest (cf. Williams [1944] 1972:124). At the same time, however, support for the antislavery cause in these former colonies remained intact, and this support played a pivotal role in the later abolition struggle.

The formation of the British Empire meant an ever-expanding involvement in black slavery and in the slave trade between West Africa and the Americas. The first effect of this extension concerns the profits of this growing involvement. As Britain gained substantially from slavery and the slave trade,[3] maintaining both was thus in the national interest (Craton 1974; Drescher 1986). This interest was an important barrier for antislavery activities, especially because not only were the slave trade and the overseas plantations positively valued, but the slave trader and the West Indian planter were also "[i]n the England of George II . . . socially respectable" (Davis 1966:154).[4] The second effect was the emergence of two different labor systems: i.e., formally free labor in Britain and forced labor in its colonies (Drescher 1986). Moreover, this occurred when forced labor in northwestern Europe was disappearing and in most cases was already something of the past (Davis 1966). Furthermore, in Great Britain this disappearance was accompanied by a rising positive valuation of freedom that made the world no longer safe for slavery. The result of all this was an anomaly that contained a potential contradiction. This was especially the case in Great Britain, where the number of black slaves coming from the West Indies was growing during the eighteenth century, negatively affecting the main protection of British slavery, its geographical insulation (Drescher 1986).

5.3 FROM COMMERCIAL TO INDUSTRIAL CAPITALISM

Eighteenth-century Britain was the arena in which the economic forces freed "by the Civil War and the Glorious Revolution from anachronistic parasiticism" clashed, and a new economic order, capitalism, was forged (Smith 1991:177).[5] Although the shaping of the basic conditions for this order, especially the relations of production, had taken place in the previous century,[6] the eighteenth century was—alongside the age of reason and of compassion—"the age of *commercial* capitalism" (Porter 1990b:187). Britain's economic life was infused, in all aspects, with capital and new capitalist values and relations prevailed. As Smith contends, attitudinal changes were rather important in this transformation of society. Actors in economic life, such as farmers, artisans, merchants, and entrepreneurs, became more and more oriented to:

- Making profits in order to invest these profits to make more profit in order to invest these profits, etc., in other words, a life dedicated to the endless cycle of profit and investment. This orientation is depicted by Weber as the spirit of modern capitalism, which focuses on "the earning of more and more money . . . as the ultimate purpose [in] life" ([1920] 1976:53).
- Viewing "things in life"—useful products, agreeable services, products of art, etc.—as goods or commodities that could be made or

performed *and* sold for a profit, i.e., things of utility came to be seen primarily as having (money) value in exchange rather than being useful—or as Marx states—as having use value (Marx [1887] 1965, see especially Chapter II, pp. 84–93).

This capitalization of social life could be seen, above all, in the realms of production, trade, and the conditions for both. First, the sphere of production was increasingly capitalized. In agriculture, enclosure demanded considerable outlays of capital for "new roads, fencing, walls, hawthorne hedges, farmhouses, barns, cottages and perhaps drainage systems" (Porter 1990b:208). This was also the case with regard to applying innovations in agriculture. The agricultural undertakings in the colonies, especially the big plantations, also demanded large amounts of capital. The same applies to the industry in Great Britain itself, where in the bosom of the traditional, guild-organized, artisanal mode of production the figure of the capitalist entrepreneur developed.[7]

Second, the economic queen of eighteenth-century Britain, commerce, drew a lot of capital into its activities. As described above, Great Britain in the eighteenth century was primarily a mercantile nation, a dominance to which most other realms of society—production, the military, politics, the arts, etc.—were geared. According to Smith, "England's domination of world commerce during the first quarters of the eighteenth century was unprecedented" (1991:187). The internal trade of Britain had, in the preceding century, developed from a regional network into a national one (Lie 1993). Trade with other countries—first northwest Europe, then the Mediterranean, and finally other parts of the world—grew quickly in this period; this demanded capital as well. In this, the colonial trade had an important place: it provided an outlet for British agriculture and industry; it supplied British citizens with dearly wanted tropical products; and it made the profitable reexport of colonial products possible.

Third, the conditions that fostered the growth of production and of trade needed their share of capital. One of the most important conditions was the physical infrastructure, i.e., roads, canals, docks, and ships. All these were vastly improved during the eighteenth century. The same was true for the financial structure, i.e., banks, credit facilities, paper money, etc., which profited from the existence of a favorable political and legal infrastructure. Finally, the burst of inventions, especially toward the end of the century, demanded much capital to apply them in the new factories and workshops.

The beginning of the eighteenth century witnessed an economic life—in agriculture, industry, and trade—that was still highly traditional and essentially rurally based. Up to the 1740s, there were only limited changes in this situation and, most importantly, the changes occurring in technology were nominal. As Porter states, "Improvement occurred through the piecemeal modification of existing technologies within traditional employment structures" (1990b:196), and in his view the economy at the beginning of the century was "continuing on a plateau" (p. 205). The situation in agriculture was, however, somewhat different as the gradual growth of the seventeenth century continued, regardless of the regular conjunctural ups and downs. In the words of Smith, "During the late seventeenth and eighteenth centuries, English agriculture continued to improve" (1991:178).

From the mid-1740s, the situation changed, bringing with it more rapid demographic and economic growth. The population started to grow again, which boosted demand and cheapened labor, leading then to economic growth. In the 1770s, this growth was further stimulated by technological innovations, particularly in the textile and iron industry, by scaling up the production units, and by extending the division of labor. Equally helpful were the improvements in transportation, e.g., the building of canals, the reconstruction of docks and harbors, and the constructions of (mostly turnpike) roads. Alongside these developments, enclosure was speeded up, which fundamentally altered the physical and social landscape of rural England. The enclosure movement further rationalized agriculture and boosted output and profits. "By the mid-eighteenth century it [Great Britain] was essentially a highly prosperous commercial economy, with an equally efficient (and unique) agricultural sector" (Rubinstein 1993:34).

From the late 1770s onward the pace of economic growth quickened.[8] The trends of the previous decades, such as road and canal building, enclosure and improvement of agricultural techniques, and the development of the financial infrastructure, continued, but the sheer magnitude of the cumulative effects of these developments caused the onset of a vast and rapid transformation of society. The rise in population lasted, which was especially important, and—as Porter makes clear—the quickening of the economic growth and the population increase sustained each other; they "went hand-in-glove" (1990b:311). In this period emphasis began to shift from agriculture to industry, the reason why this period is referred to as the Industrial Revolution.[9]

New in this period were technological breakthroughs in certain industries: the mechanization of the cotton industry, e.g., Arkwright's water frame (1769), Hargreaves's jenny (1770), Cartwright's power loom (1785); the emergence of a new technology of coal and iron, e.g., the substitution of coke and charcoal and the large-scale production of wrought iron; and in all industries, at the end of the century, the replacement of human, animal, wind, and water power with steam power after

James Watt perfected the steam engine in 1769. This breakthrough led to more and better products, new applications (e.g., iron ships and bridges), and, above all, to labor-saving devices. New technologies combined with improved industrial organization boosted the output of products and the productivity of labor. The rise in labor productivity cheapened production costs and therewith lowered the prices of the finished products (and thus enlarged demand).

However, the technological breakthroughs would not have had these effects without the existence of the firm foundation described above, of which the most important elements were the presence of accessible natural resources like coal and iron; a growing population (and thus a growing labor force); the agricultural capacity to feed this growing population; the favorable infrastructure; and the advantages connected with a dominant position in an evolving world economy, especially the growing outlets for the increasing output and the influx of capital coming from trade and from the colonies (and, with that, from the trade in African slaves and the employment of their labor; see, among others, Inikori 1987; Solow 1987). Summarized, three types of interrelated economic changes were taking place: the rise of capitalist relations, the commercialization of society, and the onset of the Industrial Revolution.[10]

In this constellation of conditions one central element is missing, viz., the figure of the capitalist entrepreneur. The entrepreneurs forged a new world with the means just described. In the view of Porter, "their personal innovating role often proved decisive [and] entrepreneurs were ploughing virgin fields, having to excel as capitalist, financier, technocrat, works manager, engineer, merchant and salesman all in one. Only in England did entrepreneurs become so prominent so early" (1990b:320). At the end of the eighteenth century then, the capitalist transformation of Great Britain was completed, an industrial society was born, and Britain was on its way to becoming the main commercial power and workshop of the world.

Black slavery "played a major role in the early development of the New World and in the growth of commercial capitalism" (Davis 1966:10). The capitalists incorporated this system of forced labor—though alien to its free-market core—into their market-oriented behavior with little trouble. In the words of Temperley, "Slavery might be socially regressive but economically it made sense" (1977:95). Slavery played its role in the emerging capitalist system in two ways. First, the trade in African slaves provided, on the one hand, a profitable outlet for British products and, on the other, a commodity for trade in the Americas. Second, slavery formed the basic system of labor in most colonies, especially those most highly valued. In the eighteenth century "there was no competitive alternative to slave-grown cotton or sugar" or to other tropical products

(Drescher 1986:9). The growing involvement of Britain in the trade in slaves and in the exploitation of their labor was not only indissolubly connected with the growth of the first British Empire, but also with the development of capitalism within Britain itself. This combination of empire and capitalism led, moreover, to the aforementioned anomaly (and potential contradiction) regarding the dominant labor system in the imperial possessions—slavery—and the dominant labor system in the metropolis—formally free labor.[11]

The transformation of British society in the eighteenth century was great. First, there was the geographic transition. Although Britain "was still essentially an agricultural community in the 1780s" (Briggs 1959:36), its urbanization, especially due to the growth of the new industrial towns, was progressing at a fast pace. Moreover, the economic focal point was shifting from southeast England to the north.

Second, the conditions of life were also changing rapidly. On the one hand, conditions were deteriorating for many, among other things due to low-paying jobs, to working long hours in poorly equipped factories, to living in bad housing and in other unhygienic circumstances, and to a lack of social security facilities. On the other hand, enormous fortunes were amassed by the happy few, the old elites and the newcoming colonial and industrial ones, who imparted a portion of their gains to a retinue of factors, agents, clerks, overseers, shopkeepers, servants, etc. The growing prosperity of a part of the population can, among other things, be deduced from the rising importance of fashion and from the commercialization of leisure activities; Britain became a bustling consumer society (Oldfield 1995).

Third, the relations of production started to change as well. There was, for example, a gradual shift in the dominance of property in land— the basis of social and political power in eighteenth-century Britain—to property in industry (Nisbet 1966). The emergence of the factory and manufacturing also meant that people, above all artisans, increasingly lost control over their work: "industrialization . . . spelt the iron cage of working six days a week, every week" (Porter 1990b:336).

Fourth, capitalism and industrialization contributed to the breakdown of the traditional order: as Dr. Johnson tersely remarked, "Gold and silver destroy feudal subordination" (citation: Briggs 1959:15). In particular, the unmitigated drive for wealth and for advantages in the market threatened the old order, in which daily life was embedded in the regionally bounded structures of rural society. The more closely knit relationships inherent to this society were increasingly transposed to the impersonal, cash nexus–based relations of modern society; as a consequence, face-to-face contacts gave way to contacts between anonymous roleplayers related to each other via the upcoming media, especially newspapers and magazines. In Toennies's metaphoric depiction, *Gemeinschaft* was on its way to being replaced by *Gesellschaft*.

Briggs describes the profound transformation of eighteenth-century Britain in the following manner:

> The changes of the late eighteenth century were social and intellectual as well as technical and economic. They were associated with a great increase in population, a further expansion of trade, the emergence of new social groups—both "captains of industry" and factory labour—the creation of new political pressures and new social institutions, new modes of thought and action, and, above all, the foundation of a new view of society. (1959:20)

One of these transformations we have singled out because it was of importance to antislavery. This concerns the emergence of new social categories,[12] namely, the middling classes and the mostly urban proletariat. Modern society witnessed the rise of industrialists, entrepreneurs, and merchants, a large part of whom did not originate in the old elites. It also saw the emergence of the lower middling stations in society, such as clerks, shopkeepers, and small traders. Parts of these upcoming new middle classes proved to be rather susceptible to the nonconformist, especially evangelical message; their members joined, in fairly large numbers, nonconformist and evangelical groupings. These groups were later to play an important role in the abolition movement; they provided the movement with its leaders and functioned as conscience constituencies from which the movement mustered its support.

The proletariat was on the whole excluded from civil (i.e., social, political, and economic) society and its members were neglected as well by the official Anglican church. After the 1770s, Wesley and his Methodists made up for this neglect, and by incorporating the lower classes into the Methodist denomination they drew an important part of the proletariat into the social fabric of society as well. As we will see later, Methodism became one of the pillars of the abolition movement and in so doing brought this part of the proletariat into the conscience constituency of the abolition movement.[13]

5.4   OLIGARCHIC RULE

Politically, the most important effect of the Glorious Revolution was the circumscription of the power of the English monarchy: "absolutism was finished" (Ashley 1973:251).[14] Parliament became the center of political power, in the words of Plumb, "Parliament and its control had become the way to power" ([1950] 1968:39), although the king retained many of his prerogative powers, especially the power to dispense of the ever-growing spoils of the developing first empire. The result was the emergence of an elliptical political system with two interdependent hubs around which political influence and power could be wielded, viz., the king and his ministers, and Parliament. Much of eighteenth-century British political history concerns the struggle for power among the political elites, e.g., the question of the Hannoverian succession, the competition between the landed Tories and the Whig magnates, or the Stuart monarchy as in the Jacobite uprising of 1745. Most of these struggles do not have direct bearing on (anti)slavery and therefore will not be dealt with here.

There was, however, one structural development that proved to be important for antislavery. The two-hub political system as it emerged at the end of the seventeenth century was inherently unstable, as it was neither a constitutional monarchy nor an absolutist state. Anyone who aspired to rule Britain needed the prerogative powers of the Crown as well as a majority in Parliament. This problem was solved in the first half of the eighteenth century by developing an oligarchic system in which the king cooperated with the aristocratic elite (or at least with a part of it). They used, on the one hand, the "plums of office," such as peerages, bishoprics, commissions, sinecures, or plain money to buy the allegiance of people, and, on the other, they worked the system by which members of Parliament were appointed or elected. The House of Lords was manned by peers and bishops of whom quite a few were appointed by the Crown: a clever way to secure allegiance and thus political influence in one go. The members of the Lower House, or the Commons, were elected by the people, but the election system—based on election districts or boroughs and counties—was never changed in accordance with the vast and rapid demographic changes of the eighteenth century. As Plumb states, "The right to return members to Parliament bore no relationship to the distribution of population or the size of the town" ([1950] 1968:38); consequently the peer or squire of the borough or county could—through bribery, deceit, or force—control the seats of that borough or county.[15]

The result was a political system based on aristocratic rule in which power, influence, and the spoils of the imperial state were appropriated by a limited group of people: "England was for the few—and the very few" (Ashley 1973:247). As Colley (1992) makes clear, the British elite was relatively homogenous, compact, very rich, and powerful. Moreover, England and later Britain was controlled[16] by warring clans and factions, which offered opportunities and openings to the "young" and "ambitious" involved in "endless political intrigue and patronage hunting" (Plumb [1950] 1968:37). Two main characteristics of this system stand out:

1.   Oligarchic rule, i.e., a patronage and clientele system that reserved political power for the aristocratic elite gathered round the king, "the Court was the heart of body politic" (p. 51). This system is often referred to as "Old Corruption" (Corrigan and Sayer 1991). Most of the citizens of Great Britain, especially the rising middle classes in Britain *and* its colonies, were excluded from political influence.

2.   A certain measure of openness of the political system to outside influence, i.e., outside the dominant oligarchic clans. This meant that the British political system was structurally conducive to political actions carried out by individuals and groups not belonging to the reigning elite. They could "buy" seats in Parliament, ally with other members of Parliament, and thus form a bloc on behalf of a specific interest.[17] Other means of regular influence were lobbying and petitioning. For the "real" outsiders there was only the street. They tried, when necessary, to affect government policies by contentious actions: e.g., bread and food riots, strikes, destroying machines, mobs and several other kinds of contentious gatherings (see, for example, Porter, especially 1990b:98–102; and Tilly 1981).

This oligarchic political system kept the country stable and relatively quiet during the first seventy years of the century. Moreover, it fostered the economic transformation of Britain into a capitalist society and the commercial metropolis of the world. This impression of peace and stability on the British isles was, nonetheless, deceptive. As Porter states, "beneath the perfectly powdered wig, emotional and psychological disorder seethed" (1990b:98). Social disorders regularly manifested themselves in all kinds of contentious activities. Again Porter: "Disorder pockmarked Georgian England—foreigners were astonished at the licence permitted to people [however, its] political fabric—endlessly abused, spat upon, pulled, torn, tattered and patched—was never ripped to pieces" (pp. 103–4).

Below the surface of peaceful stability—interspersed with disparate contentious actions—grew an unarticulated feeling of uneasiness with existing society. This was, above all, the case in the layers of society excluded from political decision-making and/or from enjoying the advantages brought about by commercial capitalism. It took a specific event, however, to trigger these diffuse feelings, to articulate them, and to transform them into concrete demands and issues. This event was produced by John Wilkes, a social and political adventurer. In 1763,

Wilkes publicly denounced a speech of King George III in the well-known 45th edition of his journal, the *North Briton*. Wilkes's arrest and the ensuing dispute as to the legality of his arrest involved him in a "feud" with the authorities. This prolonged struggle, in the name of civil liberties, transformed Wilkes and the number 45 into symbols of liberty;[18] and the diffuse feelings of unease into a demand for political reform. "For the first time for decades fundamental and profound questions were raised in British political life" (Cannon 1973:61). Plumb summarizes the importance of Wilkes for the cause of political reform in the following way:

> Wilkes by his actions and by his legal battles had confirmed important liberties, but his influence was more profound than this. He brought Parliament into great disrepute. He demonstrated by his actions its unrepresentative nature; its dependence on the Crown; its corruption and prejudice-facts known for decades, but never so amply demonstrated; nor had the danger to personal liberty, so inherent in such a system been so clearly proved. ([1950] 1968:123)

Wilkes's crusade—enhanced by the American Revolution waged in the name of liberty and sympathetic in the eyes of quite a few Britons—led, moreover, to the emergence of the public meeting and of societies in defense of civil liberties. It developed, in time, into a movement for parliamentary reform,[19] which operated with varying success. Its main goals were to do away with patronage and corruption, and to bring about a more equal representation in Parliament by extending the suffrage and eliminating the system of the "rotten boroughs." According to Colley, "from the 1780s did this kind of criticism [on the functioning of politics] enter the mainstream of political discourse in Britain" (1992:152). At the same time, other related movements arose and accompanied the movement for parliamentary reform. These were (1) radical reform clubs organized by workingmen that in time strived toward radical social reform, and (2) associations directed at the repeal of the religious barriers for dissenters and Roman Catholics. All in all, "reform was in the air by the 1780s" (Porter 1990b:121).

The actions of the political and social reformers also introduced a transformation in the way protests were carried out. Between the 1770s and the 1830s, as Tilly (1982) shows, the old parochial and patronized forms of collective actions (actions rooted in the fact that participants were members of the same local community with its own mores and customs *and* directed at the local authorities[20]) gave way to organized (often nationwide) collective action formats, i.e., to the social movement. This became one of the standard formats of nationwide political action in this period. Characteristic of this type of collective action is the sustained challenge of authorities: in Tilly's terse depiction, "a sustained series of interactions between powerholders and persons successfully claiming to speak on behalf of a constituency lacking formal representation, in the course of which those persons make publicly-visible demands for changes in the distribution or exercise of power, and back those demands with public demonstrations of support" (p. 26). It is, according to Tilly, also a new phenomenon because the challengers use new means in their struggle. They deliberately form associations, they have at their disposal new repertoires of means of action, and, in their actions, they make extensive use of the media of that period, such as papers, periodicals, pamphlets, and tracts.

The most important reason for the emergence of this new political phenomenon was the already mentioned ongoing transformation of Great Britain from a regionally organized *Gemeinschaft*-type of society to a national *Gesellschaft*-like society, with large extensions overseas (see Section 5.3). This transformation had two somewhat contradictory effects: (1) the transformation of England as a collection of relatively autonomous regional communes into a national community, Great Britain;[21] and (2) simultaneously the extension of individualism. This led, first of all, to the replacement of traditional, communal organizations with voluntary associations (Tilly 1982). Second, it meant that relatively direct personal contacts were superseded by mediated relations between people no longer intimately known to another. This mediation occurred primarily via newspapers, magazines, and other products of print (see Section 5.6). Third, it meant, as Colley succinctly states, "the forging of the British nation" (1992:1).[22]

The rise of the social movement as a new political technique was, moreover, aided by the sometimes explosive growth of grievances, making Great Britain, especially after 1760, quite a contentious society. The unchecked expansion of capitalism led to appalling poverty, to child labor in mean circumstances, and to the rise of a socially and politically marginal proletariat. At the same time, the oligarchic tendencies of the ruling aristocratic elite were at their peak, excluding, above all, the emerging middle classes from their share of political power.

The related increase in contentions was itself, however, equally important. It provided possibilities to "experiment" with new formats of political action and facilitated political activists' learning on the job, leading to a completely new collective action repertoire (Tilly 1982). For example, the association format was pioneered by supporters of Wilkes, who founded the Society of the Supporters of the Bill of Rights, and was developed further in the parliamentary reform movement following Wilkes's "one-man-guerilla." As Plumb makes clear, the Wilkes agitation produced more, such as new methods of contention and a deliberate use of the new media. The social movement was thus an interesting political innovation that in the 1780s was a structural resource in the making: on the one hand, ready to be used for political action, on the other hand, ready and able to be improved by its use in action.[23]

For antislavery, politics in eighteenth-century Britain shaped three important conditions. First, although politics was the reserve of an aristocratic oligarchy, influence from outside these circles was, in a certain measure, possible. The political system was conducive to campaigns, such as the later abolition campaigns, and to organized interests that could facilitate as well as constrain the antislavery cause (see, for an important constraint, the organized West Indian Interest). Second, the emergence of a new and important political instrument, the modern social movement, meant the coming into being of an important resource for those who campaigned for nonrepresented interests, such as the cause of the African slaves. Third, the development of other grievances into actions, campaigns, and movements for political and social reform helped to shape a reform-minded climate from which the antislavery activists could profit. Moreover, antislavery could also profit from the support that these (partially) like-minded movements—leaders as well as members—could give to the abolition movement.

5.5 CHURCH AND CHAPEL

British society was a Protestant society. As Colley (1992) shows, Protestantism became a core element in British collective conscience during Britain's rise as a nation in the eighteenth century. It was even: "the foundation that made the invention of Great Britain possible" (p. 54). Protestantism gave the British people (at least a majority of them) a framework to interpret their daily experiences and acted as a powerful cement to hold the still diverse parts of Britain together. Protestantism was, however, a worldview rather than a deeply felt religion. As Colley and Porter stress, many Britons were callous about performing their religious duties, but there were in Dr. Johnson's words "in reality very few infidels" (cited in Porter 1990b:168).[24]

Eighteenth-century religious life in Great Britain was, on the organizational level, structured by two oppositions. First, there was the antithetical relation between the Anglican and the Roman Catholic churches. The Anglican church was seceded from the Roman Catholic church by Henry VIII and made the official church of England. For Henry VIII and his successors, the Anglican church was a political instrument. When it evolved, moreover, in the direction of Protestantism, its opposition to Rome became—ideologically and structurally—part of the birth of Britain as a nation and of the struggle for world power. This made being

Protestant a condition for being British and being Catholic the opposite. Second, there was the division within Protestantism itself between the official church and the dissenting sects of the seventeenth century, the religious Dissent. These sects did not conform to the legal obligation to perform their religious duties in the Anglican church and were therefore negatively treated.

De facto, worshipping outside the established church was tolerated. There were, however, laws that gave the Anglican church, de jure, a religious monopoly and that effectively excluded Roman Catholics and—less far-reaching—Dissenters from official life. Both oppositions structured the field of religion into these three parts:

1. The official (or established) Anglican church of England.   This church "was the nation's largest and wealthiest institution" (Porter 1990b:172). It formed an integral part of (political) society and, as Gilbert states, "In much of England Anglicanism and society [were] virtually coterminous" (1976:12). Despite its central position in social life the official church failed to keep a "a positive hold on the hearts and hopes of ordinary parishioners" and religious attendance declined considerably during the eighteenth century (Porter 1990b:174).

2. The Dissent.   The dissenting sects of the foregoing turbulent period, such as the Quakers, Baptists, Presbyterians, and Unitarians, had been attractive for quite a few, especially the socially and economically privileged. After the Glorious Revolution, however, their pull steadily declined and, on the whole, "the Nonconformists . . . were content to remain on the defensive" (Ashley 1973:239; see also Gilbert 1976:14–17).

3. The Roman Catholic church.   This church did not only share in the general religious decline of the eighteenth century, but was, moreover, particularly negatively affected by political and social exclusion. This exclusion combined with the gradual evaporation of the prospects of a Catholic restoration in Britain produced a permanently marginal position for Catholics in British society. Remaining Catholic became, therefore, rather unattractive, above all for the Catholic elite. It transformed Catholicism into "a small and diminishing stream of English religiosity" (Gilbert 1976:47).

For the cause of antislavery in Great Britain, Catholicism was unimportant. "Old dissent" did not play an impressive role in this respect either. There were, however, two important exceptions: the developments within the Quaker community (see Sections 4.3 and 6.2) and the role of the dissenting academies with regard to radical thinking and reform (see Section 4.5). The Anglican church also accepted slavery as a fact of life. Still, it affected antislavery in a major way. Its internal developments in relation to the vast transformation of British society shaped the conditions for the Evangelical revival that later played a pivotal role in the antislavery and abolition struggle.

The central problem confronting the Anglican church in the eighteenth century was its relation to politics. The monopoly of religious practice demanded, first of all, "the determined and continuing support of the Crown, of Parliament, and of those who wielded social and political influence in local communities" (Gilbert 1976:4). As Gilbert shows, the support given was not sufficient, neither financially nor politically. The dependency of the church, moreover, involved the clergy to a large extent in daily politics. Many positions in the established church—from curate to archbishop—were filled by the (political) patronage of squires, peers, and the Crown, meaning that the loyalty and interest of the patronized clergy lay less with the ordinary parishioners than with the local and national powerholders.[25] What was more, the alliance of the church with the vested political interests made it vulnerable to attacks from social and political reformers in the second half of the century.

The effect of all this was a church failing its main task, viz., taking care of the spiritual welfare of all people in Britain. On the one hand, the Anglican church was too content with the way things were; spiritual profundity and interest were lacking, resulting in a religious shallowness that reduced the attraction of the church to a great extent. On the other hand, the clergy was too often physically absent or the skills clergymen needed for the care of souls were plainly deficient. This meant that, in too many cases, parsons were nonresident (sometimes replaced by underpaid curates) and "in many parishes . . . many individuals and even entire communities were without the cure of souls" (p. 7).[26] This unsatisfactory situation was further exacerbated by the transformation Britain was undergoing after the 1760s, especially the rise and redistribution of population, urbanization, and industrialization. The Anglican church was already insufficiently equipped for its spiritual tasks before this point in time, but things became even worse. The result was an ever-growing gap between spiritual need and religious supply, which was eagerly filled by itinerant ministers like George Whitefield and John Wesley (starting as early as the 1740s), whose activities forebode the coming Evangelical revival.

5.6 THE MEDIA

The rise to societal prominence of the media in the eighteenth century is one of the striking aspects of the transformation of Britain toward modernity. In the new *Gesellschaft*-like society (see Section 5.3) media

became the chief means of communication; in the words of Black and
Gregory, "The century and a half after 1600 saw a great explosion in the
world of print and the development of new forms, itself a sign of a
changing society" (1991:6). Important conditions for this rise were increased literacy and growing prosperity, especially among the emerging
middling classes (Plumb [1950] 1968; Altick [1957] 1983; Hunter 1990).
The most important factor was, however, the enlarging scale of people's
social life, i.e., from the encompassing local community to that of the
British nation in an expanding economic and political world system.
This "mediazation" of society was, moreover, amplified by cultural
changes, previously outlined (see especially Section 4.4.), and by a growing commercialization of the cultural realm (Porter 1990b).

In this section the focus will be placed on the media functioning in the
sphere of politics, as the abolition struggle was mainly waged in the
political arena. In eighteenth-century politics, media became especially
important as means for (1) authorities to communicate with the public,
(2) the public to keep abreast of current events and—no less important—of that which could and should be done, and (3) political entrepreneurs to mobilize their constituencies. Media also became in this period
the means for thinkers, writers, journalists, etc., to expose what was
going on in society and politics, *and* often provided a way for earning
money as well.

In eighteenth-century Britain, several types of media developed, each
with its own function. Three of these functions may be discerned:

1.   Bringing news.   This function was mainly carried out by newspapers, which proliferated very rapidly from the beginning of the century. The first daily newspaper, the *Daily Courant*, appeared in 1702. It was
soon followed by a host of other papers, in the metropolis as well as in
the provinces (Plumb [1950] 1968; Altick 1957; Ashley 1973; Cannon
1973; Speck 1983; Porter 1990b).

2.   Giving information on topics of general interest.   This was chiefly the province of magazines, periodicals, tracts, almanacs, and to a
lesser extent books (chapbooks included).[27] Well-known periodicals
were the *Tattler* (1709), later the *Spectator, Gentleman's Magazine* (1731),
and the *Monthly Review* (1749). In these periodicals, as in the other forms
of publication, a plethora of topics regarding art, philosophy, politics,
travels, science, etc., were dealt with, making this medium especially
important in forming opinions (Plumb [1950] 1968; Altick 1957; Ashley
1973; Cannon 1973; Speck 1983; Porter 1990b).

3.   Mobilization of constituencies.   Print was used more and more
to mobilize people for political purposes. The political pamphlet—a format with a long tradition—was probably the most typical medium in

this respect. Other important mobilization instruments were advertisements in newspapers and periodicals, announcements of meetings, and more general calls for action (Plumb [1950] 1968; Altick 1957).

The reach of the media was not confined to the circle of subscribers and buyers, but was considerably enlarged by the practice of reading tables in coffeehouses and by the innovation of the circulating library (Altick 1957; Speck 1983; Porter 1990b).

During the eighteenth century, the media became key facilities for political action, not in the least for actions on behalf of people and causes outside the sphere of regular politics. Furthermore, media proved to be— alongside the voluntary association—one of the core elements of the newly emerging political action format, the social movement. Media were also important for those who acted against slavery. From the beginning of the century (for example, John Hepburn's tract in 1715), a number of Quakers published tracts against slavery, of which Benezet's became the most well-known and influential. Others such as Sharp, Wesley, and Clarkson used the same method for spreading the antislavery message. Media also played a prominent role in the later abolition campaign and proved to be a valuable facility for the abolition movement.

5.7 EARLY MODERN BRITAIN AND (ANTI)SLAVERY

Williams's thesis, *"The capitalists had first encouraged West Indian slavery and then helped to destroy it"* ([1944] 1972:169), may now safely be paraphrased in the following way: the structural transformation of British society in the eighteenth century enlarged the involvement of Britons in slavery, while at the same time helping to shape important conditions for its demise. The cultural changes highlighted in Chapter 4, Britain's road to world power, the expansion of commercial capitalism at home and abroad, and the first steps toward industrial society, all brought into being a new type of society. The communal society of the disparate regions (still in many respects a *Gemeinschaft*) was giving way more and more to a national (in some respects even global) society in which relations between people became depersonalized, mediated, and cash nexus based, i.e., Toennies's *Gesellschaft*.[28] These processes did not, however, shape all the conditions for antislavery on their own, but were helped by two other systemic developments: the rise of political oligarchic rule and the failings of the official church. Both caused stagnation which was further exacerbated by the rapid transformation of the "old" society into a "new" one, making the political and religious organization even less adequate to perform its tasks.

For antislavery, these developments created two important constraints: (1) slavery became a national interest and doing away with it
involved more than the "robbing" of some nabobs, and (2) the West
Indian Interest took advantage of the conduciveness of the political system and formed a formidable bloc in Parliament. The transformation of
British society, however, shaped important facilities as well. First, the
political system was no less conducive to antislavery actions than to the
slavery interest. Second, a new and powerful political instrument came
into being: the social movement. The rise of the voluntary association as
an organizational format and the increasing mediazation of society were
especially important in this respect.

Still, one of the most important systemic factors with regard to antislavery may have been the coincidence of the growth of capitalism, on
the one hand, and the increase of political and religious stagnation, on
the other. Strongly stated, capitalism created new groupings, the middling classes and the proletariat; politics excluded these groupings; and
religion left them out in the (spiritual) cold. The result was a growing
demand for reform and renovation on social, political, and religious
terrains, voiced by these newly formed groups. Antislavery—first abolition, later emancipation—proved to fit in very well in this climate of
renewal and revitalization and could, moreover, draw on an anomaly
and potential contradiction, i.e., free vs. forced labor, shaped by the
same forces that shaped the new British society. Favorable systemic
conditions (as well as cultural ones) were, however, not enough to bring
about the actions to end the slave trade. They had to be transformed into
an actual set of opportunities and conditions, an action-structure, that
could make a movement campaign to end the slave trade possible. Three
events that occurred in the second half of the century were essential in
this transformation. These events will be dealt with in the next chapter.

NOTES

1. In mercantilism, trade did not mean exchange between (formally) free
parties, but obtaining wealth by taking it from others in a zero sum game between countries. In the words of Drescher, "Mercantilism was a political economy based on a view of the world as a system of closed, hostile economies. It
assumed the need to control and favor one's own domestic and imperial enterprises" (1977b:135). In Wallerstein's minimal definition, "[m]ercantilism involved
state policies of economic nationalism and revolved around a concern with the
circulation of commodities, whether in terms of the movement of bullion or in
the creation of balances of trade (bilateral or multilateral)" (1980:37).
2. There is no need to delve any deeper into this topic here.
3. The question of how much Great Britain gained is a hotly debated one.

We will not go into this as it would lead us far astray. There is, however, consensus that the gain in the eighteenth century was substantial. For a recent work on this topic, see Inikori and Engerman (1992).

4. As Williams contends, "The West Indian colonies were still [in 1783] the darlings of the empire, the most precious jewels in the British diadem" ([1944] 1972:126).

5. In this section we have used as literature Briggs (1959), Porter (1990b), Smith (1991), Brown (1992), and Lie (1993) alongside the antislavery literature already mentioned.

6. See, for example, among many other authors on this subject, Wallerstein (1980), Lie (1993), and De Vries (1976).

7. See Smail (1992) for a detailed study of this process in the textile industry in Halifax, Yorkshire, at the beginning of the eighteenth century.

8. As Mokyr (1993) and Harley (1993) show, the growth pattern was quite diverse. In the traditional economic sectors, growth was generally slow. Agriculture formed an exception: here growth was larger. The modern sector of the economy, such as cotton and iron, displayed a different pattern. Here important technological changes took place (see below) that accelerated economic growth, but as Harley makes clear, "Modern economic growth became fully established in Britain only in the railway age" (1993:208).

9. As Porter makes clear, this "revolution" was not the application of "a 'programme' engineered by factory owners but rather . . . the cumulative outcome of millions of individual actions throughout the system" (1990b:311–12). Moreover, its main point is to be found in the nineteenth century. The question as to whether there has been a real turn at all (for a denial, see Wallerstein 1989) or only a continuation of long-term trends will not be taken into consideration. For a very enlightening essay on the arguments pro and contra such a revolution, see Mokyr (1993).

10. The last form of change in this period was still regionally bounded and did not affect—at that time—a large part of the British labor force, but it touched Britons also "indirectly as consumer, user, or spectator" (Mokyr 1993:15).

11. As Drescher states, at the end of the century not only was the potential contradictory character of this anomaly important, but also the connotation that "being involved in slavery" had with pollution and corruption. This fed the antislavery sentiment as "antagonists could always hark back to that inescapable whiff of pollution" (1986:18).

12. Drescher warns, however, (in a personal comment), of not attaching too much importance to these new social categories with regard to their effect on abolition. As he shows in *The Long Goodbye*, this relationship seems to have been rather complicated, especially with respect to the role of urbanism (see 1994b:51–53). The causes of antislavery are, according to him, not so much to be found in the capitalist industrial revolution but rather in political (cultural and structural) factors such as the emerging modes of social and political mobilization (p. 68).

13. Other proletarian workers joined the more radical workingmen's clubs that stood positive toward the abolition cause as well (Fladeland 1982).

14. This section is mainly based on Plumb ([1950] 1968), Ashley (1973), Cannon (1973), Porter (1990b).

15. The underpopulated and the uncontested boroughs were called the "rotten boroughs." Porter comes to a conclusion similar to Plumb's when he states, "In short, Georgian government became exceptionally secure against the electorate. A diminishing number of seats actually came up for contest, and of those that did, a majority of boroughs could be fixed in advance" (1990b:111–12). Cannon typifies the situation as follows: It was an oligarchy at the peak of its aristocratic power in 1761, the year in which "only 4 counties out of 40 were contested, and 42 boroughs out of 203. Almost two-thirds of the English boroughs were under patronage" (1973:49–50).

16. This rule is tersely typified by Plumb: "The government machine in alliance with the major borough patrons could be certain of victory at any general election; and so, winning the heart of the electorate became of diminishing importance to eighteenth-century politicians. In opposition, they exerted all their skill to win over patrons of importance, then to provoke a ministerial crisis, and in the resulting intrigues to capture the Treasury, a manoeuvre of great strategic and tactical complexity, frequently attempted and rarely achieved" ([1950] 1968:40).

17. The West Indian Interest was a prime example of such an organized interest group which "bought peerages and political power" (Davis 1966:154). In order to further their interests even more, they also sought allies among the landed aristocracy and the commercial bourgeoisie of the seaport towns. It was by no means the only "interest cluster" in Parliament; for a description of the diversity of organized interest in Parliament see Briggs (1959:108). The same author even depicts "Parliament [as] essentially a chamber not of 'parties' but of 'interests'" (p. 116).

18. As Goodwin states, "He personified as no one else the successful defence of the legal, constitutional and civic liberties of the ordinary citizen. . . . 'Wilkes and Liberty' was more than a mere political slogan" (1979:44).

19. Christopher Wyvill and the Yorkshire Association—originating in the dissenting academies—played an important role in this development. See, for a detailed account of the history of parliamentary reform, among many others, Cannon (1973) and Goodwin (1979).

20. Tilly mentions the following examples of these types of actions: "food riots, attacks on moral offenders, election brawls, and demands of workers on their masters" (1982:25).

21. See, for example, Lie (1993), who describes the commercial transition of England from a society with predominantly isolated local marketplaces to a national "market" society.

22. This process comprised three simultaneous processes: enlarging the scale of the community in which people lived, struggling for world dominance, and fending off the internal Stuart threat.

23. As Temperley concludes, the British abolition campaign was a prime example of how these new techniques of political action were developed (see especially 1965:349). More accurately, abolition and the development of the social movement as a new political technique of contention went hand in glove in a dialectical fashion; as Drescher states, "The popular mobilizations and innovations of the 1780s and early 1790s had crystallized the modern social movement" (1994a:166).

24.   Alongside Porter (1990b) we have used Plumb ([1950] 1968) and Gilbert (1976) in this section.

25.   According to Plumb, "It meant . . . that bishops became first and foremost politicians, and politicians are rarely men of the spirit" ([1950] 1968:43). Porter observes in this respect that the independent spiritual leadership of the church was missing because of the patronage system, "for prelates were generally thick as thieves with the politicians who were their nursing fathers" (1990b:173). At the local level the situation was often not much different where "the parson was subordinate to the squire" (Gilbert 1976:4) and "the squire set the tone" (Ashley 1973:239).

26.   As Porter, Gilbert, and Plumb also make clear, the situation was not as bad everywhere in the country; many parishes were attended by dutiful parsons, and in the words of Porter, "If few parsons were saints, few were utterly scandalous" (1990b:174).

27.   Oldfield (1995) points to an interesting development in this respect. The provincial book trade grew considerably, which eased the availability of books all over the country.

28.   This process was, however, far from being completed. As Porter states, "[M]uch of society was still encased in small face-to-face communities. In 1800, fewer than one person in five lived in towns of more than 20,000 inhabitants" (1990b:345).

6

From Potential to Actuality
The Episodic Context

6.1 INTRODUCTION

Favorable conditions are, in most cases, necessary but not sufficient for bringing about change. Change—social as well as cultural—has to be organized. It needs, as Zaret (1989) states, an organizational context, i.e., actors who deploy the activities that bring forth the changes. In the case of cultural changes, this means actors engaged in discourses that change meanings. Change needs, according to Zaret, an episodic context as well, i.e., the occurrence of historical events that shape the situation that makes these organizational activities possible. This was also the case with antislavery, which primarily involved changing morality, moral meanings as well as rules. It needed actors who would not only struggle for declaring slavery and related undertakings immoral, but who would see to the introduction of rules that would make it illegal as well. In the terms of Becker (1963), the cause of antislavery needed moral entrepreneurs. It needed, moreover, a situation that would facilitate (and thus not constrain) antislavery actions: an opportunity structure conducive to abolition and antislavery actions.

In the case of the abolition of the slave trade, the situation did not only demand active and skillful entrepreneurs with plentiful resources, but an active conscience constituency as well. As slavery involved the national interest in the eyes of many powerful politicians and as the slavery interest itself was politically powerful, the abolition entrepreneurs would (and did) need pressure from outside the political system to force the abolition issue onto the social and the political agenda. As we have seen before, in this period a new political instrument for generating and applying this kind of extrainstitutional pressure was in the making, namely, the social movement. One of the important aspects of this collective action format was the associational way of organizing constituents as a means to wield this extrainstitutional power. In the case of abolition, this constituency had to be a conscience constituency because the beneficiaries of the abolition themselves were not living in the metropolis, where the necessary decisions had to be taken, and moreover they lacked the power, the very reason for their becoming slaves, to fend for themselves.

There were three events in the period before the onset of the first abolition campaign that proved to be essential in shaping a positive situation—in terms of people and resources—for that campaign. Anstey (1980) points to two of them as he identifies what was responsible for the dynamics of the antislavery drive at the end of the eighteenth century, viz., Quakerism and Evangelicalism.[1] In Section 4.3 we have already dealt with the early developments concerning slavery in the Society of Friends. In Section 6.2, we will treat the turn of the Quakers to antislavery as an important historical event. In Section 6.3, we will look into the effects of the Evangelical revival on antislavery and abolition. This was another historical event that had decisive consequences. Alongside these events, a court case against a runaway slave took place: the Somerset case. This acted as a triggering event. This case is the subject of Section 6.4. Together with the cultural and social changes described in the previous chapters they shaped an opportunity or action-structure that made the abolition crusade possible. The state of this structure as it was just before the onset of the first abolition campaign will be evaluated in Section 6.5.

6.2   THE TURN OF THE QUAKERS TO ANTISLAVERY

Although the antislavery issue gradually grew in strength from the end of the seventeenth century onwards, it did not automatically reach a central position on the Quaker agenda concerning the rules and norms of daily behavior. For this, as Davis (1975) makes clear, specific decisions were needed. Benjamin Lay had already done his utmost with his violent rhetoric and his eccentric and shocking behavior[2] to force antislavery onto this agenda, but it took the efforts of less conspicuous figures to develop antislavery into *the* test of religious truth and purity. As Davis shows, John Woolman and Anthony Benezet "were instrumental in convincing the Society of Friends that antislavery was a test of religious truth" (1966:330).

John Woolman became seriously involved in the antislavery question during a tour on which he visited fellow Quakers in Virginia and North Carolina. The confrontation with slaveholding Quakers, both on this tour and during his earlier work in Pennsylvania, crystallized in the antislavery tract *Some Considerations on the Keeping of Negroes,* which

Woolman published in 1754 after an eight-year delay. His involvement in the antislavery cause led him to a lifelong friendship with Anthony Benezet, a Quaker schoolmaster in Philadelphia, who was opposed to slavery as well. They embarked on an antislavery crusade within the Society of Friends, which came to a sudden success by a triggering force, the Seven Years' War. This war confronted the Quakers with the question of the compatibility of politics and morality, i.e., politics demanded them to fight or at least to pay taxes for the war effort and their moral rules forbade them to do so.[3] This confrontation led to a severe crisis, which the Quakers met by withdrawal from politics and by a drive to self-purification that led to a Quaker revival, eventually coinciding with the Evangelical revival in Britain. Part of this purification was concerned with Quakers severing all ties with any involvement in slavery as "a means of reasserting the perfectionist content of their faith" (Davis 1966:332). Slavery became condemned for its sinfulness, not in the least because of the luxury and idleness it produced.

Benezet became one of the most important abolitionists in relation to the formulation of the abolitionist message. From 1762 on he wrote several influential pamphlets and tracts against slavery and the slave trade. In these he not only incorporated the religious line of reasoning from the Quaker tradition against slavery, but also many empirical data on the conditions of life in Africa, on the ways the slave trade was executed, and on the conditions of daily life on the plantations. Moreover, he selectively incorporated the ideas and themes of the Enlightenment that had direct and indirect bearing on the subject of slavery as those were represented in the work of Montesquieu, Hutcheson, Wallace, and other writers mainly of the Scottish Enlightenment. Benezet is important because his work was widely distributed in Great Britain and because he had a decisive influence on the writings of other abolitionists, such as Granville Sharp, Wesley, and Clarkson. He was, above all, the connection between the progressive Enlightenment cast of thought and the antislavery message of the abolitionists, who were primarily religiously oriented. Benezet did this by adding "[t]o the original Quaker position, based on the simple logic of love, . . . the assertion of natural right and the sanction which resulted from bringing slavery and the slave trade within the orbit of providentially sustained retributory justice" (Anstey 1975:232).

The turn of the Quakers to antislavery became one of the pivotal events in the genesis of the abolition movement because of the way they solved the eternal dilemma of all religious virtuosi, viz., realizing their religious ideals *inside* or *outside* the world[4] by living at the same time inside *and* outside the world. This internally contradictory solution was reached and maintained in two interlocking ways.

First, the Friends organized themselves as a distinctive grouping that forged a separate identity for its members through rules concerning behavior, dress, speech, marriage, etc., in order to insulate the Quakers from the corrupting world. The organizational and disciplinarian activities of the Society of Friends directed at the latter were stepped up during the century as the success of their worldly activities brought the Quakers wealth and in its wake worldliness and religious apathy.[5] This resulted in the extension of communications between the Friends and in a more important role for the Quaker meetings, i.e., in a growing internal international network that linked the Quakers on both sides of the Atlantic.

Second, in order to survive as a dissenting sect, they organized relations with the outside world more and more through these meetings, which in time were transformed into specialized committees (see, for example, Davis 1966:329, on the evolution of the London Meeting for Sufferings). The latter were especially active in shaping outside society (above all through political lobbying) in such a way that Quakers could deviate from the standards of everyday life and still remain accepted.

As we have already seen, the involvement in the corrupting practices of daily life produced tensions, Woolman's daily dying, that were controlled by directing the impulse resulting from these tensions toward concrete objectives, in this period antislavery. At the same time, the need to entertain fruitful relations with this same corrupting world produced a communications network (arising from the internal Quaker network) that made the Society of Friends an international pressure group that was unparalleled in eighteenth-century Britain.

The Society of Friends in England and in North America influenced each other reciprocally on the question of slavery and slave trade, which strengthened the drive against these dismal practices. In America this led to a ban on members engaging in the slave trade in 1761 and to a ban on members holding slaves in 1774 and 1776 (Craton et al. 1976). The American Quakers directed their influence not only toward their brethren, but toward non-Quakers in Great Britain as well. It is the first attempt to mobilize consensus on the issue of slavery and the slave trade. Benezet took the lead here by making contact with the archbishop of Canterbury, Burke, Wesley, and Granville Sharp (Anstey 1975). In 1783, Benezet even approached Queen Charlotte with a letter accompanied by several antislavery books and tracts. In this letter Benezet pleaded for royal interference in the slave trade, which he depicted as "this flagrant Violation of the common Rights of Mankind" (Bruns 1977:491). The British Quakers—under strong pressure from the American Friends—formed two committees to organize the drive against slavery and the slave trade, and they were the first to petition Parliament against the slave trade (1783). They also formed local networks with local agents to spread the antislavery message, printed a pamphlet[6] especially written for their antislavery actions, and lobbied the political elite on this topic by spreading this pamphlet and Benezet's writings among the elite, among which the king, the queen, the Prince of Wales, and the leading ministers in the cabinet. The Quaker influence pertaining to the antislavery issue was rather important; in the words of Davis, "By 1786 it was not accidental that the Quaker testimony was commonplace knowledge in Great Britain, or that a pamphlet by Benezet should be readily accessible to anyone who cared to read it" (1975:224).

The turn of the Society of Friends toward antislavery was important for the genesis and working of the abolition movement in three respects:

1.   The Quakers, especially through the writings of Benezet, helped to shape the antislavery and abolitionist message that was used in the ensuing campaigns.
2.   The Friends initiated the abolition movement with their activities in Great Britain between 1783 and 1787. They were also well represented in the Abolition Committee, which started the campaign against the slave trade in 1787.
3.   The Quakers, together with those inspired by the Evangelical revival (see the following section), became the carriers of the abolition movement. They delivered and mobilized the resources, especially their organizational networks needed for reaching the goal of the movement, the abolition of the slave trade.

Quakerism became an important part of the set of conditions that made the abolition movement possible, or as Davis states, "By the 1780s the British and American Quakers could provide what no other group seemed capable of: decision, commitment, and most important, organization" (p. 215).

6.3   THE EVANGELICAL REVIVAL

As we stated in Section 5.5, the established church failed in its main function: catering to the spiritual needs of important sectors of British society.[7] Structurally, there were not enough clergymen in some parts of the country and the traditional parish system, the *squirearchy*, sometimes even fell into complete disarray. Culturally, the church had sunk into a torpor, refused to reform, and furthermore its attitude to life had become worldly. In short, the church had little to offer to those who "needed revelation and salvation" (Plumb [1950] 1968:45).[8] The shallowness of official religion led some people, notably Wesley, to search for a more vital religion, and the itinerant preaching, among other things, that Wesley initiated resulted in time in a religious revival; in the words of Porter, "[F]rom the 1770s a powerful Evangelical revival got under way" (1990b:176). This revival is to be seen as "a revolt against abstract and ossified theology; they [the evangelicals] strove to awaken men to the inadequacy of a worldly life, and to make the quest for true holiness a constant concern" (Davis 1966:387).[9]

In the Evangelical revival, the dissenting undercurrent in religious life that was present inside as well as outside the Anglican church became more visible, especially in the sphere of public religious practice. It is therefore no surprise that it also presented itself in organizational form both within and outside the Anglican church. Within the established church, the so-called Clapham sect was the center of the Evangelical movement, with members like Henry Thornton, Rev. John Venn, William Wilberforce, and Granville Sharp. Outside the church, the Methodists—founded by John Wesley—were the most important Evangelical denomination.[10] The secession of the latter into a dissenting denomination was, however, a gradual process that was caused as much (if not more) by the established church itself as by the dissenting forces within Methodist circles.

The Evangelical revitalization of religious life revolved around three notions: sin, redemption, and retribution. Man was (again) seen as a sinner because he was by nature prone to concerning himself exclusively with his own pleasures and interests. Self-interest and self-centeredness were the essence of the Evangelical notion of sin. Man could, however, be redeemed from this state of sin and its awful consequences if only he would turn to God, repent, and open his heart to God's divine grace. This meant on the one hand an appeal to let God touch one's soul so that conversion and salvation became possible. On the other hand, it meant that one should listen to God's duty call (in one's heart, in the Bible, in sermons, etc.), in other words, to actively look for what one's duties in life are. But to turn God down, i.e., to not accept his grace and not cooperate with the work of his Providence, called for retribution and punishment.

Although the Evangelical revival was a reaction to a religious life shaped by reason, its thought remained in touch with the main intellectual and religious currents of the eighteenth century. First, the notion of Providence as moral government retained—and even strengthened—its central position in Evangelical belief. Evangelicals saw the hand of Providence operating everywhere and in very specific ways pointing to evils that had to be eradicated immediately. Moreover, alongside the idea of the general Providence of God the Evangelicals also distinguished a form which they depicted as particular Providence. The latter meant that

Evangelicals saw their own life as being directed in specific or particular ways. Second, the Evangelicals accepted the central eighteenth-century values—liberty, happiness, and benevolence—which they transposed to their own setting. Liberty is Christian liberty, i.e., freedom from sin; promoting happiness is the right end for everyone, but in its true form it is obtainable only in the afterlife; and benevolence is doing well, but it is only complete if it is informed by Christian love and humility.[11] Taken together, a cast of thinking that Anstey typifies as follows:

> All in all the Evangelical mind was a dynamic thing. It accepted much of the moral philosophy of the day—notably the belief in liberty as a cardinal virtue, in benevolence as the duty of men and in happiness as a proper goal. . . . Their ability to transpose, to supercharge, these values stemmed from a desolating conviction of their own sin, the assurance that that sin was forgiven and could be overcome by the grace of God, and by the consequential assurance that they could overcome the sin of and in other men by that same grace. Anterior to this was a greater sense of the horror of evil just because they had come to see its enormity in themselves. They believed in Providence as a divinely sustained moral order, which included judgment on the nation that sinned, and this belief gave them a satisfying and coherent philosophy of history, whilst their lively sense of a particular Providence ruling and directing their own lives was also their inescapable summons to mould the world to a righteousness which would avert deserved national disaster, relieve the mundane sufferings of men, and pave the way for the salvation of their eternal souls. (1975:198)

The turn to the dark sinful side of mankind, the hope of salvation, and the threat of retribution were all clothed in an overwhelming emotionality that instilled an unremitting zeal for bettering themselves and the world in those who were spiritually awakened by the Evangelical clarion call.[12] The Evangelical revival was clearly not confined to personal salvation and reform, but extended to saving Britain by reforming it as well. The resulting crusading spirit was directed at several causes, of which antislavery was one of the first and foremost.

The Evangelical revival did, however, not automatically lead to antislavery attitudes and actions. Nonconformists accommodated, for example, to the existing situation of slavery in the colonies. Yet, important notions in the Evangelical cast of thought were congenial to antislavery ideas. First, the prominence of the law of love strengthened by the idea that God had come for all men facilitated feelings of empathy with the suffering slave. Second, the notion that one was called to active engagement in realizing God's kingdom of love coupled with the threat of heavenly punishment if one refused to do so facilitated an active involvement in the fate of the slave.

What was needed to activate this posture against slavery was, however, a confrontation between the blatant contradiction of this institution and one's beliefs without at the same time being overwhelmed by the sheer facticity of it. This situation was realized in Great Britain in the second half of the eighteenth century. In the relatively free situation of that country, Evangelical-minded people met black slaves in the streets and in advertisements in newspapers, read tracts about the dismal reality of the slave trade and slavery and about their injustices, and got involved in court cases regarding runaway slaves, either directly, e.g., as defending counsel, or indirectly through accounts in the newspapers.

Granville Sharp was the prime example of the Evangelical who got involved in defending runaway slaves against the claims of their owners (see the following section). He did, however, not restrict himself to these legal activities, but became—in writing and in acting[13]—one of the main antislavery activists. Wesley was converted to the antislavery cause by reading Benezet's tracts and he subsequently wrote his own very influential antislavery tract, *Thoughts upon Slavery* (1774).[14] Both played an important role in putting the Evangelical revival on the antislavery track. They shaped an antislavery message for which they drew on the Bible, especially the Old Testament, and on the main themes of eighteenth-century philosophical and theological thinking. In this, they were helped greatly by the work of Benezet and other Quakers who drew on the same sources.

The Evangelical revival brought forth two kinds of resources for the cause of antislavery and the coming abolition campaigns:

1.   The shaping of a specific Evangelical message against slavery and the slave trade that contained (1) a description of involvement in slavery as wicked and sinful, (2) an order to immediately do away with it, and (3) the threat of God's retribution for the British nation. In this message, the Evangelical notions concerning sin, redemption, and retribution that applied to individuals and nations alike were combined with the more hopeful eighteenth-century thought regarding liberty, happiness, and benevolence. This made the Evangelical abolitionists certain that "the African slave trade entailed monstrous burdens of national guilt, which would either lead to horrifying retribution or afford an opportunity for moral regeneration" (Davis 1975:311).

2.   The shaping of an organizational base for antislavery activities. The revival gave the antislavery and abolition cause:

    a.   Its leaders.   The Evangelical revival provided antislavery with the moral entrepreneurs for the coming crusades. The revival within the Anglican church appealed foremost to members of the (higher) middle classes, who possessed

the necessary intellectual, political, and financial resources. The revival instilled in them, moreover, a dogged
persistence in their task as leaders of good causes due
to the particular Evangelical conception of (particular)
Providence.

b. Its mobilization potential. The Evangelical revival was
organized in its own specific networks. Methodism especially was successful in organizing and coordinating the
life and thinking of many people. Above all, it appealed to
the members of the lower middle classes and the working
classes, who—as we have already seen—were drifting
more and more toward the margin of civil and political
society. Porter typifies Methodist organization as follows:
"Methodism became the century's most fertile new national organization [and it] proved fertile in many directions"
(1990b:177–78). One of its greatest successes with regard
to the cause of abolition, was that it drew people into the
campaign that otherwise most probably would have
stayed out.

The effects of the Evangelical revival on the cause of antislavery can be
summarized by taking a statement of Drescher, who depicts these effects on British antislavery as a whole in the following manner:

> In religious perspective British anti-slavery movements, in their heyday,
> paid homage to the increasing power of nonconformist values and modes
> of association. They provided the basis for a cross-class and cross-national
> appeal to a common standard of human rights. In their independence
> from state support and subordination they were also more flexible chan-
> nels for the rapid mobilization of public opinion against a traditional eco-
> nomic institution than the established religious and political organizations
> of unreformed Britain. (1980:57–58)

6.4   THE SOMERSET CASE

In the episodic context in which the movement toward the abolition
of the slave trade arose, a third historical event was important. This
event concerned the existence of black slavery on British soil and the
legal battle it invoked. The growing involvement in the trade in slaves
from the sixteenth century onwards, and later in slavery especially in
the colonies in the West Indies, led to the entry of black Africans into
Great Britain. They came as servants, soldiers, seamen, and sometimes
"even as prosperous and fêted individuals," but most of them came as

slaves, "the human property of a homecoming [from the colonies] Englishman" (Walvin 1973:47). Although black Africans lived all over England—sometimes free, often enslaved, sometimes prosperous, but more often poor—most of them lived in London, where a free black community grew. In the 1750s, they had, in any case, become very visible for contemporaries and their presence was more and more perceived as a social problem.[15] As Walvin describes the situation:

> The black population of England by the mid-eighteenth century had begun seriously to worry contemporaries. It was large, growing, virtually unknown to white society and desperately poor. . . . More alarming still for those disturbed by black settlement in England was the increasing speed and scope of immigration. Contemporaries seemed gripped with a fear that the country was beset by a tidal wave of black immigrants. (pp. 46–47)[16]

The growing British involvement in slavery was not the result of a conscious policy but the (by-)product of two interrelated systemic developments in the eighteenth century: the forming of the British Empire and the unfolding of capitalism (see in this regard Chapter 5). At the same time, however, bondage in Britain had disappeared and "Enslavement . . . was exceptional to the norm [of British society]" (Drescher 1986:173), i.e., structurally, it was no longer an existing relationship and culturally slavery was seen as being antithetical to the core of Britishness and to living in Britain. Moreover, contrary to the colonies in the Americas, slavery was for the British people not a racial fact but one of geography; human beings could be slaves only in faraway places. The entry of black slaves in the metropolis itself thus meant, as Drescher (1986) aptly states, the crossing of the borderline between bondage and freedom; it meant transferring slave relations to a society in which the social conditions for such relations were lacking. It revealed a double contradiction: (1) forced labor was contrary to the British system of formally free labor, and (2) slavery was a negation of the British ideal of liberty.

Quite naturally these contradictions produced confusion[17] concerning the presence of black slaves on British soil, which showed itself in a fragmented and divided public opinion. It was, moreover, exacerbated by changes in the intellectual climate of the eighteenth century (see Chapter 4 on the latter). The confusion was especially visible in four areas: the legitimacy of slavery and the slave trade, the image of the black African, the acceptance of black Africans in British society, and the legal status of slavery in the metropolis.

First, the legitimacy of slavery and the slave trade was questioned more and more, above all, in intellectual circles, while at the same time both were accepted as world-historical facts. The self-evident character of the factual situation often superseded ambivalence and doubt. Second, on the one hand, the black African continued to be seen as a human being; on the other hand, he was dealt with as a commodity and as chattel. The latter implies a less than human status. Third, black Africans were accepted in eighteenth-century Britain, as may be derived from the fact that there were mixed marriages, that runaway slaves were helped by (mostly poor) whites, and that relations between white and black workers, often servants and sailors, were generally good. At the same time, however, there was discontent with the influx of black Africans, alarm about miscegenation, and instances of hostility and even of racial hatred.[18] Fourth, the legal situation regarding slavery in Britain itself was rather ambiguous. There was, on the one hand, the popularized version of British law stating that its "air was too free for a slave to breathe" (cited in Drescher 1986:26); there were no statutes sanctioning slavery and in some cases courts ruled that everyone who set foot on English soil was free. On the other hand, there were authoritative legal opinions, such as the York-Talbot opinion of 1729, that declared the opposite (Walvin 1973:111–13).

The situation regarding slavery in eighteenth-century Britain is succinctly typified by Drescher as he states that "[s]laves in Britain were socially and legally anomalous" (1986:27). There were neither statutes nor social norms sanctioning the institution of slavery, which meant that in Britain both masters and slaves lacked protection. Masters had trouble in reclaiming runaway slaves and "in the metropolis masters simply could not count on the help of either the white citizenry or the magistracy to enforce their claims in persons" (p. 33). They therefore hired men to kidnap the runaways and to bring them aboard a ship bound for the West Indies. Slaves were generally not protected against these illegal practices, as in most cases neither the magistrates nor the public intervened on their behalf.[19] This ambiguous situation led to several court cases in which slaves tried to gain or maintain their freedom and in which slave owners tried to induce "the courts to become active agents of slave control" (p. 36).

In this context of uncertainty one man, Granville Sharp, created a triggering event, the Somerset case. Sharp, a remarkable and eccentric figure, descended from an unbroken line of clergymen and theologians; his grandfather was archbishop of York and his father an archdeacon. Due to adverse circumstances in his family he was apprenticed to a draper in his early youth, but this humble start did not withhold him from remarkable attainments (Howse 1952). If Sharp set himself to a challenging task, he was indefatigable and his exceptional intellectual gifts came to the fore.[20] In 1765, Sharp came into contact with slavery through a runaway slave, Jonathan Strong, whom he met in his brother's surgery. Strong's condition was very bad due to a series of savage beatings by his masters and "Sharp's prickly sensitivity was outraged by what he saw and heard" (Walvin 1973:117). Sharp helped the young man recover, found him a job, and defended him later in court against the claims of his master.[21] From then on Sharp threw himself completely into the cause of antislavery. He wrote (in 1769) a tract on the injustice of tolerating slavery in England, made contact with the antislavery Quaker Anthony Benezet, and saw to it that a tract against slavery by Benezet was reprinted in Britain. "By 1768 Sharp was accepted—by both black and white alike—as the principal white defender of black interests in England" (p. 119).

In the beginning of the 1770s the Somerset case took place, which soon became the battleground for the struggle on the question of slavery in Britain. James Somerset was a slave who was brought to England by his master, Charles Stewart. He ran away, was recaptured by his master, was placed on board a ship bound for the West Indies, and was released on a writ of habeas corpus. When Sharp became involved in this case, he and his humanitarian friends tried to use the case to "finally shatter the legal pretensions of the slave owners" (p. 121). The latter, in turn, sought to use the same case in their efforts to obtain legal backing for their property rights in slaves, joined forces, and supported Stewart, Somerset's master, with their wealth and influence. The presiding judge, Lord Mansfield, tried to avoid taking a decision, but in the end he decided that "English law did not allow the master to seize his servant to be sold abroad" (Drescher 1986:37). Somerset was thus a free man[22] and from then on deportation of runaway slaves to the colonies was no longer sanctioned by law.

The main difference between the Somerset case and earlier court cases regarding runaway slaves was the extensive coverage of the former by newspapers. The newspapers not only covered the Somerset case but, on this occasion, published other material regarding slavery as well, such as brief histories of slavery and excerpts from the writings of Benezet. The public interest in the case was enormous; in the words of Walvin, "From the first hearing of January through June, the court had been packed by interested parties, supporters and reporters" (1973:123). This public notoriety gave the Somerset case its triggering effect. It made the evils of slavery clearly visible for contemporaries, although these evils—as is the case with most triggering events—were openly present all along.[23] It gave, moreover, "the distaste for claims to property in persons an opportunity to crystallize" (Drescher 1986:39). The Somerset case together highlighted the anomalies and contradictions of slavery, brought the abstract and distanced evils of slavery to the people's doorstep, gave slavery its ugly face, and enlarged the public consciousness about the injustice and undesirability of slavery. Moreover, it drew more people into the orbit of those already active against slavery and the slave trade. This case did not, however, lead to collective actions against this evil. The Somerset case was, according to Drescher, "a skirmish, not a battle" (p. 49).

6.5 THE ACTION-STRUCTURE OF ABOLITION REVIEWED

It follows from our conceptualization in Chapter 3, that the action-structure within which the abolition movement was to operate must have played a pivotal role in changing the public definitions of slavery and the slave trade. We hypothesized that it could play this role because this structure—as any other action-structure—contained the resources, facilities, and constraints for the actors who committed themselves to waging the abolition campaigns. In this section we will take the first step in finding out whether the conceptualization of Chapter 3 is sound by assessing the state of the action-structure on the eve of the first abolition campaign, which started at the end of 1787. The state of the action-structure at this point in time provides the link between the historical developments described in Chapters 4 and 5, the episodic context depicted in this chapter, and the organizational context of the first abolition campaign, which will be analyzed in the next chapter.

As far as the internal elements of the action-structure, the cultural and structural power of the abolition movement, are concerned the important point is that there was not an abolition movement to speak of until the end of 1787 (see Drescher 1986:65, especially note 50, p. 207). Before that date, the Quakers had already undertaken collective actions against slavery and the slave trade, but they acted more as a pressure group than as a social movement. In these actions the Friends predominantly used the rather formidable resources they had at their command, but they were less active in mobilizing new resources specifically for the cause of abolition. The most one can say is that they initiated a protomovement. They foreshadowed, as it were, the coming abolition movement as they pioneered the methods that were subsequently used in that movement, such as the forming of networks of local agents and the petitioning of Parliament. Most importantly, with their actions the Quakers laid the foundation for the interpretive packages that were later used in the abolition struggle.

The conduciveness of the action-structure proved to be more important for the takeoff of the first abolition campaign. First of all, the preceding historical developments and events affected the culture of British society. The Enlightenment together with providential theology put forward notions regarding reason, right, and Providence and shaped a cultural climate in which themes like liberty, happiness, benevolence, and progress became dominant. These notions and themes pervaded all realms of society and put a premium on social reform and change. This way they highly facilitated collective actions directed at change. Although the ideological defense of existing societal arrangements remained intact and maintained widespread support (and thus put important constraints on collective actions directed at change), change had the edge on the status quo.

The aforementioned developments and events also had consequences related specifically to the cause of abolition. First, slavery was not easy to reconcile with the cast of Enlightenment thought, especially after Montesquieu's elaborations.[24] Under the influence of enlightened thinking, ideas changed so much in all cultural realms of British society that these were more and more at odds with the institution of slavery. In the 1780s, slavery and the slave trade could no longer be defended, intellectually and philosophically. The antislavery implications of the Enlightenment became especially clear in literature and economic theory.

Second, the Evangelical revival, which made antislavery the core of a drive to moral regeneration, combined with the turn of the Quakers to antislavery as *their* test of religious purity and truth (both, moreover, in relation to the above-mentioned more general cultural trends) undermined the classical and Christian justifications of slavery. This resulted in a cultural and religious climate that "directly challenged the traditional Christian view of slavery. God was [now seen as] a benevolent and constitutional ruler who desired the happiness of his subjects; He would not think of sanctioning perpetual and unmerited punishment of any kind" (Davis 1966:401). This new view did a great deal to shift the thought on the subject of slavery.

Third, the cultural changes mentioned above undermined, as Davis points out, "traditional religious and philosophical justifications for slavery" (p. 446). This weakening of the existing justifications of slavery helped to revive the basic contradiction of slavery that Davis puts forward, the contradiction between the notion of the slave as a thing and instrument of his master and the notion of the slave who is also a human being.[25] At the same time, another potential contradiction arose: the existence of two mutually exclusive labor systems in Great Britain. Such contradictions have the tendency to alert people to the injustice and untenability of situations revealed by the contradictions, especially when assisted by triggering events like the Somerset case. This, in its turn, facilitates collective action.

Fourth, the cultural trends of the eighteenth century further shaped the image of Africa and Africans. The overall image of Africa remained unfavorable. Its inhabitants were seen as human beings who were primitive and culturally backward. Their recognition as human beings contributed to reviving the aforementioned basic contradiction[26] and made empathy with the dismal fate of the black slave possible; both could facilitate antislavery actions. The fact that blacks were depicted as culturally inferior and backward, moreover, fit in well with ideas so popular among Evangelicals regarding their providential tasks in helping their less fortunate fellowmen. At the same time, the image of the West Indian planter deteriorated and with it all links with the institution of slavery became more and more corrupted. This weakened an important constraint on antislavery activities quite considerably.

Fifth, the ongoing discourses about slavery among philosophers, economists, theologists, Quakers, Evangelicals, etc., produced the tools for building the interpretive packages that were later used in the abolition struggle. Especially important in this respect were Montesquieu's work, Smith's economic condemnation of slavery, the literary theme of the noble Negro, the Quaker tradition culminating in Benezet's monumental antislavery writings, and the tracts of Wesley, Sharp, and Clarkson, which brought the antislavery message home to the Britons. Probably the most important cultural tool in this respect was forged by the changing meaning of sin. The vision of sin as a state of self-inflicted spiritual slavery and of external bondage as a product of sin gave way to the identification of slavery as a sin in itself. This made the elaborate Christian fund of ideas concerning sin available for abolitionism.[27]

The cultural conduciveness of British society to change, reform, and antislavery must, however, not blind us to the existence of four important cultural constraints. First, slavery was a self-evident fact of life for the British public until the end of 1787. Neither the widely publicized Somerset case, the atrocities of the Zong case (see Chapter 7, note 48), the activities of the Quakers, nor the actions of men like Sharp and Wesley changed the matter-of-fact character of slavery. As Drescher puts it, "Until then [the end of 1787] slavery and the slave trade remained at the prepolitical level of unsavoury but unassailable" (p. 65).[28] Second, the conception of a British national interest of which the colonies and slavery were indispensable elements hindered antislavery considerably in becoming a public issue. Third, there were rules in the political culture that restricted participation in politics to members of the social elites, which constricted the range of potential initiators and leaders of collective action to a rather great extent. The same rules excluded dissenters from official life, which acted as another constraint since antislavery was foremost the province of dissent. This last constraint became, however, less and less important as this exclusion became factually less strict toward the end of the century. Fourth, the principle of the right of property posed another far from negligible hindrance to abolition actions.

The structural or systemic conduciveness of British society to collective (political) actions in general and to abolition campaigns in particular is equally important as its cultural conduciveness. The political structure of Great Britain in the last quarter of the eighteenth century offered important opportunities for collective action. First, the system's partial openness made political activities possible while its partial closure delivered "causes without voice" in the sphere of politics; an important part of the "stuff" social movements are made of. Moreover, the system remained open for the cause of abolition as this drive was not seen as a threat to the stability of the political structure (Davis 1975). Second, the political elites in Britain were divided on important political questions such as the necessity of social and political reform and the need to do away with slavery and the slave trade. This division facilitated access to political decision-making. Third, the simultaneous existence of several causes without a voice,[29] especially parliamentary reform, was an important facility for the abolitionists as the supporters of the other causes often supported abolition as well. Fourth, the coming into being of the social movement as a new way to influence political decision-making was another important asset for the abolition movement.

The mediazation of British society due to the vast structural transformations also gave important facilities to social movements in the last part of the eighteenth century. Media became more and more the focal means of communication for elites as well as publics. For social movement organizations and moral entrepreneurs, they provided the channels to reach constituencies and the general public alongside the channels provided by the networks in which people were organized; the media became key facilities for political action. Media also provided the public with information about events and developments in society. In view of all this, they occupied an important position in society and were—when the lively interest in media products is taken into account—highly valued. Finally, the routines of the media were such that they regularly paid attention to (anti-)slavery and abolition.

The combined developments in the economic realm and in the religious sphere, i.e., the Evangelical revival and the Quakers' turn, were not only important in cultural terms but had systemic effects as well.[30] They were responsible for creating the potential for the abolition movement. Economic changes set in motion the forming of the middle and the working classes [the proletariat included], part of which the Evangelical movement and the Society of Friends turned into:

1.   The leaders of the abolition movement.   The Quakers initiated the founding of the central social movement organization, the Abolition Committee, by erecting the London Meeting of Sufferings directed at attacking the slave trade. The Evangelicals provided the other important leaders such as Wilberforce and Sharp.

2. The mobilization potential of the abolition movement. The existing networks of the Evangelicals and Quakers offered the conscience constituencies, which could easily be mobilized. Here the example the Quakers set was important as well. They set up an organization of local agents to organize the antislavery drive and to dispense antislavery material. This example was readily followed by the Abolition Committee.[31]

The opportunity structure of Great Britain in the 1780s was not only characterized by its systemic facilities; it contained important constraints as well. First, the core of the political elite was against curtailing slavery and the slave trade. Above all, the king, his relatives and other members of the aristocracy—a formidable bloc in the House of Lords—were outspoken adversaries of antislavery measures because they regarded slavery as being central to the interests of Britain. Illustrative in this respect is the position of Pitt, who stood practically alone when he tried to do something about the slave trade in 1787 and 1788. Second, the slave interest was well organized, in Parliament as well as in society, and had plentiful financial resources and political influence at its disposal. The West Indian Interest had the means to organize the resistance against antislavery actions and to obstruct them. It had—in any case—the ability to limit the effectiveness of abolition groups considerably.[32]

Historical developments and events in the eighteenth century had shaped a situation in Britain that made collective actions against slavery and the slave trade possible. In 1787, three of the key ingredients of Anstey's tentative model of the reforming impulse were present: "the preparation of the ground by changes in philosophical and theological ideas; the slow germination of reform in the bosom of a denominational community; the impetus for reform coming from an new, or newly rediscovered, religious dynamism" (1980:36), alongside other cultural and systemic facilities. Although the situation was favorable, abolition would not be a walkover as serious constraints and limitations still remained.

Furthermore, a favorable social situation is not enough. At least two conditions have to be met if such a situation is to develop into a movement and collective actions: a cause and agency.[33] Abolition (and antislavery in general) was a feasible cause in the 1780s alongside others such as parliamentary, religious, and social reform. As we have seen above, there were candidates present to act on such a cause and in the British situation there were important ingredients favoring abolition as a cause to live and to fight for. Although Rice is right in concluding that "[t]he eighteenth-century abolitionist movement . . . was rooted in a series of profound intellectual changes which affected the whole of the

western world" (1975:392), particularly important in the British situation
were:

- the contradictions inherent in slavery, which had become visible
through a conjunction of developments and events;
- the initiative of the Quakers to attack the slave trade in Great
Britain;
- the extraordinary fit between abolition and developing notions
among the Evangelicals regarding Providence, sin, redemption, and
retribution;
- the fact that abolition was less threatening for the powerholders
than reform.

Still, as Davis rightly states, "The question of abolishing slavery [the
slave trade included] was ultimately a question of power" (1975:49). We
will look further into this question in the next chapter.

NOTES

1.   In this chapter we follow Davis and use the term *Evangelical* to indicate
both the Evangelicals within the established church and those outside it.
2.   As Davis (1966) points out, for Lay (and for Sandiford as well) slavery
was not just one of the various unrelated evils, but the source of all iniquity,
whose eradication justified rhetoric like "The very worst part of the old Whores
Merchandize [slaves], nasty filthy Whore of Whores, *Babilon's Bastards*" (cited in
Davis 1966:291) or plunging a sword into a hidden bladder filled with red juice at
a Quaker meeting to demonstrate what involvement in slavery entailed.
3.   This dilemma had already originated in the bloody wars against the
Indians in the North American colonies, which dismayed the Friends considerably.
4.   As Weber shows in his work and especially in his illuminating essay
Religiöse Heilsmethodik und Systematisierung der Lebensführung ([1920] 1975), this
dilemma is a multifaceted and very complex one. Religious virtuosity *in* the
world often entails either trying to change the world and in the end being
crushed by its forces or accommodating and gradually blending into the overwhelming background of the middle of the road religion of daily life. Leaving the
world, on the other hand, puts the religious ideal out of reach of many aspiring
virtuosi and may moreover lead to their becoming tolerated and thus ineffective
curiosities.
5.   As the saying goes about the Quakers, They came to America to do good
and they did well. (Thanks to Michael Krass, who was raised in the heart of
Quaker land.)
6.   The goal of this pamphlet of William Dillwyn and John Lloyd becomes
immediately clear by looking at its title, *The Case of Our Fellow Creatures, the*

Oppressed Africans, Respectfully Recommended to the Serious Consideration of the Legislature of Great-Britain, by the People Called Quakers (cited in Davis 1975:224). Twelve thousand free copies of this pamphlet were distributed in Britain in 1784 (Craton 1974).

7. There were, however, at the same time quite a few for whom "living in the Enlightenment England afforded a relaxed, emotionally frank breathing space" between the moral strictures of the previous era and of the coming (Victorian) era (Porter 1990b:258).

8. This section is mainly based on Plumb (1950), Briggs (1959), Ashley (1973), Gilbert (1976), and Porter (1990b), alongside the already mentioned antislavery studies.

9. As Gilbert shows, the Evangelical communities executed social functions as well, especially for those who were left out in the "anomic cold" of the rapidly transforming society of the second half of the eighteenth century.

10. For a detailed exposition of this process, see Chapters 7 and 8 of Anstey (1975). As Anstey shows, the role of Philip Doddridge and William Law was especially important for the cause of antislavery as their work foreshadowed the major Evangelical themes and greatly affected the life and work of the later abolitionists.

11. See Anstey (1975:162–64) for the elaboration of this transposition. According to Davis, "true virtue [in the eyes of the Evangelicals] was to be found in a transcendence of the self, or . . . in a [general] disposition to love." Benevolence was thus in this way the ultimate ideal of the Evangelicals as well (1966:385–86).

12. The Evangelicals, especially Wesley's Methodists, put an emphasis on a personal and often emotional belief culminating in the notion of "New Birth as an instantaneous transformation of the soul" (Davis 1966:386). The soul was seen as being alienated from God and from oneself by sin. This soul could only be saved through conversion that in Methodist circles was ritualized as a "drama" of salvation (Mathews 1980). The emotionality is likewise apparent in religious activities as love feasts and "tear-jerking" open-air sermons. As Hurwitz shows, the Evangelicals were, moreover, not content with their own spiritual rebirth but pressed their fellowmen—sometimes rather compellingly—"to accept God's boundless grace and [to do] God's work on earth" (1973:17).

13. In 1779, for example, Sharp attempted to launch a parliamentary examination into the African trade. He did this by canvassing twenty-two out of twenty-six bishops and archbishops. Another example is his attempt to initiate the prosecution of those responsible for throwing the slaves overboard the slave ship *Zong*. In both cases, Sharp was not successful (Anstey 1975:245–46).

14. Wilberforce—the leader of the abolition campaign in Parliament—became an Evangelical only shortly before the onset of the campaign. Clarkson—another major figure in antislavery—got involved via a different route: through writing a prize-winning essay about slavery and through his publisher. The latter introduced him to abolitionist circles just before the campaign started.

15. Drescher (1986) clearly disagrees with Walvin (1973) regarding the problems that the African presence in Britain engendered. He sees this presence as being less problematic than Walvin does and he brings forward several indica-

tors that show the absence of high social tensions between blacks and whites in Britain.

16. The panic about, above all, nonwhite immigration is not the only striking resemblance between the last part of the eighteenth century and the corresponding part of the twentieth. The vast and rapid economic transformation of society is another example (see also the end of Chapter 9). To delve into these resemblances any deeper would, however, demand a different book.

17. Walvin (1973: especially Chapters 3, 4, and 6) and Drescher (1986:12–49) portray this confusion rather well. Their differences in valuing the attitudes toward and the treatment of black Africans especially reflect—inadvertently—the confusion alluded to.

18. Racism is, however, something from a later date. As Curtin states, "Race as such was a *mark* identifying the group—not a *cause* of the group's other characteristics" (1964:36). Only after the rise of the anti–slave trade movement did negative racial stereotyping develop.

19. As Drescher cites an early legal decision, "[T]he law took no notice of a negro" (1986:27).

20. For instance, "He studied Hebrew to confute a Jew, and Greek to confute a Socinian, and to such effect that he made original contributions to the study of both languages" (Howse 1952:20).

21. The way Sharp operated in this case is illustrative of the kind of person Sharp was. In the Strong case, Sharp was not satisfied with the legal advice he received. Although he had no legal training, Sharp "flung himself into his own legal research to prove the lawyers wrong and produced such an impressive legal paper that the counsel of Strong's master could only drop the case" (Walvin 1973:118).

22. We will not deal with the question of whether this decision meant the end of slavery on British soil as this is not relevant for the effect of the case regarding the abolition of the slave trade, i.e., its triggering effect. See on the former, among many others, Walvin (1973:124–29) and Drescher (1986:40–49).

23. For instance, people saw advertisements in newspapers about slave auctions, padlocked collars, and runaway slaves.

24. At this point, one has to keep in mind that Enlightenment writings on slavery were not all clear-cut but were inherently ambivalent. They often boiled down to a condemnation on the abstract level and an acceptance in concrete circumstances. On the whole, however, this cast of thought gravitated toward an antislavery point of view.

25. According to Davis, "The inherent contradiction of slavery lay not in its cruelty or economic exploitation, but in the underlying conception of man as a conveyable possession with no more autonomy of will and consciousness than a domestic animal" (1966:62). As Davis also makes clear, the fact that a slave is more than a thing was already recognized by the existence of laws that authorized punishment of slaves by their masters and that gave certain protection to slaves and by the practice of sexual relations between masters and slaves (for a more extensive treatment of the basic contradiction of slavery, see Davis 1966).

26. The slave as a human being is a core argument of Granville Sharp against slavery. In 1769 he argued that a black slave cannot be deprived of his

liberty as a horse or dog can because a slave "differs from a horse or a dog in . . . *his humanity*" (cited in Craton et al. 1976:211).

27. For Davis this change of meaning is a necessary condition for the abolition and antislavery struggle. He states: "Since sin was traditionally thought of as a kind of slavery, and external bondage was justified as a product of sin, any change in the meaning of sin would be likely to affect attitudes toward slavery. . . . The point is that men could not fully perceive the moral contradictions of slavery until a major religious transformation had changed their ideas of sin and spiritual freedom" (1966:292).

28. Drescher (1986) abundantly illustrates that slavery was not a public and political issue in the late 1770s and 1780s (pp. 61–66), although there was a lively interest in the subject among a considerable part of the British reading public (Davis 1966). Indicative for the general indifference was the fact that the slave interest did not even bother to react to initiatives like those of the Quakers.

29. Anstey mentions in this respect, parliamentary reform, economical reform, Catholic emancipation, and abolition (1975:357).

30. In Great Britain of the eighteenth century, religion played the same role concerning the supply of the mobilizing ideology and the organizational basis for collective action as, according to Snow and Marshall, religion does today in many Third World countries (1984).

31. As Davis shows, the cooperation between Quakers and Evangelicals, "most notably with the Wilberforce-Thornton syndicate of reformers . . . 'was very important.' It was this latter group that appropriated Quaker programs and Quaker modes of organization as means of reforming and 'saving' the nation" (1975:246–47).

32. Anstey comes, however, to the conclusion "that West Indian opposition in itself was never remotely strong enough to arrest the progress of abolition. A more generalised but deep-rooted sense of the importance of the West Indies for British prosperity among the political nation, especially as represented in Parliament, was the critically important obstacle" (1975:407).

33. This means (1) the presence of material out of which a cause may be constructed and (2) decisions of actors because, as Davis contends, "No matter how 'ripe' the time, there would be no coalescing of antislavery opinion until specific decisions and commitments were taken by individual men" (1966:489).

7

The First Abolition Campaign
The Organizational Context

7.1 INTRODUCTION

In Chapter 6 we saw that the Quakers took the initiative to attack the institution of slavery in the 1780s, through which they formed "the major link in the transition from abolitionist thought to action" (Drescher 1986:62). This initiative proceeded from an internal religious revival in which antislavery had become one of the key issues. This revival—interestingly enough—foreshadowed and partly coincided with "the great evangelical awakening of the late eighteenth and early nineteenth centuries—the Evangelical crusade within the Church of England, the triumphs of Methodism on both sides of the Atlantic, and parallel movements within the Baptist and Presbyterian churches" (Davis 1975:246). On its own, the Quaker initiative did not lead to a public discourse on slavery and the slave trade, but this changed when it fused with the religious awakening in Great Britain; particularly when the Quakers actually joined forces with the rising Evangelicals during 1787.[1] After 1787 the period began in which "popular pressure was effectively deployed as a means of altering national policy" (Drescher 1986:3).

In May 1787 the Abolition Committee[2] was formed out of the Quaker's Meeting of Sufferings. Founding this committee was predominantly the initiative of the Quakers, who drew in Sharp and Clarkson, with whom they had cooperated well before 1787.[3] Granville Sharp became its chairman, which contributed greatly to the legitimation of the committee's activities. As Anstey remarks, "No others at that time could have brought such lustre to the anti-slavery cause in Britain, such was his achieved reputation" (1975:247). Thomas Clarkson became involved in the work of the committee when he was looking for a suitable publisher for the popularized version of his prize-winning essay. He coincidentally met James Phillips, member of a Quaker antislavery committee, who not only published Clarkson's tract but also introduced him to other people involved in antislavery, such as William Dillwyn and Granville Sharp. This introduction brought Clarkson in contact with more abolition-minded people, such as the Middletons, and their combined pressures led him "to give up his considerable prospects of ecclesiastical preferment and devote himself to the abolitionist cause" (Anstey 1975:249). One of the first undertakings of Clarkson on behalf of this cause was to canvass for support among men of note. This led him to the man who would become one of the key figures of the abolition movement: William Wilberforce, the future leader of the political campaigns for abolition.

May 1787 was not only the month in which the Abolition Committee was founded, but it was also the month in which Wilberforce announced his decision to take up the question of abolition in Parliament.[4] This decision[5] was the effect of the influence of people like the Middletons, Clarkson, and above all his friend Pitt, who in the words of Wilberforce, "recommended me to undertake its [abolition] conduct, as a subject suited to my character and talents" (cited in Howse 1952:12).[6] One of the major reasons for applying this pressure was that although the Abolition Committee was blessed with the presence of dedicated and brilliant men, it lacked an advocate to put their cause forward in Parliament (Furneaux 1974:70). In Wilberforce the abolitionists found a man in whom all the needed personal qualities and relational resources—talent, position, and perseverance—were united.

Wilberforce[7] descended from an old family of prosperous Hull merchants. He was not only wealthy, but also intellectually gifted, eloquent, at times witty, and charming. His background and his gifts ensured Wilberforce a solid position in the civil and political society of the 1780s and he could (and did)—well connected as he was—participate in the leisured life of Britain's elite. Two steps that Wilberforce took were of crucial importance to abolition. The first step was his decision after completing his studies at Cambridge to pursue a political career. In the elections of 1780–1781 Wilberforce became M.P. for Hull. The second step regards Wilberforce's conversion to Evangelicalism. The seeds for this far-reaching step were sown during a mundane undertaking: his voyages to the continent with Isaac Milner, his former tutor and later fellow Evangelical. During these trips Milner and Wilberforce read religious books and discussed these, from which a profound spiritual crisis arose.[8] The decisive moment arrived when he again came in contact with John Newton, a converted former captain of a slave ship who was now a vicar. This led to a protracted period of torment and soul-searching and ultimately to Wilberforce's decision to lead the demanding life of a "real" Christian without fully giving up "the world."

The year 1787 marks the completion of Wilberforce's conversion and the beginning of his career of usefulness, which centered upon two key causes: moral reform and antislavery. As Wilberforce himself put in his diary in 1787, "God Almighty has set before me two great objects, the suppression of the slave trade and the reformation of manners" (cited in Walvin 1980:149). At about the same time Henry Thornton took the initiative of forming a group out of the Evangelicals of note within the established church. This group of leading Anglican Evangelicals is commonly known as the Clapham sect, named after the place where most of them lived and where they congregated.[9] Howse refers to this group as "the brotherhood of Christian politicians," which neatly captures its central aspects, viz., leading a practical Christian life of good works and being active in reforming society in the direction of the Evangelical ideals. The latter meant in practice that the Clapham sect as it "consisted of no ordinary persons" (Howse 1952:20) functioned as the headquarters of several Evangelical crusades. Abolition was one of them and it was important for the cause of abolition that the abolition movement and the Clapham sect developed alongside each other. The last ultimately became the most effective abolition group politically.

The years 1785–1787 form the period in which the trends and events of the preceding eighty to ninety years culminated in putting into place the basic condition of the abolition campaigns, viz., the founding of the Abolition Committee—the social movement organization (SMO) of the abolition movement—and the "appointment" of Wilberforce as the political leader of the cause. This small band of dedicated men had its roots in three resourceful networks: the Society of Friends, the developing Clapham sect, and the Middleton-Ramsay circle. The movement organization and Wilberforce also had an important link with the Methodist community in the person of Wesley, who was the first religious leader of importance to support the case against slavery. Another important link was the connection with the sphere of politics in the persons of Pitt, the prime minister, Fox, the leader of the opposition, and Grenville, the future prime minister.

The extension of this support base was one of the goals of the first campaign of the abolition movement. Another goal was convincing society that the slave trade was an evil that had to be eradicated. This meant that the campaign also had to be executed at the political level, as this was the only way to effectively end the slave trade. In this chapter we will not look at the first abolition campaign chronologically as this has already been done exhaustively (see in this respect, especially, Anstey 1975). Instead we will systematically look at the campaign from different angles. An unfortunate consequence of this choice, however, is that some elements of the campaign will be presented more than once. We will begin with a systematic description of the main activities of the abolitionists and their adversaries between 1787 and 1792 (Section 7.2).

The implication of that campaign, the public discourse on the slave trade and slavery, will be the subject of the section thereafter (Section 7.3). Here we will focus, above all, on the cultural side of this discourse. Following that is Section 7.4 on the effect of the first campaign on public thought regarding slavery and the slave trade. Finally, we will conclude this chapter with the events that brought the first campaign to a rather abrupt halt.

7.2   THE CAMPAIGN

The campaign to end the slave trade in Great Britain that started in 1787 was the first of a series of antislavery campaigns. It was not only the first popular movement against slavery in the history of mankind but was also part of the transformation of the patterns of collective action in Britain (Tilly 1982). The latter implied a great deal of experimentation and innovation, which gives the abolition campaign its rather "modern" outlook. It consisted on the one hand of building on the activities that the Quakers had started and on the other of developing further the new political techniques that were in the making at that time. We will begin this section by describing the abolitionist side of the campaign, proceed with presenting the way their opponents reacted, and end with a concluding note.

7.2.1   The Abolitionist Activities

From the beginning, the actors involved in the abolition movement directed their energies toward both Parliament and public. They aimed at a parliamentary decision to outlaw the slave trade and saw the mobilization of the public as one—albeit an important one—of the means to reach this goal.[10] Their activities represented a combination of consensus and action mobilization, collective action as a social movement, and political action in the form of a lobby and pressure group. Together, the activities of the abolitionists brought the abolition cause into a spiral of mobilization (Klandermans 1988).

Grass Roots Organization.   For the Abolition Committee, the importance of some kind of grass roots organization was clear right from the beginning. As early as July 1787 the committee started with setting up a system of local correspondents to disseminate the committee's publications and to promote the abolition cause in their areas. This system was largely the continuation of the Quaker's antislavery organization in Britain, but was extended further and developed into a network of local abolition committees. This committee system became the heart of organized antislavery and, above all, took care of raising money, managing the petitions, and more generally organizing public support (Oldfield 1995).

The grass roots organization reflected on the one hand its origins in the existing religious—predominantly dissenting—networks and on the other the connections of the abolition movement leaders among the elites of British society. The result was an abolition network composed of very diverse sectors of society.[11] It contained men of note such as the prominent M.P. Charles James Fox and the well-known man of letters and scientist David Hartley; members of the middle classes; as well as—particularly through the Methodist connection—many members of the lower middle and the upcoming working classes. As Drescher makes clear, the skilled artisans formed an especially important constituency in the first phase of the abolition movement or, in his words, "on the basis of the evidence at hand it appears that abolitionism struck an especially responsive chord among the artisanry during the early industrial revolution" (1986:133). In addition to this recruitment in the male world, the abolitionists very consciously drew women into the abolition network (Walvin 1985; Oldfield 1995).

The Gathering of Information and Knowledge of the Slave Trade. In 1787 the Abolition Committee took the decision to gather information on the slave trade, even before it was known "that there was to be a Parliamentary inquiry" (Furneaux 1974:73). On the one hand, it meant the continuation of a tradition within abolitionist circles (cf. the work of Benezet) while, on the other, accurate evidence was needed from 1788 onwards for the investigations of the Privy Council and the Parliament. This herculean task was primarily executed by Clarkson, who studied the Custom House Papers in London (p. 73), went on several journeys of investigation in Britain, and did an admirable job as detective in the ports of London, Bristol, and Liverpool.[12] Together, his efforts resulted in a wealth of facts concerning the economics of the slave trade, its importance, and the circumstances under which the trade was carried out.[13] The evidence presented a gruesome picture of the slave trade, of both the plight of the black slaves and the sailors who manned the slave ships.

The Mobilization of Public Opinion. At a very early stage the abolitionists devoted part of their energies to mobilizing public opinion, which in their case meant arousing the general moral feeling of the nation. In this respect, the Manchester Abolition Committee took the lead, turning the original London initiative, a more low-key anti–slave trade lobby, "into the prototype of the modern social reform movement" (Drescher 1986:67). The mobilization of public opinion meant even more; it was, according to Drescher, a historical turning point because "it was the mobilization of public opinion which ushered in the consciousness that one was in a new period in the history of slavery; not in the sense of inaugurating an era of uninterrupted victories but in the sense that the terms of public discourse about the institution in Britain were dramatically and forever altered" (ibid.).

The abolitionists used five means to mobilize public opinion: the production and distribution of tracts and pamphlets, the creation and marketing of visual material, organizing lectures and meetings, getting favorable notice in the press, and setting up petition campaigns. We will deal consecutively with the first four means below and will look into the fifth one separately, because mobilizing opinion was only a secondary goal of petitioning.

1.   The production and distribution of written material.   The Abolition Committee arranged that antislavery tracts and pamphlets were (re)produced and distributed. Clarkson reworked his famous essay in 1787 into a pamphlet called *A Summary View of the Slave Trade and of the Probable Consequences of its Abolition*. Another pamphlet was written "by the reverend John Newton in which he effectively attacked the trade in which he had once participated" (Anstey 1975:257). This production and distribution was executed on a relatively large scale from the late 1780s onwards; as Drescher shows on the basis of research by Joyce Bert, Lowell Ragatz, and P. C. Lipscomb, "Just before the American War of Independence about three antislavery tracts were published each year. Output rose to an annual average of under six in 1783–7, and then soared to over 46 per year in 1787–1792" (1986:207). Another activity of the committee involved the more restricted dissemination of special editions of larger works, especially those of Benezet and Clarkson.[14] These publishing activities also led Wesley to the publication of a new edition of his *Thoughts upon Slavery*.

The abolition campaign also inspired sympathetic writers to write against slavery and the slave trade, mostly in the form of poems.[15] Well-known examples are the Liverpool abolitionist William Roscoe, who wrote (originally anonymously) *The Wrongs of Africa*, the Claphamite Hannah More with her influential *The Black Slave Trade*, and the renowned Evangelical poet William Cowper, who wrote the widely known *The Negro's Complaint*. This last poem became even more widely known as it "was set to a popular tune and evidently designed as propaganda jingle" (Anstey 1975:259). The abolition cause profited, moreover, from the literary work of former slaves who had had the chance to learn to write and read English. These writings, particularly those of Sancho,

Equiano, and Cugoano, were amply used in the abolition campaign. The last two authors also played an active role in mobilization activities (Walvin 1973).

The scale of these efforts was relatively large as can be seen in the amount of money the committee spent in the first fifteen months of its existence (more than one thousand pounds) and the quantities produced and distributed (e.g., fifteen thousand copies of Clarkson's *Summary View*). The output of written antislavery material rose exponentially from 1787 onwards and the campaign was "accompanied by a flood of polemical writings which reached its high point between 1788 and 1792" (Craton 1982:104). Sypher reports that the Abolition Committee "was responsible for the printing of 25,526 reports and 51,432 pamphlets and books between May, 1787, and July, 1788" ([1942] 1969:19). Striking in the material produced by the abolitionists, especially in the tracts and pamphlets, was the ample use of statistics and empirical data on slavery and the slave trade. The people of Britain had to be convinced by facts.

2.   The creation and marketing of visual material.   The abolitionists also used nonwritten material to mobilize support and to arouse public opinion. As Oldfield (1995) makes clear, they shaped a visual culture in which the abolition message was expressed. The most famous specimens of this material were (1) the medallion Josiah Wedgwood designed and produced depicting a kneeling slave in chains with the words Am I Not a Man and a Brother? (over two hundred thousand copies sold, it functioned as a sort of campaign button; Craton 1974:262), and (2) the schematic plan of a loaded slave ship drawn by Clarkson that sold even better (Drescher 1986:78). The abolitionists created other cultural artefacts as well, such as token coins and medals. This assemblage of icons, symbols, and other visual means made abolition fashionable and brought it directly into the reach of people; it shaped a visual abolition culture of which the figure of the kneeling slave was the core (Oldfield 1995:179).

3.   The organization of lectures and meetings.   Walvin (1985) calls the lecture a crucial factor in the abolition campaigns. Right from the start, the abolitionists organized a vast amount of lectures and other antislavery gatherings all over the country and created several lecture circuits with speakers renowned for their oratory qualities. Missionaries who could give eyewitness accounts of the atrocities of slavery were also very useful in these circuits. The champion of these lectures was Clarkson, who traveled thirty-five thousand miles between 1787 and 1794 on seven lecture and research tours all over Britain. These lectures and gatherings drew huge audiences and were—if the meeting place was full—often repeated. Organizers never had trouble finding suitable meeting places; as Walvin observes, "Town halls, guild halls, music halls, Leeds coloured cloth hall, chapels, churches and so on all pro-

vided anti-slavery with a venue" (1985:36). The capacity of this abolition-ist tactic to mobilize people is illustrated by Walvin's description of Clarkson's first tour in 1787–1788: "[H]e [Clarkson] was regularly stag-gered by the crowds packing his lecture rooms [and this tactic was partly] responsible for the transformation of the concept of black free-dom, from the preserve of a small handful of propertied, educated men of sensibility—Wilberforce and his friends—into the stuff of mass, dem-ocratic politics" (p. 35).

4. Getting a favorable notice in the press. Alongside—and partly in cooperation with—the other tactics directed at mobilizing public opinion, the anti–slave trade activists were quick in seeking ways to attract the attention of the press. In the 1780s, there was already a well-developed system of national and provincial newspapers accompanied by magazines and periodicals. These media paid attention to antislavery publications and quite a number of them, especially provincial news-papers, were inclined "to publish items favourable to the abolition" (Anstey 1975:257).[16] The abolitionists also used another method to get media attention. They announced petitions, lectures, and other antislav-ery meetings in advertisements that prompted the media to be present at those occasions and to cover them.

All in all, the abolition movement actors, i.e., the London and the local committees alike, succeeded in getting access to newspapers and magazines.[17] Particularly from the end of 1787, an explosion in news-paper attention for the cause of abolition occurred. As Drescher docu-ments in a note:

> The new version of *The Times Index*, for 1785–9, illustrates [the explosion of newspaper attention]. From January 1785 to September 1787 there are 19 items entered under "slave trade" or about 18 items every two months. Items relating only to the *abolition* of the slave trade appeared *once* every *ten* months between January 1785 and September 1787. From September 1787 to December 1788, abolition-related items appeared at a rate of 90 every ten months. All told, in the 2¾ years before October 1787, only four of fifteen items in *The Times* were related to abolition. The other were simply traditional trade reports. In the 15 months beginning October 1787, 136 out of 140 items were related to abolition. During the first trimester of 1788, before the subject was mentioned in Parliament, more than half of the items consisted of announcements of the various abolition petitions. The "slave trade" items in *The Times* of London 1787–9 were [over-whelmingly on moral and political activities against slavery] (items include correspondence, reports, petitions, etc.). (1986:207)

Petition Campaigns. The Manchester Abolition Committee took the initiative[18] to apply petitioning Parliament as a means of mobilizing public opinion in order to put pressure on individual M.P.s and the cabinet. In this respect, it functioned as the social movement organization (Drescher 1987). Petitioning was an existing political format for expressing demands mostly "emanating from some [privileged] interest or corporate group (nobility, clergy, freemen, corporation members, and so on)" (Drescher 1986:74). It was, among other things, widely used in the earlier struggle for parliamentary reform.

Before the onset of the abolition campaign, the inhabitants of Manchester had already changed the character of petitioning somewhat by using this political technique not as status group but as an assembly of inhabitants of a certain locality. As inhabitants of a newly industrializing region, they acted to avert the economic disadvantages of government policies. The use of this technique for abolition purposes changed it further. It made petitioning one of the standard formats in the developing collective action repertoire (cf. Tilly 1982). Manchester could play this role because, on the one hand, it had the expertise to organize mass petitions and, on the other, it was as a newly developing town relatively free from the old corporate social order.[19]

The petition campaigns began with a formal public meeting in which the resolution, i.e., the content of the petition, was passed. Such meetings were generally announced in newspapers and were often covered by those papers. The Manchester Abolition Committee also took the initiative to publish the resolutions in advertisements, an initiative that was readily followed. After the meeting the resolution was circulated in order to get more people to sign and often additional meetings were organized. In all cases, people were canvassed for signatures in order to demonstrate that the petition expressed the general consensus.

In the first petition campaign of 1788, the Manchester Abolition Committee was actively engaged—and successful—in drawing other cities and counties into the campaign. As Drescher states, the slave interest was overwhelmed by "the resounding echo Manchester's petition elicited from all parts of England [and the resulting total of one hundred and one] was an unprecedented levy of petitions for the decade between the Peace of Versailles and the second abolitionist wave in 1792" (1986:71). Manchester assembled by far the most signatures (over ten thousand), which represented about two-thirds of its eligible men. As far as statistics are available, some of the other towns and counties reached comparable results.

The second campaign of 1792 was coordinated by the London Abolition Committee, which, however, kept a lower profile so as to avoid giving the impression of an orchestrated process. As Drescher states:

> In most respects the pattern of 1788 was repeated, but on a more comprehensive scale. The abolitionists capitalized on their virtual monopoly of popular support. The total number of petitions quintupled from 102 to

519, the largest number ever submitted to the House on a single subject or
in a single session. Every English county was now represented, although
the most massive support still seemed to emanate from the North. (p. 80)

From 1788 onwards, petitioning became a key instrument of abolitionist
politics and it made an important contribution to placing the abolition
issue at the top of both the public and the political agenda. The abolitionist petitions outnumbered all other petitions between the late 1780s
and the 1830s and the number of people who signed was unprecedented: 60,000–100,000 in 1788 and 380,000–400,000 in 1792 (Blackburn
1988:144). As Walvin points out: "Indeed, in the key phases of antislavery, when anti-slavery pressed most persistently at Parliament's
doors, the petitions reflected a staggering level of support and organization [and] attracted more names than any other contemporary issue"
(1985:37).

Parliamentary Activities.   From the beginning, it was clear to the abolitionists that the abolition of the slave trade could only be attained by
legal measures, i.e., by parliamentary decisions. This meant (1) putting
abolition on the political agenda and (2) producing a majority in both
houses of Parliament. The first was brought about by Wilberforce's announcement in 1787. The second, in Wilberforce's eyes, would not pose
much of a problem.[20] Rather naive, he thought that the recent arousal of
the nation's moral feeling with regard to the evil of the slave trade would
suffice. He was, in the words of Howse, "strangely unaware of the real
power of the interests he opposed" (1952:32).

At the same time, however, according to Anstey, "more sobering
thoughts evidently supervened almost immediately, for . . . Pitt and
Wilberforce agreed that more factual information, which, they automatically supposed would necessarily discredit the slave trade, must be
sought" (1975:267). Pitt chose to do this through a committee of the
Privy Council, which would assemble evidence and hear witnesses
about the African slave trade. This strategy caused considerable delay in
the introduction of the abolition motion because this was only possible
after completion of the Privy Council report. Such was the case in April
1789, and on 12 May 1789 Wilberforce introduced the abolition motion
and delivered his first parliamentary speech on the subject of abolition.

Until that moment, the parliamentary activities of the Abolition Committee had consisted of assembling evidence and witnesses for the inquiry of the Privy Council and lobbying for support among members of
Parliament. The move of Wilberforce in May 1789 was the next logical
step. It proved, however, to be fundamentally a nonevent because abolition "quite simply was not argued substantively but shelved on the
ground that the Commons must hear their own evidence on the matter—and this *despite* the very lengthy and thorough report of the Privy

Council" (p. 271). This decision delayed the substantive discussion of the motion for nearly two years. Even worse, in April 1791 the abolition motion was finally defeated—despite the energy Wilberforce, the Abolition Committee, and others had put into producing conclusive evidence concerning the evil of the slave trade and garnering support of M.P.s—by 88 to 163 votes.[21]

7.2.2 The Antiabolitionist Reaction

The opposition to abolition developed more or less as a countermovement in reaction to the abolitionist attack. It undertook similar activities as the abolitionists did. The institutional heart of the opposition was the London Society of West Indian Planters and Merchants in which the West Indian planters living in or near London and the London merchants trading to the West Indies were assembled. This society, mostly through its executive committee, the Standing Committee, took the lead in the opposition to abolition. Important members of this committee were Stephen Fuller, its factual leader, planter, and agent for Jamaica; Lord Penrhyn, chairman of the committee and M.P. for Liverpool; and Edward Long, the Jamaican historian and founder of the racist view on slavery. In the first phase of the abolition campaign, the West Indian Interest mainly operated as a pressure group influencing the political system. Later, when the abolitionist pressure mounted higher, they also took the "movement road." Below we will first deal with the parliamentary activities, then with the attempts to support these activities by petitioning, and finally with the antiabolitionist mobilization of public opinion.

Parliamentary Activities. Wilberforce's announcement of parliamentary action against the slave trade of 1787 coupled with the information that the prime minister would back Wilberforce's initiative pushed the West Indian Interest into action. The Standing Committee formed a subcommittee to take necessary action regarding "the present application to Parliament on the subject of Negroes."[22] The defense against the abolitionist attack in Parliament proceeded along two lines.

1. Influencing the inquiries. The antiabolitionists, particularly the slave traders of Liverpool, produced evidence regarding the way the slave trade was executed and provided (and groomed) witnesses, first for the inquiry by the Privy Council and later for that of the Commons. Initially, the antis held the floor in the Privy Council inquiry and were able to sketch an idyllic picture of the slave trade and a grim one of Africa. This rosy portrayal, however, had to give way to the harsh facts brought forward by the abolitionists.

2. Lobbying.   The slave interest lobbied from the beginning of the attack for support in Parliament and in the Cabinet. As Anstey states, "[T]he West Indians could claim an impressive bloc of support at this time [1788/9]" in the Commons, the House of Lords, and the cabinet (p. 289). As to the last, Drescher remarks, "In 1788, Pitt represented little more than himself in the Cabinet" (1986:4).

In the new Parliament (1791), however, the antiabolitionists lost an important part of their support and this was one of the reasons to start a propaganda campaign.

Petitioning.   In 1789 the West Indians decided to use petitions as a weapon in the parliamentary struggle and in May of that year petitions arrived in Parliament from seventeen different opposition groups, among which twelve from Liverpool (Porter 1970). At this point, the antis clearly lagged behind the abolitionists in the amount of petitions as well as in the amount of signatures.

The Mobilization of Public Opinion.   It was not until 1792 and 1793 that the West Indians engaged in a propaganda campaign in an attempt to sway the public opinion to their side. Just like the abolitionists, the antis attempted to get favorable notice in the press and also wrote and distributed pamphlets and tracts.

1. Getting favorable notice in the press.   The antiabolitionists provided material for publication in the newspapers, national and provincial, wrote letters to the editors, provided rebuttals to abolition pieces, and even paid editors to insert their contributions in the papers.
2. Written materials.   The subcommittee of the Standing Committee sponsored the writing of pamphlets in which the point of view of the slave interest was defended and distributed these.[23] Examples of these are *An Abstract of the Evidence favourable to the Africa trade* and *A Defence of the Planters in the West Indies.* Alongside these materials inspired by the Society of West India Planters and Merchants, other publications appeared as well, such as a reply to Ramsay's tract and a tract based on scriptural arguments by—as was later to appear—a former Jesuit expelled from Spain.

The countermovement mounted by the slave interest developed, just like the abolitionist movement, along the lines Klandermans (1988) mentions, viz., through processes of consensus and action mobilization. The antiabolitionists, however, acted only in part as a social movement. They were, moreover, not very successful in their mobilization efforts.

7.2.3   A Concluding Note

The Abolition Committee succeeded in creating a movement directed at the abolition of the slave trade. In its first campaign it mobilized constituencies all over Britain and aroused the general public. Although the first abolition campaign was directed from the beginning at arousing the general public, its "main thrust . . . had been to work on the 'political nation' and in this way to produce a favourable vote in Parliament" (Anstey 1975:273). The main defense of the slave interest consisted likewise in securing enough parliamentary and governmental support to prevent abolitionist successes. The defeat in Parliament in 1791 led the abolitionists to another attempt to mobilize the public, this time consciously directed at putting extraparliamentary pressure onto M.P.s, peers, and cabinet ministers. At the same time the antiabolitionists mounted a campaign to mobilize public opinion because, on the one hand, their support base in Parliament was declining and, on the other, they feared the effect of the continuing popularity of abolition in the long run.[24] The abolitionists were successful in their mobilization (see the more than five hundred petitions in 1792), far more than the antis in their campaign. The abolitionists' success in Parliament was, however, restricted. They got the promise of gradual abolition, a promise that the House of Lords was able to pass over the horizon.

7.3   THE ABOLITION DISCOURSE

The activities of the Abolition Committee turned a latent issue into a public discourse. The committee succeeded in placing the abolition issue on the societal (systemic) agenda. The immediate and overwhelming response in British society to the initiatives of the abolitionists shows the rapid ascendance of abolition as a topic of discussion. The abolitionists were able to give abolition a prominent place on the political agenda as well. Drescher shows that abolition, contrary to contemporary expectations, superseded India as the major political question at the end of the 1780s. As Drescher states: "By early 1788, however, India and the slave trade were rapidly exchanging places as objects of legislative attention" (1986:66).

Abolition was at the same time an *ideological* struggle and a *political* one. The ideological struggle was part of the late eighteenth-century religiously inspired general social movement to reform society in the direction of a true Christian one. In that movement a world free of slavery was a goal of which everyone—primarily the British nation— had to be convinced. The abolitionists truly believed they were the ones to tell the world what was going in Africa, the Middle Passage, and the West Indian colonies, to show what was wrong, and to make clear why this was so. Like Luther, they believed: "Here I stand, I can do no other."[25] The political struggle was necessary for reaching the ideological goal but here the emphasis was placed on winning, i.e., attaining a majority in Parliament. This second goal meant that their activities were also governed by considerations of suitability and practicality as effectiveness is the norm in political struggles.[26] The abolitionists had to win enough political support and avoid scaring off politicians. They also needed to generate broad support in society in order to put the world of politics under pressure and thus to appeal to more people than merely those who were interested in religious reform.

This double-edged struggle, combined with the necessity to simultaneously win the consent of the political elites and the support of the public at large, shaped the actions of the abolitionists and, in reaction, those of the antiabolitionists as well. For the former, it was of utmost importance to keep a *balance* between the ideological and the political part of their struggle. Moreover, they had to maintain a balance between their actions directed at the political elites and those directed at the public. The antiabolitionists were primarily driven by the need to *defend* their interests against the abolitionist attack. The lead in this defense was taken by the West Indian planters and merchants mainly because they were well aware that stopping the trade would be the first step toward abolishing slavery all together.[27] The "choices" of both contestants had a profound influence on the development of the issue arena, the content of the issue culture, and the dynamics of the issue discourse. In other words, these choices determined *who* became involved in the abolition struggle, *what* became the content of the interpretive packages used in this struggle, and *how* this struggle developed. In the following sections we will look into these aspects of the emerging abolition discourse: first into its arena, then into its culture, and finally into its dynamics.

7.3.1 Abolition Arena

The beginning of the abolition campaign meant the formation of a network of people with a positive stand toward the abolition of the slave trade who were prepared to cooperate in order to do—in one way or another—something about this. The attack of the abolitionists on the slave trade led to defensive reactions from opponents. They set up a network of their own in which those who were against abolition cooperated to stop the abolitionists. This way, a field of cooperative, competitive, and conflictual relations arose: the arena in which the abolition struggle took place and in which the abolitionists self-evidently took the central place (cf. Gamson 1988; Hilgartner and Bosk 1988; Klandermans 1992).

The Proabolition Network. The formation of the Abolition Committee meant the fusion of the existing, mostly informal networks of people who opposed slavery and the slave trade. As the first abolition campaign developed simultaneously along two tracks, the political and the societal, the network of the abolitionists also developed in both directions.

In the political world, the abolitionists built a stronghold within Parliament and the cabinet, prominent members being Wilberforce, Pitt, Grenville, and Fox. The activities of this abolition kernel, especially of its leader Wilberforce, led to a proabolition group in Parliament of, according to Anstey (1975), about thirty members. Alongside this group of committed abolitionists there were other M.P.s (about forty) who voted—sometimes occasionally—in favor of abolitionist measures.[28] As we have seen, support for abolition in the cabinet was practically restricted to the person of Pitt.

The abolition movement also created a network in society. Following the Quaker initiative of local agents, the movement formed a system of local correspondents and "Within two months of its formation the Committee had correspondents in 35 of the 40 English counties whilst names had been suggested for Edinburgh and Glasgow" (p. 261). This system readily evolved into a network of well defined local associations that organized the "propaganda" and the parliamentary petitions. These local committees succeeded in creating a massive following because the abolition message had a broad appeal. The abolitionists attracted men of note; found ample support in University circles; appealed to religious people from all denominations, especially from dissenters like Methodists and Quakers;[29] and drew adherents from all social classes, above all, artisans. The result was a following that came from propertied circles, artisans, and the lower upcoming working classes alike, a broad basis of conscience constituents.

Other network links also proved to be important. The cultural and systemic changes in eighteenth-century Britain "crystallized into the campaigns . . . for the repeal of the Test and Corporation Acts, the abolition of the slave trade and the enactment of parliamentary reform" (Ditchfield 1980:101). Those who were engaged in actions for political and religious reform were also often active in the abolition movement and they brought with them the resources of organizational expertise, experience in political action, and—particularly in the case of Protestant dissent—access to the grass roots of society. This helped the abolitionists considerably in their attempts to mobilize public support and to secure influence in Parliament.[30]

The Counterabolition Network.   The opposition to abolition was formed by the West Indian Interest. This was an already existing loosely organized alliance of returned planters, merchants trading to the West Indies, slave traders, and landed proprietors. This bloc took care of virtually representing the West Indian colonies in Parliament and government.

The abolitionist attack forced the slave interest to organize a more specific network that could avert the threat. The core of this network was the London society of West India Planters and Merchants, which organized the defense. According to Furneaux (1974), the antiabolitionists commanded about sixty votes in the Commons. Anstey (1975), however, estimates the number of "real" West Indians to have been about the same as the "hard core" abolitionists, but the number of (loose) supporters higher, about sixty. Both acknowledge that the West Indians had an impressive bloc of support in the House of Lords that consisted of the great landowners and members of the Royal Family, the king included.[31] The last also meant that they had an important say in the cabinet.

In the larger society, the counterabolition network was rooted in the existing network of planters, merchants, and slave traders. As Porter contends, in British society there "was a larger group of men with West Indian interests who occupied financial, political, and official administrative positions in the kingdom. They were merchants, lawyers, annuitants, creditors, heirs and husbands of heiresses, ranging from Dukes to petty tradesman. Few had ever seen the West Indies" (1970:17). They were, most importantly, men of business, which gave the West Indians a measure of influence on elite opinion, particularly in the City of London. There were attempts to extend this network further into society, especially in the slave ports, but even there these attempts were only successful to a limited extent.

The abolitionists were clearly more successful in co-opting existing networks (submerged structures in the words of Klandermans 1992:94) into the abolition struggle and thus won the battle of numbers. This gave them systemic power in society. The antis, however, succeeded—for the time being at least—to generate enough political leverage to prevent major legal infringements of their interests. Davis describes this balance of power between abolitionists and the West Indians very neatly. He contends that the West Indian bloc was not powerful enough "to stifle discussion [or] bury the question in a Committee on colonies. . . . On the other hand, the antiabolitionists controlled the procedural routes to legislation" (1975:102). They could prevent abolition from becoming a governmental measure. Together, the abolitionist and the proslavery networks were interlocked in a dynamic antagonistic system to which we earlier referred as an arena or a multiorganizational field (Gamson 1988; Hilgartner and Bosk 1988; Klandermans 1992).

7.3.2 Abolition Culture

The dualities that faced the Abolition Committee as the entrepreneur of the abolition cause were also reflected in the interpretive package—the cultural weapon—that the abolitionists put forward. The necessity of balance made the package, above all, complex. The same applied to the package of the counterabolitionists, which—as a consequence of their defensive posture—generally became the mirror image of the abolitionist package.

The Abolition Interpretive Package. This package was built around two themes: the immorality of slavery and the slave trade, and the impracticability or impolicy of these practices. The first was the dominant theme, particularly in the first phase of the abolition movement. It embodied the true and deep-rooted feelings of the religiously inspired abolitionists, and it was also very suited to arouse public opinion and thus mobilize support. This suitability is clearly indicated by the content of the 1791–1792 petitions as studied by Drescher. He states, "All petitions in the sample demanded abolition first on grounds of humanity. The overwhelming majority did not even bother to raise the issue of policy" (1990:567). The second theme was a subsidiary one and was often used in a more politicostrategical way, especially to win support in the world of politics. It became particularly important in the phases where the emphasis was placed on the parliamentary "road to success," although the abolitionist M.P.s justified their voting predominantly with moral arguments (Drescher 1990). Drescher's study shows that both themes were—as two distinct sets of arguments—always present in the case the abolitionists presented.[32] Thus they formed one package and it would therefore not be an adequate procedure to treat them as separate packages.

1. *The Immorality Theme.*[33] This theme is a very complex one that has been elaborated on by many abolitionist writers and activists. In this theme, the three elements worked out in Appendix B are nevertheless clearly discernible.

A. *Framing.* The slave trade (and as logical sequel slavery) is depicted as a horrible, barbarous, bloody, and evil activity that transgresses all boundaries of morality and legitimacy. Three citations of Baxter, Benezet, and Wesley present the kernel of the immorality frame very clearly:

> To go as pirates, and catch up poor Negroes, or people of another land, that never forfeited life or liberty, and to make them slaves, and sell them, is one of the worst kinds of thievery in the world; and such persons are to be taken for the common enemies of mankind; and they that buy them and use them as beasts for their mere commodity, and betray, or destroy, or neglect their souls, are fitter to be called devils incarnate than christians: It is an heinous sin to buy them, unless it be in charity to deliver them. Undoubtedly they are presently bound to deliver them, because by right the man is his own, therefore no man else can have a just title to him. (Baxter cited in Benezet's *An Account of Guinea*, 1771; see Bruns 1977:166)

> An Evil of so deep a Dye, and attended with such dreadful Consequences, that no well-disposed Person (anxious for the Welfare of himself, his Country, or Posterity) who knows the Tyranny, Oppression and Cruelty with which this iniquitous Trade is carried on, can be a silent and innocent Spectator. How many Thousands of our harmless Fellow Creatures have, for a long Course of Years, fallen a Sacrifice to that selfish Avarice, which gives Life to this complicated Wickedness. (Benezet in his *Pamphlet on Negroes in Africa*, 1762; see Bruns 1977:80)

> I would to God it [the slave trade] may never be found more: that we may never more steal and sell our brethren like beasts; never murder them by thousands. Oh, may this worse than Mohammedan, worse than pagan abomination be removed from us for ever. Never was anything such a reproach to England, since it was a nation, as the having a hand in this infernal traffic. (Wesley cited in Anstey 1975:240)

Notable in the framing of the slave trade as an immoral undertaking is the use of metaphors that associate this lawful economic activity with criminality. Sharp speaks of "rapine theft" and Benezet and Wesley describe the trade as man-stealing and the death of slaves during the Middle Passage as murder. Writers also refer to slavery and the slave trade metaphorically as a sin and a sign of human depravity and wickedness; as Walvin shows, for abolitionists "slavery was a deep and abiding sin and wickedness, an affront alike to man and God, and a religious insult" (1985:39). The way the institution was framed related, moreover, quite well to the changing image of the West Indian planter with its "inescapable whiff of pollution" (Drescher 1986:18; see also Section 4.7).

Also notable is the use of vivid depictions and visual images to convey the cruel and wicked character of the slave trade. Benezet, for example, sketches the scene as children are forcefully separated from their parents: "Mothers are seen hanging over their daughters, bedewing their naked breasts with tears" (Bruns 1977:178). Newton portrays the torture of slaves aboard ships: "I have seen them agonizing for hours, I believe, for days together, under the torture of the thumbscrews" (Sypher [1942] 1969:75). Others described how children were mercilessly thrown overboard or otherwise killed if they did not stop crying, or how slaves who refused to eat were forcibly fed. Clarkson assembled the instruments of torture and they were shown at lectures and meetings. One of the most explicit visual images that made the horrid situation aboard a slave ship clear at a glance was the schematic plan of the slave ship drawn by Clarkson, especially if it was accompanied by the vivid and detailed description by the former slave captain Newton (pp. 75–76).

This immorality frame was primarily rooted in religion (Walvin 1985) and was as such part and parcel of the Evangelical awakening with its emphasis on sin and guilt. As Hurwitz (1973) points out, this relation with religion applies to the content of the frame as well as its rhetorical form. It was, however, as we will show below, related to Enlightenment thought as well.

B. Reasoning. The slave trade was immoral, illegal, wicked, etc., for three reasons.

First, slavery and the slave trade were depicted as practices that were contrary to natural law as conceived by God. Natural law states that everyone is born free and that this freedom cannot been infringed on without consent.[34] Therefore, human beings cannot be objects of trade and cannot be bought or sold. In Wesley's words:

> It cannot be, that either war, or contract, can give any man such a property in another as he has in his sheep and oxen. . . . Liberty is the right of every human creature, as soon as he breathes the vital air; and no human law can deprive him of that right which he derives from the law of nature. (cited in Sypher [1942] 1969:71)

Or as Benezet stated this point:

> God gave to Man Dominion over the Fish of the Sea, and over the Fowls of the Air, and over the Cattle, &c. but imposed no involuntary Subjection of one Man to another. (Bruns 1977:121)

In the abolition package the focus is, quite naturally, placed on the slave trade. This trade is an evil as it is contrary to God's commands, plans, and intent. Benezet exhorts those involved in this trade to:

> refrain a Practice so inconsistent with thy Duty, both as a Christian and a Man. Remember, the first and chief Commandment is, *Thou shalt love the*

Lord thy God with all thy Heart. And that the Second like unto is, *Thou shalt love thy Neighbour as thyself.* (p. 89)

This first reason is clearly religiously inspired. The influence of the philosophy of the Enlightenment is indirect, i.e., through processes of elective affinity (*Wahlverwandtschaft*) between religious and philosophical developments. It was, however, not unconditionally formulated, as this could easily lead to a radicalism a la Paine.[35] Most abolitionists were in favor of keeping the existing hierarchies intact and were against infringements upon authority; they were generally more conservative than radical (for a different opinion, see Oldfield 1995:42–43).

Second, the practices of slavery and the trade in slaves were delineated as being contrary to the natural and inborn human trait of benevolence. Men (normally) sympathized with the fate of their fellowmen and strove toward their own happiness and that of others. People involved in slavery were portrayed as being unnaturally hardened by their desire for wealth; their avarice and greed had corrupted their true human nature and estranged them from their own humanity. Viewed in this way, involvement in slavery meant an affront to humanity, because it implied an insensitivity to human suffering and misery. Moreover, denying the trait of benevolence was a threat to civilized society as benevolence preserved society from anarchy. As Davis states:

> By the 1770s there was a widespread consensus, on the level of moral theory, that slavery not only violated natural law but represented the supreme denial of those benevolent instincts which preserved society from anarchy. The eighteenth-century "man of feeling," the ideal of so much literary, religious, and philosophical writing, had been trained to empathize with human suffering. Convinced that reason and national interest should not require unending misery and slaughter, he would respond automatically to empirical exposures of the slave trade. (1975:526)

This second reason was, like the first, an offshoot of the eighteenth-century changes in religion and theology combined with the more secular philosophical reappraisal of nature as the universal standard of truth and virtue. All together, benevolence had become an important cultural theme in the philosophy, religion, and literature of the eighteenth century.

Third, the slave trade and slavery were portrayed as gross injustices. Greed and avarice, the sources of slavery, had overcome equity because slavery and the slave trade violated the natural equality of all human beings. As Benezet asks his readers:

> When and how, has this Man [a slave] forfeited his liberty? Does not

Justice loudly call for its being restored to him? Has he not the same Right to demand it as any of us should have, if we had been violently snatched by Pyrates from our native Land? (Bruns 1977:92)

Wedgwood's medallion underscores this statement of equality rather forcefully by the graphic representation of this reasoning in the rhetorical question: Am I Not a Man and a Brother?

This conception of justice as equity is a typical product of the Enlightenment. Infringements on the natural rights of individuals need, in the enlightened vision, a legal foundation or "title" and, moreover, a balance between what one gets and what one gives up. Justice as equity is also an important element in the new economic thinking with its emphasis on contract and therefore the notion—the slave trade as being inequitable—fits in admirably with capitalist developments.

C. *Consequences.* The abolitionists showed what the inevitable consequences of acting immorally would be and what people had to do to avert these. Slavery and the slave trade were such enormous violations of God's design and commands that retribution was inevitable. This retribution threatened not only the people directly involved in the evil of slavery but also the British nation as a whole. The British people not only tolerated this evil but took advantage of it and were thus collectively guilty. The abolitionists therefore demanded that individuals sever all ties with slavery and the slave trade *and* that the British government, as the representative of the nation, at least end the trade as soon as possible. Only then would the pending disaster be averted.[36] As Sharp warned the Archbishop of Canterbury in a letter of 1769:

[T]he unlawfull practice of buying and Selling the Persons of the unfortunate Natives ought by all means to be prohibited if the Government is concerned, otherwise the British Government is answerable for all those unjust Wars which distract those wretched Countries, and which may draw heavy judgments upon this Kingdom. (Craton et al. 1976:239)

At this point, the influence of the Evangelical revival, with its strong emphasis on God's wrath and retribution for those who do not repent, is very visible.

2. *The Impolicy Theme.* This subsidiary theme is less complicated than the immorality theme and is directed at exposing the errors in the defense of slavery and the slave trade, viz., that these contributed greatly to the wealth of the British nation and were thus in the national interest. When we look at the impolicy argument in the same manner we looked at the immorality argument, we discern the same elements.

A. *Framing.* In an open letter to Granville Sharp, an anonymous

adherent of Adam Smith's free-market vision typified the colonial mercantilist system as follows:

> [T]hat the West Indian islands, so far from being of the importance com-
> monly described to them, have . . . long been and while the present sys-
> tem remains, must continue to be, a dead weight about the neck of this
> country, to stifle its efforts and distract its strength. (cited in Davis
> 1975:355)

The abolitionists framed the slave system in much the same way, as
being unprofitable and inefficient, in other words: as a waste.

B. Reasoning. Slavery was unprofitable and inefficient because it
was founded on faulty assumptions regarding the nature of man and
society. This reasoning was disseminated, above all, by Adam Smith,
and the abolitionists made ample use of his work. Davis cites Adam
Smith as follows:

> "[T]he experience of all ages and nations" demonstrates that the labor of
> slaves, "though it appears to cost only their maintenance, is in the end the
> dearest of any. A person who can acquire no property, can have no other
> interest but to eat as much, and to labour as little as possible." (p. 352)

These arguments were mainly derived from the ascendant economic
theory, especially put forward by Adam Smith, which attacked the mercantilist economic policy with its monopolies and a dominant government, and instead strongly propagated the blessings of the free market
complemented by a restricted role for government.

C. Consequences. The main consequence was that the nation was
less wealthy than it would have been without a slave system protected
by monopolies and subsidized by the British taxpayer. In the end, ordinary citizens, particularly those of the middling classes, were the victim.
In the words of Adam Smith:

> The prosperity of the English sugar colonies has been, in great measure,
> owing to the great riches of England, of which a part has overflowed . . .
> upon those colonies. (cited in Davis 1975:352)

The logical solution for Britain was abolition, or as Clarkson put it:

> [A]n end to the slave trade would greatly benefit the national economy by
> preventing the annual loss of thousands of seamen; by encouraging the
> development of the cheapest markets for the raw materials needed by
> industry; by opening new markets for British manufactured goods; by
> eliminating a wasteful drain of capital and a cumbersome system of credit

. . . ; and by creating in the colonies a self-sustaining labor force that would in time consume more British produce. (cited in Davis 1975:353)

Summarized, ending this trade would not only be the right thing to do, but would also be in the national interest, or as Temperley has it, "Freedom meant prosperity; freedom meant progress" (1977:109). This interrelatedness of the two abolition themes made the abolition package "a double-edged sword confronting the authorities of the metropolis" (Drescher 1986:143).[37]

The Counterabolition Interpretive Package.   From the beginning of the first abolition campaign the antiabolitionists had little to offer on moral grounds against the abolitionist attack; as Anstey puts it, "[N]o serious defence of the slave trade on grounds of justice and humanity is attempted by the opponents of abolition" (1975:310). Instead, they concentrated their defense on the point where the political elites—particularly the high aristocracy and the landed interest—were the most susceptible, viz., the impact of abolition on the position of Britain and on the existing social order. The justification of slavery was only secondary to this main theme and generally played a marginal role. This emphasis on the "policy" aspects of the trade turned the counterpackage into a mirror image of the abolition package; in the parliamentary debates, "the two sides were virtually inversions of each other" (Drescher 1990:571). Again, as in the abolition package, the two themes formed one package and will be treated accordingly.

1.   *The Policy Theme.*   In this theme the elements of framing, reasoning, and consequences are clearly visible.

A.   *Framing.*   For many defenders of slavery and the slave trade, slavery was self-evident; it was a fact of life and "a Condition of Mankind in Africa, from the earliest Times" ("At a General Meeting of the PLANTERS, MERCHANTS, and Others, interested in the WEST INDIES, held at the LONDON TAVERN, May 19, 1789," cited in Anstey 1975:293). Moreover, "The use of Negroes has been the universal practice from the infancy of the colonies in all the islands, British or foreign" (eighth resolution of the West Indian Interest; cited in Porter 1970:56). Slavery and the slave trade were, according to the West Indians, matters of expediency and sound policy comparable to other economic activities or, as Mr. Grosvenor stated in the 1791 parliamentary debate, "He acknowledged it was not an amiable trade, but neither was the trade of the butcher an amiable trade, and yet a mutton chop was, nevertheless, a very good thing" (cited in Anstey 1975:310). The antiabolitionists did little more than reiterate what had been the essential rationale and frame of reference for British-sponsored slavery all along, viz., "its apparent contribution to the collective wealth and power of the empire" (Drescher 1986:20).

B. *Reasoning.* The core element of the reasoning was the assertion that slavery was in everyone's interest, including the black slaves. The antiabolitionists discerned three groups of interests in relation to slavery and the slave trade.

First, the trade in slaves and the use of their labor was depicted as being essential for the national interest. According to the West Indians, the strength of the British Empire depended to an important degree on slavery. Black slaves could endure the harsh conditions of the West Indian climate, whereas white laborers could not, and their labor was therefore necessary to exploit the potential riches of the colonies. In this respect, the trade in slaves was not only necessary for the required labor in the West Indies, but also for replenishing the slave stock because natural causes and accidental calamities led—even among African slaves—to a decrease in their number (Porter 1970:58). Wholly in line with the then dominant mercantilist economic theory, the antiabolitionists argued that the wealth produced by slaves was the source of British power and an important contribution to the well-being of the British people. This mercantilist dogma was the most powerful argument the defenders of the slave trade could evoke. It comprised, according to Davis, the following notions:

> [T]he slave trade was a source of naval power and a great "nursery" for seamen; as a form of state-regulated exploitation, the slave colonies were essential to a favorable balance of trade and were the main source of the nation's economic surplus. (1975:351)

In this way, the antiabolitionists employed the wisdom of mercantilist theory regarding the slave trade and colonial slavery, as was tersely voiced by Malachy Postlethwait, who wrote in 1746:

> The *Negroe-Trade* and the natural Consequences resulting from it, may be justly esteemed an inexhaustible Fund of Wealth and Naval Power to this Nation. (cited in Davis 1966:150).

Second, the West Indians argued that their legitimate interests were at stake. The abolitionist attack interfered with their right of property— the Holy Grail of the developing civil society; in the words of Davis, "[S]laves were defined by law as property, and property was supposedly the foundation of liberty" (1975:267). In their opinion, they deserved— like any other citizen—protection from the abolitionist encroachment. They had also invested much capital in the colonies, relying on the British government who had encouraged these investments in the past.[38] As the West Indian planters and merchants put it in a petition in 1792, "[T]he system of peopling the West India colonies with Negroes, obtained by purchase in Africa, has long and repeatedly received the national sanction" (Craton et al. 1976:270). On this point, they found that they deserved protection as well. Moreover, the slave interest pointed out that abolition would interfere with the interest of unfettered commerce between Britain, Africa and the West Indies. They stressed that not only everyone was entitled to the form of trade he saw fit, but that that trade brought wealth to many in the metropolis. The West Indian Interest put the kernel of its argument down in nineteen resolutions, which together boiled down to "the protection of either property or commerce" (Porter 1970:66).

Third, being brought to West India as a slave was also in the interest of the slaves. They would otherwise be killed as captives of war, be employed as slaves by (barbarous) African masters, or die from hunger as Africa was overpopulated. In order to support this reasoning, the antis took great care to portray the prevailing conditions in Africa as bleakly as possible.

The whole policy reasoning was very cleverly articulated by Fuller, an important representative of the West Indian Interest, in the following way:

> In certain vast regions of the Africa Continent, where the Arts are almost as little known, of rural as of civil cultivation, inhabitants grow faster than the means of sustaining them; and Humanity itself is obliged to transmit the supernumeraries, as objects of traffic, to more enlightened, or less populous countries; which, standing in constant need of their labour, receive them into property, protection and employment. Whatever branch of commerce contributes thus to the mutual convenience, and even subsistence, of Nations . . . must insensibly . . . interchange intellectual cultivation with the culture of the ground. (cited in Anstey 1975:293)

C. *Consequences.*   The abolition of the slave trade would, according to the antiabolitionists, lead to a life of misery and want for the inhabitants of Great Britain. This country would lose its dominant position in the world to France and abolition would mean the end of the empire. It would cause the ruin of the West Indies and of everyone in Britain who depended on its revenues or on its possibilities for commerce. These consequences were vividly portrayed in a pamphlet that Wilberforce cited in his first abolition speech in 1789. The pamphlet summarized the gloomy consequences of abolition as follows:

> "I [Wilberforce] have in my hand the extract from a pamphlet which states, in very dreadful colours, that thousands and tens of thousands will be

ruined; how our wealth will be impaired; one third of our commerce cut off for ever; how our manufacture will droop in consequence, our land-tax will be raised, our marine destroyed, while France, our natural enemy and rival, will strengthen herself by our weakness (*A cry of assent [was] heard from several part of the House)*" (cited in Anstey 1975:313–14; italics added by Anstey)

2. *The Justification Theme.* A defense of slavery on nonmaterial grounds was also sought in antiabolitionist circles. Generally, this defense proceeded along two lines, referring either to the bible or to the supposed inferiority of the black Africans.

2a. *The biblical argument.* This argument was most forcefully put forward by "Reverend Raymond Harris" (a former Jesuit who had been expelled from Spain), who attempted to shift the dispute to abolitionist terrain, viz., the scripture. Hereto, he:

(a) *Framed* slavery and the slave trade as lawful activities.

(b) *Reasoned* that they were lawful because God had positively sanctioned slavery in the past. Harris contended that no practice could be inherently illicit that God had at any time—in one way or another—approved of.

(c) Thus, as *consequence* the abolitionists were flying in the face of God's word as revealed in the bible.

In this way the abolition debate became a dispute about the authority of scriptures, an authority that was also generally uncontested by most abolitionists. Davis succinctly describes Harris's attack as follows:

> Having boxed his readers within this framework of orthodox Protestant assumptions, Harris proceeded to show that slavery had been positively sanctioned by God during the period of natural law, in the time of Abraham and Joseph; during the period of Mosaic law; and during the earliest Christian dispensation. Throughout his argument, Harris adhered to the central premise that intrinsic lawfulness is unaffected by changing dispensations. Thus it was immaterial that Mosaic law limited the servitude of Jews to six years; if the practice had been unlawful, God would not have allowed it for one hour. (1975:544–45)

The biblical argument was, however, also related to the eighteenth-century theological dispute regarding the role of Providence in society and the "Reverend" cleverly drew on the Deist point of view (see also Section 4.3).

2b. *The racist argument.* This argument was based on the work of Edward Long, an absentee planter and Jamaican official. He wrote the

History of Jamaica (1774), in which he mixed a selected choice of certain widespread assumptions with existing colonial stereotypes to arrive at "a gross caricature designed to persuade the reader of the Negro's innate inferiority" (Craton et al. 1976:260). Long's work systematically reproduced all the myths invented by planters to justify slavery. As Lewis rightly puts it, "[H]e exposes the central principle of racism, which is to stigmatize a whole racial group in order to justify and facilitate its exploitation" (1978:52). The fact that he presented these myths and stereotypes as scientific facts not only undergirded planters' beliefs and justified their behavior toward the black slaves, but also shaped—partly through the abolition discourse—later racial stereotypes, even to this day.

The elements of framing, reasoning, and pointing to the consequences can also be found in this argument, as is shown below.

A. Framing. The black African was portrayed as subhuman, somewhere between the orangutan and the white man. As Long phrased it:

> When we reflect on the nature of these men, and their dissimilarity to the rest of mankind, must we not conclude, that they are a different species of the same *genus?* (cited in Sypher [1942] 1969:41)

The West Indians added to this general denial of humanness a long list of negative characteristics: "stupid, incredibly lazy, cowardly, mendacious, grossly sexualistic, and possessed of an animalistic nature" (Lewis 1978:49).

B. Reasoning. The assumed animalness justified slavery and the use of black Africans as beasts of burden, justly serving man like other animals. Their savage and subhuman nature, moreover, made them less sensitive to pain and hardship and thus better suited to the harsh circumstances in the West Indies.[39]

C. Consequences. Abolition would lead to the downfall of planters and slaves alike, the former because black Africans would cease laboring without being forced and were likely to rebel, the latter because they could not take care of themselves without the severe, paternalistic leadership of the planter.

Two sets of citations give a fair idea of the racist argument. The first set comes (1) from the work of William Beckford, Jr. (Sypher [1942] 1969) and (2) from a counterabolitionist pamphlet *West India Trade and Islands: Commercial Reasons for the Non-Abolition of the Slave Trade in the West India Islands, etc.* (Rice 1975:220). Beckford was more a "picturesque" writer than a historian and presents the idealized benevolent paternalistic view of the planter that is more or less a form of racism in disguise. The pamphlet asserts black Africans' unfitness for freedom. The second set is a limited selection of quotes (out of an abundance of possible ones) from the work of Long and renders the undisguised racist vision:

> A slave has no feeling beyond the present hour, no anticipation of what may come, no dejection at what may ensue: these privileges are reserved for the enlightened. [Negroes] have not the least idea of personal delicacy, or shame [they] seem not to have any moral feelings, the tenderness of sentiment, or weight of thought [they] are savage in the cold revenge of spilling blood. (cited in Sypher [1942] 1969:41–42)

> [Black Africans if emancipated] like those of Virginia, New York, etc., will die in the Streets, unprovided and unprotected; the Ground their wretched Bed, and the inclement sky their miserable Covering, no friendly Cott, Fuel, or Bannanah Walk to call their own. (cited in Rice 1975:220)

> A covering of wool, like the bestial fleece, instead of hair. . . . Their bestial or fetid smell. . . . In general, they are void of genius, and seem almost incapable of making any progress in civility of science. They have no plan or system of morality among them. Their barbarity to their children debases their nature even below that of brutes . . . among so many millions of people, we have heard but of one or two insignificant tribes, who comprehend any thing of mechanic arts, or manufacture; and even these, for the most part, are said to perform their work in a very bungling and slovenly manner, perhaps not better than an *oran-outang* might, with a little pains, be brought to do. . . . In many respects they are more like beasts than men. (Craton et al. 1976:260–62)

As we stated before, this second theme in the antiabolitionist package was a nasty but marginal one, and as Drescher states, "Quite significantly, however, neither line of argument [racial inferiority and biblical sanction] was sustained in either polemical or Parliamentary debate" (1986:20).

7.3.3 Abolition Dynamics

An issue discourse is not simply the clash of ready-made arguments but also a dynamic in which the arguments evolve further or even arise anew. The framing of the issue in the abolition discourse developed, on the one hand, from the dynamics within the contending groups themselves, e.g., the abolitionist's religiously inspired need to reshape society. On the other hand, the themes in the discourse evolved in reaction to each other, e.g., the need of the West Indians and the slave traders to defend themselves against the abolitionist attack pressed them to develop their interest theme more fully. This dynamic of framing is the first subject we will look into below.

Another important dynamic concerns the way in which the networks in the issue arena contingently evolve. We discussed the abolition arena above, at that point dealing with its statics as well as its dynamics. There is no need to repeat it here. A third dynamic pertains to the strategies used in the discourse. Both parties developed and adjusted their strategies in reaction to each other and to the vicissitudes of the struggle. We will look into the strategical dynamic of the abolition struggle after we have described the framing dynamic.

The Framing Dynamic. From the beginning, the abolitionists framed the slave trade as an undertaking that transgressed the boundaries of morality. This moral argument was already completed before they started their campaign in 1787. Between 1787 and 1792 the abolitionists only remolded the abolition message in more appropriate forms, such as pamphlets, poems, and lectures, and distributed it. As is shown above, the antiabolitionists attempted to counter this moral attack in two ways. First, they tried to turn the dispute into a "policy" debate. The dynamics of this debate will be dealt with below. Second, they tried to answer it on its own terms by justifying slavery and the slave trade on either scriptural or racist grounds. The former involved the abolitionists in a biblical war and the latter was not left without a rebuttal.

The biblical war evolved in the context of the ongoing theological controversy between Evangelicals and deists regarding the notions of Providence and revelation (see also Section 4.3). This time, however, it became more specific as it was related to a concrete subject, i.e., slavery. Here the Evangelical abolitionists got caught between their tendency to interpret the scripture quite literally—as most of their contemporaries did, thus having to accept slavery as a possibility—and their principled rejection of the African slave trade and the West Indian slave system. They tried to find a way out of this dilemma by further developing the notion of moral progress: the idea that mankind could morally grow by following the directions of divine Providence. The abolitionists found another important defense against the scriptural antiargument in the largely undisputed assumption regarding the common ancestry of man from which they deduced the fundamental equality of all humans before God. But all in all, the abolitionist defense against the scriptural attack remained less than satisfactory (for a more detailed description of this biblical war, see Davis 1975:525–51).

The racist arguments were repeatedly rebutted in the public and parliamentary debates, particularly by pointing out that the brutishness, barbarity, and other negative characteristics of black Africans, especially the way they were apparent in the West Indies, were the product of the intercourse between Britain, Africa, and their inhabitants. As Wilberforce stated in his first abolition speech in the Commons in 1789:

[W]hen we think how in this same period all improvements in Africa had been defeated by her intercourse with Britain; when we reflect it is we ourselves that have degraded them to that wretched brutishness and barbarity which we now plead as the justification of our guilt; how the slave trade has enslaved their minds, blackened their character, and sunk them so low in the scale of animal beings, that some think the very apes are of a higher class, and fancy the ourang-outang has given them the go-by. (cited in Howse 1952:35)

In their rebuttal, the abolitionists gratefully used the literature produced by black writers as proof that black Africans were human and not subhuman, as the racist defenders of the trade claimed.

Although the abolitionist's answers to the counterattacks in the moral sphere were not always wholly satisfactory, the antiabolitionists did not get very far with their justification of the slave trade and slavery. This negative result was foremost a consequence of the lack of resonance these moral justifications had with the public's understandings and beliefs. As Barker concludes, "[T]he abolitionist debate brought into the open a weight of opinion in favour of the Negro's human integrity which had long existed. The new element in the late eighteenth century was . . . that a small minority began to argue the contrary. Such people were well aware that their claims were new and unpopular" (1978:160). The leading antiabolitionists were either aware of this unpopularity or soon found out what public opinion at this point was and decided to concentrate their defense on policy arguments.

In the policy debate, the arguments of the contestants developed— more than in the moral debate—in reaction to each other. The abolitionists brought the national interest into the abolition discourse.[40] The antis not only exerted themselves to counter this argument, but broadened the debate by bringing other interests connected to the slave trade to the fore.

First, the national interest argument put forward by the abolitionists drew heavily on the ascendant economic theory of the free market, in which slavery was depicted as an economic anachronism. Their opponents countered this argument by pointing to the dangers of abolition. In their view, abolition would:

1.   Threaten the productive capacity of the West Indies because there were no alternatives for black slaves. It would, moreover, enhance the competition of foreign countries, such as France, Spain, and the United States. Both would lead to the ruin of the West Indies, and thus abolition would put the value of these colonies for the empire—particularly their contribution to British commerce—at risk;

2. Place British dominion at sea in jeopardy, especially because the African trade functioned as a nursery for seamen.

The arguments on both sides regarding the national interest developed into a discussion that had a factual character, each side confident that facts would prove the other wrong. In answering the arguments of the antiabolitionists, the abolitionists were, however, only partially successful, and as Anstey states, their answers "were too often hopes and calculations rather than demonstrable truths. . . . [I]t *was* widely feared that abolition would have just those fatal consequences which its opponents predicted" (1975:313). In reality, the discussion regarding the slave trade and the national interest was more ideological than factual from both sides, being a mix of abolitionist and counterabolitionist dogma and factual proof. The mainstay of the national interest debate was, as Temperley (1985) shows, the redefinition of the national interest and as such the discussion was part of the more encompassing—also largely ideological—discourse between political economists regarding the value of free-market versus mercantilist policies.

In this case, the discussion took place predominantly in Parliament, although here the abolitionists continually related the policy argument to the moral argument. As a result, quite a few M.P.s and peers shared the abolitionist's moral disapproval, but voted against abolition out of fear that it would harm the national interest. In the words of Davis, "The decisive swing vote hinged largely on definitions of national self-interest" (1975:430).

Second, the antiabolitionists brought the legitimate interests of the planters, West Indian merchants, slave traders, and those who depended on West Indian revenues into the discourse. They argued, in particular, that abolition violated the sacrosanct right of property. Slaves were defined by law as property, and on that basis traders, planters, and others had invested in the African (slave) trade and in slavery in the West Indian colonies. Abolition meant a violation of legitimate trust in law and government policy and was therefore unconstitutional.

The defense of the abolitionists against this point was again problematic because the right of property (and all it entailed) was sacred for them as well. They found, however, a line of defense by differentiating between legitimate and illegitimate possession. Property rights, they reasoned, were only sacrosanct if they rested on a valid title. This was lacking in this case because slavery and the slave trade rested on usurpation born out of greed and avarice. These specific motives made these practices especially sinful and illegal. The abolitionists thus basically reiterated their moral argument against the antis' policy argument. With this, they tried to save their thesis of liberty as a fundamental and natural right as well as the thesis of property as one of the foundations of that same liberty.

In addition, the counterabolitionists pointed to the fact that talking about abolition as such increased the chance of slave rebellions, the basic fear of every planter. The abolitionist answer was simple. Slaves would not rebel if they were treated better and legally protected against all kinds of abuse. As such a policy would also lead to their natural increase, the slave trade would become superfluous. Abolition was thus a rational thing to do, and therewith in the interests of the West Indians.[41]

Third, the antiabolitionists added the interests of the slaves themselves to the abolition discourse. They contended that:

• Africa was a barbaric continent pestered by feuds, wars, and bloody massacres. The slave traders were, in fact, doing the people of Africa a favor, or as Porter phrases this argument, "The slave trade served the cause of civilization by carrying victims of barbarism to new homes, where education, discipline, and religion were available for their benefit" (1970:55). In addition, this situation, according to the antis, precluded any other trade between Africa and Britain than the slave trade.

• In contrast to barbaric Africa, the West Indies were a veritable paradise. This thesis was further strengthened by the portrayal of the planter as a benevolent, patriarchal, and kind master (Lewis 1978). However, the West Indians themselves negated this argument as they pointed out that the slave trade was needed for the repletion of black slaves due to their rapid decrease in the West Indies (see Porter 1970:58). Wilberforce ironically negated this argument by remarking that if a slave in extraordinary circumstances could purchase his freedom he invariably realized his release from "this situation of superior happiness by the sacrifice of his last shilling" (cited in Furneaux 1974:101).

• "[T]he transported African prisoner found the middle passage to be little less than a Elysian retreat" (Lewis 1978:42), or as Lord Penrhyn put it in the debate on the Dolben regulation bill "[T]he captive slave looked upon the voyage from Africa as 'the happiest period of his life'" (see Howse 1952:33).

The abolitionist answer to these arguments was twofold: First, the abolitionists pointed out that the slave trade itself caused the negative situation in Africa. Originally, Africa had been little less than a pastoral heaven. At this point the abolitionists tended to exaggerate the positive characteristics of the black African.[42] An opposite bias arose from the slave interest, which emphasized the negative aspects of Africa and its inhabitants. In short, the abolitionists conveyed an idyllic picture of

Africa against the barbaric portrait of the antis; an opposition that was rooted in the cultural myth of the noble savage[43] and in the interests of the West Indians and slave traders as expressed in horror tales about Africa and racialist theories of black inferiority.[44] In both cases, however, the building of the image of Africa was more ideologically than factually determined and was as a symbolic struggle of great importance in the battle for the public opinion.

Second, the abolitionists came with an overwhelming amount of factual proof regarding the horrible and cruel character of the slave trade. Although many of these factual statements were unanswerable, they were answered nonetheless, mostly in the form of blunt denials. The abolitionists poured out this torrent of facts on the public and Parliament alike. In both cases it convinced many, but was not enough to spur legal measures against the slave trade.

The Strategical Dynamic. As we have already seen in the description of the framing of the interpretive packages, the use of facts was an essential strategy in the abolition discourse. No less important strategically were the use of procedural tactics and the appeal to emotions.

Facts served three functions in the discourse and were used by abolitionists and their opponents alike.[45] First, the resort to facts concealed the ideological character of the discourse.[46] This is clearly visible, for example, in the national interest debate. The same was true when idyllic and barbaric pictures of Africa were placed opposite each other. Second, the abolitionists assembled facts to lift the veil of ignorance regarding the slave trade because they assumed that the Britons were unaware of its true character. Particularly the inquiry of the Privy Council—an initiative of Wilberforce and Pitt—had to yield "more factual information, which, they automatically supposed would necessarily discredit the slave trade" (Anstey 1975:267). Such information could show the enormity of the evil, prove its impolicy and therewith, in the abolitionists' eyes, convince the public as well as the authorities.[47] The counter-strategy of the slave interest was directed at proving the opposite and if this was of no avail the antis would deny their adversaries' information. Third, both the abolitionists and the antis used facts to expose the flaws in the myths and arguments of their contenders. The abolitionist showed, for example, that the slave trade was not a nursery for seamen but their cemetery or that the Middle Passage was horrible and meant death for many slaves. Their adversaries in turn pointed out, for example, that slavery had been rampant in Africa for centuries.

As their initial *procedural tactic* the abolitionists opened the political discourse on abolition with choosing for an inquiry by the Privy Council. They did so because they entertained—as we have seen—a rather naive trust in the efficacy of facts. This procedural opening of the discourse self-evidently implied a considerable delay. It also meant losing the initiative because the West Indian Interest had now been given the time to organize itself for the abolition battle. As the West Indians succeeded in commanding a considerable bloc of votes, Wilberforce depended on them for his parliamentary moves after the inquiry. They cleverly used all the intricacies (and there were many) of British parliamentary procedures to reduce the abolitionists' chance of success. On the one hand, they sometimes sought to delay the discussion of abolition motions and bills. They did so by demanding an investigation by a parliamentary committee on the report of the Privy Council. It was in this respect a clever move. On the other hand, they pressed for a vote when this held the promise of a quick victory, for example, by attempting to forestall a full presentation of the abolitionist case [see, for example, Furneaux (1974:90, 104, 105) or Porter (1970:70, 74, 75)].

Finally, both sides appealed heavily to the *emotions* of their audiences. The abolitionists used emotionally charged words, like the infamous traffic in blood, striking images, like the famous Wedgwood medallion, or presentations of gruesome facts about the trade, such as the plan of a slave ship, which made the inhumane and appalling circumstances on board these ships immediately clear. Very emotional also were the detailed and vivid descriptions of the situation on board the slave ships and of the way slaves were cruelly punished. Illustrative for such descriptions is the following citation by Benezet from an account by John Atkins, Surgeon on board Admiral Ogle's squadron:

> [O]f one *Harding*, Master of a Vessel, in which several of the Men Slaves, and a Woman Slave, had attempted to rise, in order to recover their Liberty; some of whom the Master, of his own Authority, sentenced to cruel Death, making them first eat the Heart and Liver of one of those he killed. The Woman he hoisted by the Thumbs, whipped and slashed with Knives before the other Slaves, till she died. (cited in Bruns 1977:121)

These shocking descriptions of the slave trade were often contrasted with descriptions of an idyllic Africa populated by peace-loving inhabitants. With these methods, the use of facts revealing the infamy and cruelty of the trade strengthened the mobilization of support and helped to change the opinion of the uncommitted public.

The antiabolitionists did not shun emotions either. First, they did their utmost to put the actions of their adversaries in an unfavorable light. Abolition was depicted as irrational and irresponsible. This drive would not stop at abolishing the slave trade but could unleash forces that would threaten all authority. As Anstey (1975) and Davis (1975) show, the defenders of the slave trade readily appealed to the peers' dislike of change, particularly their fear that abolition would contribute to the undermining of all authority. This fear—and the strategy based on it—become clear from the following description by Davis:

> They [the West Indians] and their proslave allies did their best to evoke fears that any humanitarian tampering with the slave system would open Pandora's box, as the Earl of Abingdon put it, and let loose democratic forces that would ultimately destroy both monarchy and rank: "The Order, and Subordination, the Happiness of the whole habitable Globe is threatened," Abingdon warned. "What anarchy, confusion, and bloodshed," Gilbert Francklyn asked, "may follow too nice and critical an enquiry into the exact portion of each man's particular liberty, the society of which he is a member may have a right to deprive him of?" (1975:345)

Another line in this strategy was to point to evils at home, such as the insecurity of British laborers, the awful poverty in Britain itself, and the flogging of soldiers, about which the abolitionists did nothing and which showed their selective indignation. As Drescher puts it:

> The counter-abolitionist propaganda touched on every sore in the British Isles [and] invoked dreadful examples of the insecurity of English labour, the awful poverty of the Irish, the pathos of the short-lived chimney sweeps, the dangers of the miners, the sale of pauper children, the abuse of apprentices, the pangs of hunger, the flogging of soldiers, the impressment of seamen, the mortality of Manchester, the uprooted of Scotland, the black beggars and the white debtors of London. (1986:157)

William Beckford pointed to this defect (and to others as well) in his *A Descriptive Account of the Island of Jamaica* (1790). He stated that the abolitionists seemed to be blind to the true interests of Britain and that if their eyes were opened,

> they might then find that their humanity began at a wrong end; and that, while they are traversing seas in quest of speculative philanthropy, numbers of their own condition and colour stand more really in want of that protection and fellow-feeling which, from motives of pure and unbiassed pity, they are anxious to extend to the inhabitants of Africa. (cited in Craton et al. 1976:266)

A third line was to invoke emotionally charged stereotypes. The West Indian planters and merchants used stereotypes that referred negatively to the fact that most abolitionists were Evangelical. The abolitionists were, for example, depicted as sectaries or "gloomy fanatics and dangerous visionaries" (Rice 1975:219). Lord Penrhyn assured the Commons that "the tales of the Middle Passage were begotten in fanaticism and

nurtured in falsehood" (Howse 1952:33). Fuller referred to the abolitionists as "enthusiasts and fanaticks" and to their arguments as "that horrid
mass of calumny" (cited in Furneaux 1974:104) and for Cobbett the abolitionists were "the hypocritical sect of negro-loving philanthropists"
(cited in Drescher 1986:252, note 41).

The emotional tone of the abolition debate was neatly captured on the
abolitionist side by Gisborne in a letter to Wilberforce on the occasion of
the passing of the Dolben Bill. This created a storm of opposition to the
abolitionists; Wilberforce was especially attacked. Gisborne wrote:

> I shall expect to read in the newspapers of your being carbonadoed by
> West Indian planters, barbecued by African merchants, and eaten by
> Guinea captains; but do not be daunted, for—I will write your epitaph.
> (cited in Howse 1952:34)

On the counterabolitionist side, comparable explanations showing the
emotionality of the debate can be found. Drescher, for example, cites
Jesse Foot, who remarked in his *A Defence of the Planters in the West Indies*
(1792),

> Is the imaginary cruelty of the *West India Planters* to be the theme of every
> *drinking club* and *psalm singing meeting?* . . . the cruelties . . . are become as
> familiar to *children* as the story of *Blue Beard* or *Jack the Giant Killer* (cited in
> Drescher 1986:213, note 31).

7.3.4 The Abolition Discourse Concluded

The abolition discourse was a game of *balanced* attack countered by a
forceful *defense.* The abolitionists maintained the balance as regards the
content of their attack (i.e., the balance between the immorality and the
impolicy of the slave trade); the balance between ideology and facts;
the balance between a matter of fact approach and emotional appeals;
the balance between the world of politics and the wider society; and the
balance between satisfying their own religious needs and avoiding the
alienation of other sympathetic publics. The counterabolitionist's defensive strategy was above all directed at not losing political support. This
is, among other things, reflected in their choice of the dominant theme
in their interpretive package; in the emotional charges at the sincerity of
their adversaries; and in the way they used the extant procedural
possibilities.

According to Furneaux, the abolitionists won the argument: "Any
impartial person reading the evidence and the debates must conclude
that the Trade was unjust, that it caused boundless misery, that it was

ruinous to Africa, of little benefit to the West Indies, and of none to the Navy" (1974:103). Nevertheless, they lost the vote.

When we interpret the outcome of the abolition discourse in 1792, we see that the antiabolitionists commanded enough systemic power to block effective legal abolition measures. They were, however, not powerful enough to halt the public and political discourse regarding abolition on their own. For this they needed the help of adverse political circumstances (see Section 7.5). When we look at the results of the discourse on the cultural level, we can only conclude that the situation was very problematic for the West Indian Interest. The effect of its defense was limited and the cause of abolition was very popular during the first abolition campaign. The abolitionists had clearly generated a considerable amount of cultural power, a fact that the West Indians recognized. As Fuller stated, "'the sentiments of a vast majority of the people of Great Britain' were hostile to the slave interest" (cited in Drescher 1986:214, note 38). Drescher rightly concludes that "the terms of public discourse about the institution [slavery] were dramatically and forever altered" (1986:67).

7.4 CHANGES IN THE DEFINITION OF SLAVERY AND THE SLAVE TRADE

Between 1787 and 1793 a real battle for the public mind took place. Before 1787 the opinion on slavery was divided and fragmented. The importance of the Afro-Caribbean slave system for Great Britain was widely acknowledged, although by the 1770s educated men in Britain were likely to regard slavery as morally and philosophically condemned. Antislavery and abolition of the slave trade were not issues on the public or the political agenda in 1780s. This is clearly indicated by the fact that in 1783 the atrocities of the *Zong* case[48] did not arouse public indignation: "The *Zong* case became the *Zong* affair only in retrospect, *after* the emergence of popular abolitionism" (Drescher 1986:60).

Another indication of the state of public thought in Britain at the time the first abolition campaign started is provided by Drescher, who notes that "Only weeks before the great petition campaign opened at the end of 1787 another [antislavery] correspondent catalogued long-simmering antislavery sensibility among the other futile 'manias' of the British" (p. 64). The same author remarks that the people who were strongly against slavery were fatalistic regarding the chances of getting rid of this institution and "Even those who condemned slavery root and branch on religious grounds saw no hope of dramatically altering the system before the age of abolition" (p. 86).

Slavery was also not an offense to the religious feelings of many Christians and even the missionary organization of the Anglican church in the West Indies owned slaves. In 1767, the Society for Propagation of the Gospel "earnestly begged" Benezet to stop (and even retract) his antislavery writing upon Benezet's request to the Society to act against the infamous slave trade (Mellor 1951:32). The ordinary attitude of Christians is well represented in a statement by Reverend Newton, when he looked back on his past as a mate and a captain of a slave ship: "During the time I was engaged in the slave trade, I never had the least scruple as to its lawfulness" (cited in Sypher [1942] 1969:74–75).[49] In general, the slave trade was seen as a practice so deep-rooted "that it is now [1778] almost a ridiculous common-place to cry out against the barbarity and cruelty of it".[50]

By 1792 this situation was completely reversed. Temperley describes this volte-face as follows:

> Yet in a remarkably short time, as we all know, opinion on these matters [the morality and expediency of slavery and the slave trade] underwent a sea change as first the slave trade and then slavery itself came under attack. Like most revolutions, it began in men's minds. What seemed self-evident to the men of the 1770s no longer seemed so to their children, still less their grandchildren. (1985:87)

In 1792, the way slavery and the slave trade were collectively defined had moved up to the abolitionist view, a change that Drescher refers to as "the cultural revolution of 1787–92" (1986:86). This transformation was unusually *rapid*—according to Walvin, "one of the most rapid transformations of collective political opinion in modern British society" (1985: 32)—and *definitive*—the terms of public debate in Britain on slavery were forever altered (Drescher 1986:67). Moreover, the abolitionist view had by then become *unassailable*; it was raised "almost to the status of religion" (Williams [1944] 1972:181). As Craton et al. assess the situation, "[T]hey [the West Indians] had not made a major impact on the popular imagination. The people had swung behind abolition" (1976:233).

The extent of the transformation of public thought regarding slavery and the slave trade may be inferred from the way:

(a)   These practices were dealt with in writing from the 1790s onwards. Illustrative examples in this respect are:

- The turn of Arthur Young, the quantifier and geographer of liberty and slavery.[51] In 1772 he depicted the slave trade as being highly important and advantageous to Britain. In 1788, the same author dismissed the thought of a defense of this trade—in a review of a reprinted book containing such a defense—because this "would be paying a very poor compliment to the understanding of my readers" (cited in Drescher 1986:86).

- The changes in books on trade. As Drescher shows, "[T]he authors of books on international trade, which as late as the mid-1780s treated the slave trade as a deplorable but integral part of the British imperial economy, began to write about the trade as one facing proximate elimination" (p. 94).
- The revolution in literature. Although in literary works, "the sentimental revolution against slavery was complete by the 1760s, as indeed was the theoretical argument against it," slavery was still treated as an inevitable evil as can be seen in *Jonathan Corncob* (1788). This notion disappeared in these works completely [Rice (1980:326); Drescher (1986) reaches the same conclusion]. The same effect was visible in children's literature; "By the turn of the century, . . . anti-slavery sentiments had made considerable inroads into the children's literature, and, if anything, its influence was increasing" (Oldfield 1989:48–49).[52]

(b)   Nonabolitionists took the existing abolitionist opinions of the general public into account. Examples can be found in:

- The world of politics. After 1788 public opinion functioned as a deterrent with regard to governmental measures that were obviously positive to slavery. Furneaux gives a clear example of the dominance of the abolitionist view. In the final debate on abolition in 1807, "It was difficult for supporters of the Trade to gain a hearing and impossible for them to impress the House [of Commons]. Many of its regular defenders including Windham remained silent, while others, like Rose and Castlereagh, did not even vote. But speeches for Abolition were greeted with enthusiasm and every telling expression in them applauded" (1974:251).
- The circles of the slave interest. The West Indian planters and merchants openly acknowledged that public thought was abolitionist and acted accordingly. They occasionally mounted a vigorous counterattack, but "the balance of expressed opinion was usually so heavily against them that merchants and planters preferred" conventional ways of lobbying and influencing (Drescher 1986:95–96).

The abolitionists succeeded in changing the framework of political discourse so completely that antislavery could no longer be treated as a fad or fashion; the "initial dismissal of abolitionism in 1788 as a 'five days fit of philanthropy,' the fad of a season, yielded to the sense that a permanent addition of policy considerations had occurred" (p. 94). As Eltis notes, "[T]he conviction that slavery was anomalous was widespread; the West Indians found almost no defenders outside those who had a stake in the slave system" (1982:196). The abolitionists succeeded despite the fact that they did not reply satisfactorily to much of the anti-abolitionist literature. An open proslavery point of view was nearly impossible and the opposition against the abolitionist proposals rested mainly on arguments of expediency. The story of the actor George Cook—as told by Lewis—illustrates the change in public opinion rather well. When this actor was hissed for appearing drunk on stage at a theater in Liverpool, the center of the British slave trade, he pulled himself together and told the public that "he had not come to be insulted by a pack of men every brick of whose detestable town was cemented by the blood of a Negro." The actor was loudly cheered for his act of defiance which says much about the change in public opinion (1978:75).

The magnitude of the transformation in the way slavery and slave trade were collectively defined during but particularly at the end of the eighteenth century may be derived from the following citations:

[T]he career of one key figure [John Newton] can symbolize the crucial transition among the majority of English Christians during the later eighteenth century; from a position that since slavery was so necessary and valuable it was obviously God's will it be accepted, to a certitude that it was God's will it be eradicated at all costs. (Craton 1974:250)

The Privy Council and Parliamentary hearings on the slave trade between 1788 and 1792, like public discourse out of doors, represented a paradigmatic leap in the relationship between the British metropolis and the Atlantic slave system. (Drescher 1986:86)

In the trivial space of a hundred years—perhaps sixty in the British case—slavery had passed from being a given factor on the social landscape, to being incompatible with the beliefs of thinking men and women in the Atlantic community. Disapproval of slavery ultimately became the kind of cultural assumption which requires no evidential support, with something of the reflexive force of the taboo against incest. (Rice 1980:319)

In May 1792 Sir Samuel Romilly wrote that "the cause of the negro slaves is at present taken up with much warmth in almost every part of the kingdom as could be found in any matter in which the people were personally and immediately interested. Innumerable petitions for the abolition have been presented to Parliament and (what proves mens' zeal more strongly than petitions) great numbers have entirely discontinued the use of sugar. All persons, and even the West India planters and merchants, seem to agree that it is impossible the trade should last many years longer." (Walvin 1981:63–64)

7.5 THE END OF THE FIRST CAMPAIGN

The first abolition campaign came to a definitive halt at the end of 1791 and the beginning of 1792. This was the consequence of a dramatic change in the political climate caused by the slave rising in the French colony of St. Domingue and the Jacobin turn in the French Revolution. The atrocities and violence of both events led to an augmenting antipathy to radical political changes, a political shift to the right, and eventually a period of political repression. Davis typifies the situation by stating, "By 1793 the official view held that any expression of political opinion through spontaneously formed associations was criminal and dangerous to the state" (1975:93).

In such a climate, extraparliamentary actions are already suspect as such, but in the case of abolition the fact that many political radicals were active in the mobilization campaign of 1791–1792 made it even worse. It was now easy for the adversaries of abolition to link abolition to political radicalism and thus place abolition in an unfavorable light. The Earl of Abingdon expresses this link very succinctly as follows:

> For in the very definition of the terms themselves, as descriptive of the thing, what does abolition of the slave trade mean more or less in effect, than liberty and equality? What more or less than the rights of man? And what is liberty and equality, and what the rights of man, but the foolish fundamental principles of this new philosophy. (cited in Anstey 1975: 317–18)

Both events produced a shift in the structure of opportunities because they temporarily (1) augmented the constraints on collective action in Great Britain and (2) precluded far-reaching changes in social arrangements by governmental measures. As the antiabolitionists could use the adverse social and political climate to block abolitionist actions, the French Revolution and the St. Domingue rising, moreover, added to the power resources (particularly the systemic ones) of the counterabolitionists. They did not, however, affect the main asset that the abolitionists had won with their campaign: the conversion of the public to the abolitionist view. The transformation of public thinking regarding slavery and the slave trade proved to be enduring. As Drescher contends,

> The creation of a climate of opinion was therefore the most important residue of frequently renewed petitions [and other abolitionist actions as well]. It became part of the consciousness of all those who played a role in shaping British policy regarding Atlantic slavery. (1986:94)

The drastic turn in the political and social climate meant that the abolitionists had no other choice but to end the mobilization campaign and dissociate themselves as much as possible from the other movements. As Anstey states:

> In this situation the struggle would have to be waged exclusively in Parliament and a new phase in the abolition movement began. (1975:278)

NOTES

1.   Evangelicals such as Granville Sharp became important partners in this undertaking. There were, however, other deeply religious people who became involved in abolition as well. They played their own important role in this fusion of forces and resources. One of these was the Rev. James Ramsay, who had been a parson in St. Kitts for nineteen years. In 1784 he "published a devastatingly circumstantial account of plantation slavery" (Craton 1974:261). Ramsay was very active in disseminating abolitionist sentiments as were his patron, Sir Charles Middleton, comptroller of the navy, his wife, Lady Middleton, and Beilby Porteus, the bishop of London, who encouraged Ramsay in these activities. They formed the kernel of a developing abolitionist network that was important in putting Clarkson and Wilberforce on the abolitionist track.

2.   In the literature different names for this organization are used. Here we will follow Anstey and use the name Abolition Committee. The first move of the committee concerned the decision to attack the slave trade, and not slavery itself or both evils at the same time. This was primarily a tactical decision. The abolitionists reckoned that their chances on success were better if they concentrated on one of these evils. Attacking only one of them would moreover suffice, since by attacking one evil the other one would inevitably be negatively affected as well. Further advantages of attacking the slave trade were the fact that such an attack would lay the axe at the very root and the fact that the right to regulate the trade was undoubtedly within the province of the imperial government. A negative aspect of attacking slavery itself was finally that it involved an open assault on property, the Holy Grail of eighteenth-century society. This could facilitate the resistance against the movement greatly.

3.   Alongside the non-Quakers Sharp and Clarkson, a third non-Quaker, Philip Sansom, became a member of the committee. The other (Quaker) members were William Dillwyn, Samuel Hoare, George Harrison, John Lloyd, Joseph Wood, Richard Phillips, John Barton, Joseph Hooper, and James Phillips (Anstey 1975:249, note 370).

4.   This was done at the famous anti–slave trade dinner at the home of Bennet Langton, at which among others Clarkson and the Middletons were present. As Anstey indicates, "It was deemed politic that Wilberforce should not at once openly take membership of the Abolition Committee, but from the very evening of the Langton dinner party it was agreed that that Committee should work closely in Wilberforce's support" (1975:253–54).

5.   As a matter of fact Wilberforce had shown his interest in the problem of slavery earlier. At the age of fourteen he had written an antislavery letter to a Yorkshire paper; later he had begun to gather information about the state of slavery in Antigua; and in 1784 he had consulted with Ramsay about slavery in the West Indies.

6.   Furneaux indicates that Pitt also urged Wilberforce to take on this matter "or the ground may be occupied by another" (cited in 1974:72). This had almost been the case at one point in the 1770s when "Burke began to interest himself in the anti-slavery cause and . . . drafted a scheme for gradual emancipation [but the strength of the West Indian Interest] deterred [him] from proceeding further" because he feared for his political career (Anstey 1975:241).

7.   In addition to the literature already mentioned, we have used Furneaux (1974) and Howse (1952) for this sketch of Wilberforce and the Clapham sect, the group of leading Anglican Evangelicals, of which Wilberforce was one of the foremost members.

8.   This crisis was provoked in particular by Dr. Philip Doddridge's *Rise and Progress of Religion of the Soul*, which they had by chance included in their luggage. Wilberforce began to dissociate himself more and more from the diversion of social life and "[t]he more he brooded the more he became convinced of his own sinfulness in having neglected the mercies of God for so long" (Furneaux 1974:36).

9.   Important members of the sect were Henry Thornton, M.P. and banker; Rev. John Venn, rector of Clapham; William Wilberforce, M.P. for Yorkshire; Isaac Milner, dean of Carlisle and provost of Queen's College, Cambridge; Zachary Macauly, founder of the Sierra Leone Colony; Thomas Babington, a country gentleman, philanthropist, and M.P.; Hannah More, philanthropist, poet, and writer; and James Stephen, a lawyer who practiced in the Prize Appeal Court of the Privy Council (Anstey 1975:157). Anstey also includes Granville Sharp, who was not a member in the strict sense (pp. 157–58). There were other Evangelicals of importance such as Thomas Gisborne and John Newton, but they did not participate in the sect itself.

10.   The Abolition Committee stated its goals as follows: "Our immediate aim is, by diffusing a knowledge of the subject, and particularly the Modes of procuring and treating slaves, to interest men of every description in the Abolition of the Traffic; but especially those from whom any alteration must proceed—the Members of our Legislature" (cited in Anstey 1975:255).

11.   As Drescher shows, the depiction often given of abolitionism as a nonconformist middle-class movement is—at the least—an incomplete one. As he states, "The likelihood is that British abolitionism was more cross-class than most accounts of abolition, whether sympathetic or critical, have usually implied" (1986:130). On the other hand, Oldfield's study (1995) shows that the grass roots support came predominantly from the provincial middling ranks.

12.   Lewis vividly describes this job in the following fashion: "We watch him [Clarkson] as he rides up and down England, visiting mainly the slave ports of London, Liverpool, and Bristol; persuading ships' captains, many of them the real monsters of the trade, to allow him to examine their ships' logs; interviewing ordinary seamen, first to tell their horrendous stories of the middle passage,

secondly to make notarized statements of their experiences, and thirdly to persuade them to appear as material witnesses before the parliamentary investigating committees, often at the price of being victimized by their employers; visiting the sordid public houses of the slave ports in order to note at firsthand the methods used by slaver captains to impress their unwilling crews; obtaining copies of articles of agreement which documented the fraud employed in that particular aspect of the trade; collecting specimens of the torture instruments to terrify, sometimes murder, refractory slaves on board passage; assiduously researching in customs houses to make notes of the muster rolls of slave vessels. . . . It was a truly herculean task, at times involving the very real possibility of . . . being murdered" (1978:40–41).

13.   As Furneaux states, Clarkson had during his investigations acquired "the names and histories of 20,000 seamen, so that the Abolitionists now knew more of the Trade than the slavers themselves" (1974:75).

14.   "[B]oth categories usually published by James Phillips, the bookseller and member of the Committee" (Anstey 1975:256–57).

15.   For a more extensive treatment of verse inspired by the abolition movement, see Sypher ([1942] 1969, esp. pp. 181–204). He shows that in these poems most of the well-known abolitionist themes were brought to the fore but this time injected with a generous dose of sentiment and sensation. As Sypher typifies this "poetic" element, "a preposterous idealization of African life, together with a heavy realism in portraying the conditions of slavery itself" (p. 203). The same elements of idealization, sentiment, and sensation also spiced the novels of the 1780s and 1790s (pp. 276–89). These novels, however, used slavery primarily in a literary fashion and thus served less as a vehicle for the abolition message.

16.   The readiness of the press to cover events and publications related to slavery has already been mentioned in Chapters 5 and 6. As Hunt (cited in Anstey 1975:259–60) has made clear abolitionist poetry was much reproduced in provincial newspapers. Sypher ([1942] 1969) shows that such attention was also present in magazines at the end of the 1780s, although this attention flagged (in the two magazines he mentions) after 1789. He also finds that after that year these magazines gave more room to proslavery publications as well. According to Porter, the picture was worse: "Many newspapers, even those supporting Pitt's government, were anti-abolitionist" (1970:52).

17.   As Drescher remarks, "Abolitionism was probably the first social movement to use provincial press on a national scale" (1986:212).

18.   This initiative does not mean that petitioning took place completely out of reach of the London committee. For a reasoned attempt to set the record straight regarding the role of the London and the Manchester Abolition Committees in the first abolition campaign, see Oldfield (1995, esp. pp. 46–49).

19.   As Drescher (1986) points out, Manchester had to experiment with new ways of organizing itself and with new venues for political participation because it was a new town not represented in the political order.

20.   Wilberforce's optimistic view can be found in two letters he wrote in January 1788, in which he stated: "There is no doubt of our success [and] I trust

there is little reason to doubt of the motion for abolition . . . being carried in parliament" (cited in Anstey 1975:267).

21. The abolitionists renewed their parliamentary efforts the next year. The abolition motion was then accepted in the Commons but only after it was amended to gradual abolition. Earlier both houses had accepted a bill, put forward by Sir William Dolben, to regulate the number of slaves on one ship. This bill was, however, only accepted after much pressure by Pitt.

22. "Minutes of the Standing Committee," 7 February 1788 (cited in Anstey 1975:288).

23. The slave interest spent £2,096 on propaganda, which was almost double the abolitionist expenses in the same period (Anstey 1975:292). Rather oddly, Porter concludes that the antis could never match the abolitionist propaganda, "[p]artly in consequence of the lack of funds" (1970:87).

24. The success of the campaign to boycott the use of slave-grown sugar in the years 1791–1792 is a clear indication of this popularity (see, for example, Drescher 1986:78–79).

25. Apocryphal statement of Luther before the Diet of Worms in April 1521 when summoned to withdraw his theses (*Encyclopedia Britannica*, 15th edition, 1985, vol. 23, p. 367).

26. The choice between abolition as part of an overarching movement to religious revitalization and moral regeneration of society and abolition solely as a clear-cut social and political goal was a difficult one. It was difficult because both choices fitted in well with the background of the initiators of the abolition discourse, the former choice with the deeply rooted conviction that religious and moral reform of society was needed in order to avert national disaster and the latter with the fact that most of the abolitionists were practical men as well, experienced in the world of politics, business, or professional activities.

27. Throughout the first campaign the slave traders played only a complementary supporting role.

28. Two points are important here. First, abolition got support from M.P.s who were dedicated to the cause of parliamentary reform. Second, being elected as an M.P. became increasingly dependent on one's stand toward abolition.

29. As Drescher (1986) points out, the religious and ideological differences were deliberately muted, so that the appeal could remain broad. During the first abolition campaign, dissent formed a minority, albeit substantial.

30. The support actually flowed more in the direction of the abolition movement than the other way around. As Drescher states more generally, "For 50 years [from the 1780s] abolitionist leaders had carefully preserved their autonomy from political parties and other social movements" (1986:147). This was partly caused by tactical considerations in order to avoid becoming associated with the Jacobin turn in the French Revolution, which was generally disapproved of in Great Britain. It rested, however, also partly on substantial considerations. Most abolitionists were strongly in favor of the existing order and propagated only reforms that pertained to individuals and not to structures (see, for example, the emphasis on the reform of manners). Oldfield, however, presents a different picture and states that many members of the Abolition Commit-

tee were political radicals (1995:42–43). Even if this is true for the committee, it certainly does not hold for the majority of the abolitionists. All in all, this implied a certain measure of ambivalence in the abolitionist movement (on this, see Davis 1975:373–75).

31.   Opposition to abolition was mostly based on direct interest or was seen as being in the national interest. Another not unimportant motive for supporting the antiabolition drive was the implicit threat of reform inherent in the abolitionist attack.

32.   As Anstey states, "Just as Clarkson's writings began with condemnation of the immorality of the slave trade and progressed to demonstration of its impolicy, so the Abolition Committee soon concluded that the general, moral case against the slave trade had been made and that the way to induce a positive readiness to end the slave trade was to demonstrate that it was impolitic as well as unjust and inhumane" (1975:260). As Drescher (1990) makes clear, the moral arguments were originally the basic ones (and remained so) throughout the whole abolition struggle.

33.   In the following, citations are sparingly used. A fuller description of the horrors of the slave trade might easily fill a volume in itself.

34.   Davis (1975) shows that there was at this point a contradiction in the abolition package: abolition was an infringement on the right of property, which itself was one of the foundations of liberty. Below we will examine the way the abolitionists dealt with this contradiction.

35.   As Davis points out, this reasoning had mostly unintentional radical implications. It could easily lead to questioning the legitimacy of the authority of government, as can be seen in an argument by Sharp, who citing Benezet stated, "No Legislature on Earth, which is the supreme power in every Civil Society, can alter the Nature of things, or make that to be lawful, which is contrary to the Law of God" (cited in Davis 1975:270).

36.   Colley contends that this argument, later on, was also positively phrased because antislavery became part of the process of the formation of the British national identity. She states, "Anti-slavery became an emblem of national virtue [and] was increasingly seized on as a means to redeem the nation, as a patriotic act" (1992:354).

37.   The notion of injustice occupied a specific place in the abolitionist package and had a specific restricted meaning that differs from the meaning Gamson (1992b) gives it. His definition—moral indignation—can be found in the abolitionist package as well but is mostly not referred to as injustice. As the impolicy theme shows, moral indignation is not a necessary component of an action frame. Another drawback of using notions like justice and injustice is that a lot of different meanings are attached to these notions which may easily lead to confusion.

38.   The West Indians (loosely) estimated this capital at seventy million pounds sterling (Porter 1970:56).

39.   George Turnbull related this justification to the biblical one by giving it a place in the "Great Chain of Being" created by God. In this chain everything and everyone occupied, quite naturally, its and his preordained place (Anstey 1975:294).

40. As Drescher makes clear, the abolitionists were wary to invoke the policy debate and only "after abolition coalesced into a broad political movement did Clarkson and his colleagues feel the need" to respond to the earlier points by the opposition to antislavery (1990:565).

41. Better treatment would obviously be in the interest of the slaves as well, and if as a consequence they worked more diligently such treatment would also be in the interest of the nation. Abolition would, moreover, be in the interest of Africa and its inhabitants.

42. As Walvin makes clear, "They [the friends of the Negro] tended to seize on half-truths and inflate them into distorted generalisations about black life. It appears, said a friend of the Negro, 'that the natural disposition of the negro is gentle, amiable, grateful, affectionate and docile'" (1973:186).

43. This myth was often supplemented by the growing tendency in all realms of society to negatively stereotype those who were involved in slavery. For instance, Davis shows that Cowper—who generally stood positive toward commerce—typifies the slave trader very negatively as one who grows "rich in cargoes of despair" (cited in Davis 1975:369). In contrast, Cowper associates the native African with pastoral innocence and natural liberty.

44. Long's theory in the 1770s may be regarded as the first systematic theory. As Drescher (1992) shows, systematic racism, especially scientific racism, is primarily a reaction to the drive to end slavery, although racial theories were not invented from scratch but drew on earlier accounts and ideas about Africa and its inhabitants.

45. As Drescher (1977a) shows, the antiabolitionists were possibly even more empirically oriented than the abolitionists.

46. The contestants were often quite sincere in their claims of factual proof.

47. Benezet's writings were exemplary in this respect. His pamphlets and tracts are replete with references to travel accounts of explorers, travelers, factors, merchants, and other authorities on Africa. He shows the deep (and for us somewhat naive) faith in the efficacy of accurate knowledge so typical for the religiously inspired abolitionists, as he states in his *Pamphlet on Negroes in Africa* (1762), "It is scarce to be doubted but that the foregoing Accounts will beget in the Heart of every considerate Reader an earnest Desire to see a Stop put to this complicated Evil" (cited in Bruns 1977:92). Eltis points to the utter certainty and self-confidence of the British abolitionists; they simply could not imagine that the "facts" could prove them wrong and when the facts did so they did not see it (1982:197).

48. This case involved a dispute over an insurance claim. The owner of the slave ship *Zong* claimed reimbursement for the loss of 133 slaves the captain of the ship had thrown overboard because he feared a shortage of water.

49. Newton was at that time not a irreligious man. His first religious conversion came when he was a slave trader: "[it] did not immediately lead him to forsake his calling, but merely to treat his slaves well and to conduct daily services upon deck from the Anglican *Prayer Book*" (Craton 1974:250).

50. This citation comes from a report of 1778 on the situation of the West Indian colonies. [See Drescher (1986:182, note 65).]

51.   See, for example, the way he mapped the regions of freedom and un-
freedom Drescher (1986:17).

52.   Drescher points to another cultural event that illustrates the transformation of the social climate very well, viz., the fact that the play *Oroonoko* was
adjusted to Manchester's new militancy when it opened there during the first
petition campaign (1986:228, note 26).

III

Confrontation

8

Social Movements and Social Construction of Meaning

8.1 INTRODUCTION

The years 1787–1792 witnessed a momentous popular mobilization for the cause of abolition and the rapid and definitive change of public thinking about the slave trade and slavery. In this chapter, we will ascertain what the relation between these phenomena was and whether our conceptual model is useful for understanding and explaining this relationship. The development of such a model is the subject of this book, which—as we made clear in Chapter 1—is directed at (1) clarifying the role of social movements in processes of meaning construction, and (2) devising a conceptual instrument for studying this role. To that end, we elaborated a model in Part I using both theoretical and empirical studies. Next, we studied existing historical works regarding the abolition of the slave trade in Great Britain. The data from this study, presented in Part II, are structured with the help of the concepts developed in Part I. This makes the final part, Part III, possible: the confrontation of conceptualization and empirical research. In this chapter, we will put the model from Chapter 3— and with that the theoretical notions of Chapter 2—to the test.

We will execute this confrontation in three steps: First, we will look into the question of whether the conditions assumed in our model were actually present in the case and, if so, to what degree. This is taken on in Section 8.2. At the same time and also in this section, we will ascertain which of the previous developments and events led to these conditions and we will look for conditions that were present but were not included in the original model. The second step involves the problem of causality, which is dealt with in Section 8.3. Here we will put three questions to the test: (1) Did the abolition campaign cause the change in thought? (2) Were the conditions we have established causally related to this effect? and (3) If so, what was the causal weight of each condition? The third step involves the revision of the conceptual model of Chapter 3 in light

of the results emerging from the earlier steps in our examination. This is
the subject of Section 8.4. After this revision we will end this chapter by
giving the adjusted model a place in a more encompassing view of
cultural change. This is done in Section 8.5.

8.2 BACK TO THE CONCEPTUAL MODEL

The conceptual model of Chapter 3 is build around three sets of interrelated factors: (1) a *cause* to campaign for, (2) the *decision to act* on that cause,
and (3) the *properties of the action-structure* within which the campaigning
actors act. We will start the examination of this model by looking at the first
two sets, which are, as we have seen, the preconditions for collective
campaigns. Then we will turn to the properties of the action-structure.

Cause

Antislavery and abolition were potential causes for collective action in
the 1780s. As we saw in Chapter 4, the philosophical and religious
developments in the eighteenth century (and before as well; see Davis
1966) revived the basic contradiction of slavery: the slave being at the
same time a thing and a human being. In the same period, the rise of
Britain as a colonial empire and commercial world power involved the
nation heavily in overseas slavery and the slave trade. It led, moreover,
to slavery on British soil at a time when forced labor had disappeared
from Britain and its inhabitants praised themselves for living in one of
the few free spots in the world. This last contradiction became especially
visible through the Somerset case.

The slave trade was a latent cause for action because it represented a situation that was contrary to the way human beings ought to be treated *and*
because it was a situation upon which the British government could act because the slave trade and the traders fell under British jurisdiction. Moreover, it was a cause without a voice because slaves were not represented in
the polity of Britain. The notion that the British government could act on
the slave trade was further strengthened by the altering views regarding
the power of man to change social arrangements. As we have seen, these
views originated in the same cultural developments we alluded to above.

Decision to Act

The decision to do something about slavery and the slave trade was—
before it was eventually taken in 1787—in the air for some years. This

propensity to act was rooted in several preceding historical developments and events. These developments and events will be treated below, under the heading Cultural and Structural Conduciveness. Although these developments and events were important in determining the decision to act on the cause of abolition, the actual decision was (and had to be) taken by specific people who could have abstained. We have here the voluntary element, agency, that is present in all social movement actions and that makes the occurrence and timing of collective action so difficult to predict.

The decision of the abolitionists to do something about the slave trade led almost automatically to the decision to counteract the abolitionist activities. The people involved in slavery and the slave trade also had a cause: their interests were threatened. The voluntarist element in their decision was, however, relatively insignificant, because they, the West Indians in particular, had a standing organization in the metropolis to watch their interests: the West Indian Interest. The moment the abolitionist threat became serious, they acted.

Properties of the Action-Structure

In Section 3.4 we elaborated four types of properties of the action-structure: two regarding the power that the movement actors bring into the campaign and two concerning the opportunities for their campaign. Here, we will deal first with the opportunity and then with the power aspects because in the abolition case the opportunities preceded the collective action and thus the generation of power.

1. Cultural Conduciveness of the Opportunity Structure. The cultural climate of the eighteenth century was largely shaped by the Enlightenment. Another important influence came from the realm of religion. Both led to an evolving climate characterized by four basic guiding values: liberty, happiness, benevolence, and reform. These values gave the century its character as the Age of Reason and Compassion. This climate favored—as a kind of filter or amplifier (Brand 1990)—themes, concepts, symbols, attitudes, etc., that were receptive to antislavery.

One of the main elements of this cultural climate was the theme of change and progress that permeated all realms of society, above all, the world of politics. But the more conservative theme of maintaining the existing social order remained important as well. Both themes kept each other more or less in a volatile balance that was easily disturbed, as is shown by the favorable reception of the French Revolution in its beginnings and by the widespread support for the counterrevolutionary measures following its violent Jacobin turn. It is clear that change as theme was more positive for antislavery activities, while a call for order was the opposite.[1] The change theme affected the basic cultural rules as well. The mood for change enlarged the access of new participants and issues to societal and political discourses. The only serious limiting rule was the one regarding property, which meant a serious bias against debates that in any way implied the curtailing of this right.

The cultural climate favored other cultural elements positive to anti-slavery as well. Enlightenment and religious thinking shaped a tool kit with symbols, doctrines, myths, narratives, images, etc. (see Sections 4.7 and 6.5) favorable to antislavery and abolition on which the abolitionists freely drew. At this point, two developments proved to be particularly useful. First, the Quaker heritage of antislavery writing, especially as it was complemented by the Evangelical notions of sin, guilt, and retribution, delivered important basic tools for the abolition struggle. Second, the world of writing in general, and that of literature specifically, contributed to the abolitionist tool kit by its themes and its format. The latter made printed matter such a perfect vehicle for the abolitionists.

On the other hand, the culture of "old" society fashioned the elements of a tool kit that the slave interest used. These were cultural elements that were, above all, related to tradition, national interest, and dominant visions regarding the way Britain should be run. The slave interest also had the benefit of the matter-of-fact character of the status quo, in which slavery and the slave trade were self-evident facts of life and self-evidently essential to the well-being of the nation.

The edge that the abolitionist tool kit had over the other depended on the basic values reigning in the period, which were more favorable to antislavery than to its opposite. It depended also on the dominance of change and order; in this respect the fortunes of the proponents of abolition were less steady. But all in all, the culture of Britain in the 1780s and 1790s was more conducive to abolition than to the defense of the slave trade. The case study has made it also perfectly clear that cultural elements play an important role in making collective campaigns—and, with it, cultural change—possible.

2. *Systemic Conduciveness of the Opportunity Structure.* British society changed considerably during the eighteenth century and this had far-reaching consequences for the conduciveness of its social arrangements to abolition. Recall each of the arrangements we distinguished in Chapter 3:

(a) The societal agenda. The historical studies we analyzed are not specifically directed at approaching abolition in terms of agendas and agenda building. However, they make clear that there were no systemic barriers that kept abolition off the agenda. Although Britain was an elite society and important members of its core were against abolition, these members could not seal off the agenda for the topic of abolition. Stated otherwise, the antiabolitionists did not control the agenda, nor for that matter did the abolitionists. At this point, it is important to note that abolition reached the agenda the moment that important people in Britain joined the Quaker initiative. The last—probably because of their status as dissenters—had not been able to do so on their own.

Something else the historical material does not tell us is who the important gatekeepers were, if there were any. There was no specific triggering event that helped abolition onto the agenda, although Pitt's coming to power opened a window for abolition. It is, however, clear that the carrying capacity was limited and that other issues, such as reform, the situation in India, and France, were competing for public attention. Illustrative in this regard is, as the end of the first campaign shows, the ease with which abolition could be crowded out.

(b)   The media.   Again, the studies we analyzed are not specifically directed at the role the media played in the first abolition campaign. Still, they make it very clear that contemporary media such as journals, magazines, and pamphlets occupied a central place in the abolition campaign. They could do so because of their pivotal position in British society. Moreover, it appears that they stood in high esteem.

Both the abolitionists and the antis had access to these media or were able to procure (i.e., buy) it. Both parties, moreover, succeeded in creating their own media, e.g., by printing and distributing pamphlets and tracts. The historical studies do not provide enough material to decide how access was divided or which party was the most successful in its own media production. One thing is clear, though: no party was continually barred from the media, although in the first phases of the abolition campaign access was more difficult to obtain for the slavery view than for the abolitionist one.

The media, chiefly print, could play their pivotal role because Great Britain was in an important measure already transformed into a *Gesellschaft* type of society in which face-to-face contacts no longer dominated as channels of communication. It seems warranted to conclude that access to the media was essential for initiating a public discourse on an issue like abolition and for participating in it.

(c)   The political system.   The development of the British political system after the Glorious Revolution led to an oligarchic system, which was positive for collective action. First, it was open to outside interests and issues, provided these were brought to the fore by "insiders" of civil society. This access was there for abolitionists and their adversaries alike. Second, this openness was limited, leading to "causes without a voice" such as abolition. It also gave birth to other causes, such as political and religious reform, which meant another source of support for abolition. Third, the system was inherently unstable, which gave challengers the opportunity to enter the public and political discourse. Fourth, a new and important political instrument, the social movement, was in the making. The existence of workable formats for contention is an important—and as such not separately mentioned—feature of a political system with regard to the feasibility of collective action.

(d)   The existence of movement potential.   One of the most important systemic developments of the eighteenth century concerns the creation of the leadership of the abolition movement and the constituencies that could be mobilized. Especially important at this point was the coincidence of the growth of capitalism and the increase of political and religious stagnation, leading to a growing demand for social, political, and religious reform.

(e)   Resistance in society.   From its beginning in 1787, the abolition campaign evoked counteractions from the slave interest.[2] This interest was shaped by the growth of the commercial empire, which gave it the resources to organize the defense against the abolitionist attack. An important resource was missing, however. The growth of this empire did not create constituencies on which the defenders of the slave trade could draw to fend off the abolitionist threat. The potential for resistance was an important constraint on the abolition campaign, although it could only hinder but not stop abolition. It was also remarkable that there were no competing organizations (or better still, that the abolitionists were successful in containing divisiveness) or large negative publics. The lack of constituencies and competing actors kept the resistance, however politically powerful it was, restricted.

The action-structure offered important systemic opportunities and facilities for both waging the abolition campaign and organizing the defense against it. If there was an advantage at all for one of the contending parties, this was only a slight one. The most one could say is that the availability of constituencies that could be mobilized tilted the scale slightly toward the abolitionist side.[3]

3. *Systemic Power: The Amount of Support.*   Both abolitionists and antiabolitionists were able to organize themselves very rapidly and they successfully tapped the resources available in society. As with every movement mobilization, this building of power was a multidimensional affair that was further complicated by the fact that abolition involved both an ideological and political struggle.

The abolitionists were very successful in their self-organization with their nationwide system of local abolition committees. This system facilitated the mobilization of resources in an important manner because it built on preexisting solidarities and co-opted existing, often religious, networks into the campaign (cf. Klandermans 1992:94–95; Tarrow 1994:150). It was also very successful in mobilizing public support. In this respect, the clever use of printed material, lecture circuits, abolition meetings, and petition campaigns was particularly helpful. This is how the abolitionists turned the existing Quaker antislavery organization into an abolition network. The Abolition Committee was also moderately successful in building a network of support in political circles. The slave interest revitalized the existing, mainly London-based organization that was already there for defending its interests. At first, the antis directed their external efforts toward the world of politics, in which they were rather successful. Later, they tried less successfully to build public support for their case.

Summarized, the abolitionists clearly won the battle of numbers. They were able to mobilize many into action and to capture the support of the public at large. In the realm of politics, on the other hand, the antiabolitionists had and kept the edge over the abolitionists. All in all, the resulting balance of (systemic) power was an unstable one that was easily disturbed.

4. *Cultural Power: The Framing of the Interpretive Packages.* Between 1787 and 1792, the abolition discourse was a veritable clash of arguments in both the public and the political realm. Here we will focus on the former as our concern is above all directed at changes in the realm of public thought. We will therefore systematically examine the interpretive packages of both contending parties with regard to the four characteristics we put forward in Chapter 3.

(a) Cultural resonance. The moral argument of the abolitionists clearly resonated with the culture of British society, which was profoundly affected by Protestantism and the Enlightenment. It showed that slavery and the slave trade were at odds with core elements of Britishness: man as a being who is naturally free, inclined to his own happiness and that of others, and—when not corrupted—engaged in progressively reforming the world to the dictates of God and reason. Both practices were thus unnatural, unjust, and sinful. This moral argument was, moreover, framed in such a way that it appealed to a wide spectrum of people, running from conservative Tories like Wesley to political radicals like Paine and was continually kept in balance so that people did not shun abolition. The policy argument that played a limited role in the public discourse was also in accordance with the emerging progressive thought regarding free trade and free enterprise, which was a characteristic element of the climate of that period.

The appeal and cogency of the abolitionist interpretive package was mainly the effect of the origin of the abolitionist arguments. On the one hand, they originated in cultural trends concerning the renewal of social thought such as the Enlightenment and the related innovating theological movement. On the other, abolition as an idea owed much to developments that had a more traditional and in some respects more conservative character, i.e., the changes in the Society of Friends and the Evangelical revival. Thus the themes that the abolitionists put forward resonated with two important undercurrents in British society that became really visible at the end of the eighteenth century. One concerned the feeling that political, economic, and social change was badly needed and showed itself off and on from the 1760s onward. The other regarded the feeling that Britain was in need of a thorough spiritual renewal, which revealed itself in the reappearing dissenting tradition, this time as the Evangelical revival inside and outside the established church. This last need was, above all, fed by an awareness of living in a sinful world and the resulting fear of God's retribution.

The formulation of the counterabolitionist arguments resonated mainly with the culture of the "old" society as this was shaped in the first seventy years of the eighteenth century by the landed and the mercantile interests.[4] This society had, however, discredited itself morally in the eyes of many Britons. The vices and disreputable behavior of the reigning elites and of the homecoming West Indians were clearly visible and at odds with the way Britain reputedly had been in the distant past, with how it should be, and with how it would become in the future. The proslavery and pro–slave trade message with its focus on the national interest and the importance of maintaining the existing order as the best of all possible ones was out of tune with the emerging cultural climate of late eighteenth-century Britain. The moral tone of the abolition discourse swept away other considerations and even restricted the effectiveness of appeals on accepted notions such as the right of property. The result was that the counterabolitionist interpretive package with its emphasis on the national interest only convinced politicians but not the public at large. Many Britons were, moreover, not receptive to racial and biblical justifications of slavery. These justifications contradicted one of the cornerstones of Christian thought with their denial of the common ancestry of mankind. They were also at odds with the emerging notions of Providence and moral progress.[5]

(b) Empirical credibility.   One of the notable aspects of the abolition struggle is the effort of both parties to "prove" their case. Another striking aspect, particularly on the abolitionist side, is trust in the efficacy of facts. As we have seen before, the use of facts functioned as a means to:

- conceal the ideological character of arguments;
- expose the flaws in the narratives and arguments of one's opponents and therewith to prove the other side wrong;
- lift the veil of ignorance from the public and politicians regarding the true character of Africa, the slave trade, and the situation in the West Indies.

The abolitionists won the battle on empirical credibility. First, the facts they used in the ideological struggle—and often in their exposing efforts as well—concurred with Enlightenment notions and the literary myth of the noble savage. This does not, however, necessarily mean that their narratives were always "truer" than those of the adversaries. Second, the gruesome character of the slave trade and slavery was difficult to conceal with so many eyewitnesses around[6] and could often only be bluntly denied.

(c) Rhetorical force.   Both sides in the abolition discourse structured their interpretive packages the same way: (1) framing or depiction, (2) reasoning, and (3) consequences. Such a structure gives an argument its inherent logic, which becomes effective in appeal and cogency as the three elements are substantially acknowledged and regarded as "true." In this respect, the contenders did not differ, since both structured their themes the same way. Still, the abolitionists had the edge over their opponents as their moral argument was the most elaborated and concurred well with the rhetoric common to the Protestant tradition so familiar to most Britons (see, for example, the way Sharp and Wesley formulated their argument). The antis could not draw on the same tradition, because their main thrust was emphasizing the policy aspects of the trade.

(d) Resolution.   At this point the results are contrary to the expectations stated in Chapter 3. The abolition package was more vaguely and less restrictively formulated than the counterpackage, which was "higher" on resolution. The former, however, appealed to a wider public or, better, to different publics because it contained something for everyone. The latter was directed at a specific section of society, got its support, but failed to win over the public at large. We have here the same result as Gerhards and Rucht (1990), who found that a more ambiguous package has the ability to attract more diverse support to a cause.[7] It seems that resolution can sometimes be a help for movement campaigners while at other times it can pose a hindrance. This result suggests that is better to leave this characteristic out of the model altogether.

The above shows that the abolition interpretive package clearly resonated better with the culture of Great Britain at the end of the eighteenth century than the counterpackage and that it was more credible in the "factual" sense. As far as the rhetorical force of the packages is concerned, the difference was smaller but success was still on the abolitionist side. The abolition package was, however, lower on resolution, which is contrary to our expectations. Three out of four characteristics discussed in Chapter 3 were thus present. Another element—emotionality—received a great deal of emphasis in the interpretive packages. The amount of energy that both parties put into appeals to emotion particularly indicates that this element might be important. It was, however, not mentioned in our model but needs—it seems—a place in it.

8.3 CAUSALITY

The data in Chapter 7 clearly show that between 1787 and 1792 two historical events coincided: (1) the relatively sudden, sharp, and lasting change in the way slavery and the slave trade were collectively defined, and (2) the first campaign of the abolition movement, which started in 1787 with the formation of the Abolition Committee and ended in 1792 due to drastic changes in the cultural and political climate. Until now we have assumed—guided by the historical studies of abolition—that both events were causally related. Now is the time to pose the question of whether this was the case, because without such a relation it would not make sense to probe the efficacy of a model in which movement campaigns occupy a central place. Below we will examine this question of causality by searching for historical alternatives.

The first alternative for the existence of a causal relation between the abolition campaign and the change in public thinking is that it is a spurious one. Both events could be expressions of the continuous gradual process of change in the way people thought about slavery and the slave trade. The change in public thinking—in this explanation—is no more than the rounding off of the long-term process that began in intellectual circles in the beginning of the century and consequently filtered through into other layers of society. When this process was almost completed at the end of the century, the cultural barriers hindering the abrogation of the slave trade were demolished, opening the avenue for political actions against the trade: the first abolition campaign.

This alternative explanation does not seem to hold, because two arguments contradict it. First, the change in public thought was so sudden and enormous—it was a veritable sea change—that no one, neither those who were all for abolition nor those who were dead against it, expected it to happen, at least not so soon. Second, the emphasis in the campaign on changing public opinion on slavery and the slave trade—and this was an important part of it—does not make sense. Why put so much energy into this undertaking if its goal was practically accomplished? The only reasonable answer is that many were not convinced. We think that both arguments weigh heavily enough to reject this first alternative explanation.

The second alternative implies that the abolition campaign was a ruse. It functioned as a facade for actors who wanted abolition for other, self-interested reasons. Williams's capitalists are one example. Other candidates could be members of the political elite who used the abolition campaign as a means for buying rest at home by shifting public attention to evils overseas. This concealing of reality could even have gone a step further. Actors who try to change institutional arrangements in capitalist societies do so in a culture and structure that is so fully hegemonized by the dominant capitalist elite that they—consciously or unconsciously—can only contribute to the goals of this elite. In the case of abolition, they did so by realizing institutional changes that in the end were beneficial for the dominant elite.

This alternative explanation does not appear to hold either, because of the following arguments: First, none of the historical studies indicate that there were any concealed actions of conspiring actors. Otherwise stated, there is simply no proof of a ruse. Second, even if the campaigning actors were successful in hiding their true motives, this does not affect our explanation. Whatever their motives, these actors overtly campaigned for abolition, and in this way they changed public thinking on slavery and the slave trade. In this case, the alternative explanation concerns motivation and not causality, and thus does not impair the causal relation between campaign and outcome. Both arguments suffice, in our opinion, to reject this second alternative as well.

The third alternative is in fact a complement to the previous two. It consists of a mental experiment in which the abolition campaign is abstracted from the course of events described in Part II. The question is whether it is probable that the change in collective definitions would have occurred in the absence of this campaign. As Drescher shows, there was no abolitionism in the countries that just like Britain had free labor at home and slave labor in their colonies but that unlike Britain had no (sustained) popular mobilization against the slave trade. In his words, "Against the Anglo-american areas one must set the virtual absence of metropolitan abolitionism in Denmark, Sweden, the Netherlands, and Portugal, the belated movement in Spain, and the sputtering combustibility of France" (1987:197). His argument that popular mobilization made the difference is even more strongly supported in a more recent study, *The Long Goodbye*. Here, he compares the Netherlands and Great Britain in terms of economics and antislavery and finds that the rise of antislavery is, above all, a correlate of "new modes of social mobilization" (1994b:68). Drescher's work also makes abundantly clear that the mobilization in Britain led to the pursued changes in public political opinion (1986, 1987). Thus it does not seem probable that the drastic change in opinion would have occurred without the abolition campaign. Moreover, chances are that the momentum present in late eighteenth-century Britain would have been lost and that abolition and emancipation would at least have been delayed considerably.

Our conclusion is that the first abolition campaign was essential in changing the collective definitions regarding the slave trade and slavery in Great Britain in the last part of the eighteenth century. We therefore concur with Drescher as he states: "The most significant immediate result [of the abolitionist breakthrough in 1788–1792] was . . . the emergence of a new attitude towards slavery and the slave trade" (1986:85; see also Drescher 1994b).

The next step in unraveling the causal relationships between the abolition campaign and the change in thinking is the question of which elements were causally important in the course of events of which the abolition campaign was a part. Because we already concluded that this campaign occupied a central place in this course of events, we can narrow down this question to two, more specific subquestions regarding this causality:

1.   What made the abolition campaign possible? The preconditions of the campaign are causally relevant because—as we made clear above—the change in the definitions of slavery and the slave trade would not have occurred at that time and in that form without the abolition campaign. Thus, the conditions that made the campaign possible are indirectly related to the result;

2.   What made the abolition campaign effective? This question has to do with the characteristics of the campaign and the actors involved in it, which made the difference between success and failure. The answer to this second question will mainly depend on a comparison of the abolition campaign with the countercampaign.

The first subquestion concerns the preconditions for the abolition campaign as shaped by historical developments and events during the first eighty years of the eighteenth century—"history" in terms of our model. Of these preconditions the most important was the *decision to act*, the agency aspect of collective action. This decision implied that:

(a)   There was a latent problem[8] that could be constructed into a *cause*—in this case the immorality and injustice of the African slave trade.

(b)   There were *actors*—moral entrepreneurs, sponsors, caretakers—present who could initiate and eventually conduct the abolition campaign. In the abolition case this type of actor was present on the scene.

This was, however, not enough to get the abolition campaign going: British society had to be *conducive* to and had to offer the *opportunities* for this campaign. The situation in the 1780s was—in terms of culture—relatively favorable for antislavery and abolition, in terms of our model, *culturally conducive.* There were important facilities present and no fundamental constraints. In terms of getting the abolition campaign off the ground, the *systemic conduciveness* of the action-structure proved to be even more important than the cultural one. In this respect, two elements stood out:

(a)   The movement potential.   The combination of leadership and potential constituencies was decisive. In 1783, the Quaker initiative was based on the same combination of elements but these were not broad enough to turn it into a movement campaign. It was the Evangelical infusion that turned this initiative into a campaign.

(b)   The political system.   The British political system had just those characteristics—relative openness, a measure of instability, a workable format for collective political action—to make a collective campaign like abolition possible.[9]

As was the case in the cultural realm, there were no decisive constraints in a systemic sense.

The same situation, however, made the counteractions of the slave interest possible. All the preconditions for a countercampaign were present: leaders who could decide to act against the abolitionist threat, a cause, and an action-structure that did not constrain pro–slave trade actions definitively. From a systemic point of view, the antiabolitionists were no less endowed for the waging of a campaign against abolition, although they were handicapped by the fact that their network of potential constituents was much narrower than the abolitionist one. But when we turn to the cultural side of their action-structure, it becomes clear that their handicaps vis-à-vis the abolitionists were much larger.

As we stated above, the second subquestion concerns the characteristics of the campaign. The basic causal assumption of our model with regard to cultural change is that cultural changes are rooted in cultural processes. More specifically, changes in meaning will only come about in

and through processes in which actors are actively engaged in constructing meanings that differ from extant ones. If social movements are involved in these processes, these different meanings are the result of
public discourses initiated or entered by social movement actors. In
these discourses alternative meanings are put forward, debated, often
amended, and in the end agreed upon or rejected. This basic assumption implies that a movement campaign can only have effect if the campaigning actors:

1.   are able to open a discourse or to enter an existing one on the
cause or issue they are putting forward;
2.   have the capability to sustain such a discourse; and
3.   can put forward their message—the construction of the cause—in
such a way that people in society are convinced that the campaigning
actors are right and thus change their thinking in that direction.

Below we will ascertain whether this pattern of causality can be found in
the abolition case.

The first barrier was easily overcome by the abolitionists. Their campaign evolved readily into a discourse because before long many people
concluded that it was time to discuss the evil of the slave trade and its
eradication or at least its amelioration, and so they did. Abolition almost
immediately reached the societal agenda as may be inferred from the
immense public interest in this topic. The abolitionists could open the
discourse on abolition because "history" had produced:

(a)   A *cultural* climate that was—especially in its basic values and
themes—*conducive* to abolition.
(b)   *Systemic* opportunities for waging the abolition campaign, above
all, the presence of and access to media, that was sympathetic to their
cause. In other words, the social system was *conducive* as well.

Although the abolitionists initiated this discourse, their adversaries
were not excluded (or could not be) from it. British society in the 1780s
was organized in such a way that the antiabolitionists were not barred
from the abolition discourse. It was culturally and systemically conducive to their countercampaign, which gave them the opportunity to put
forward their message as well.

The British abolitionists could also open the discourse on abolition
because they had the resources to do so. First, the initiators of the
abolition campaign were socially respectable and incumbents of positions with authority; they were people one would take seriously and
listen to. Second, the abolition movement was rooted in extensive reli-

gious networks, which gave the abolition campaign the power of numbers and access to other, related resources. Although their *systemic power* made it very difficult to dismiss the cause the abolitionists were campaigning for, it could not keep the slave interest out of the debate. The latter was powerful enough to enter the discourse and to prevent abolition becoming a walkover.

Taken together, the abolitionists and their opponents had the opportunities and power necessary to open or enter the discourse on the abolition of the slave trade. This was more a matter of opportunities for the abolitionists than for the antis, who entered the discourse on the basis of their power. This finding concurs with the basic assumption of Tarrow (1994), who gives political opportunities and the changes therein a central position in explaining the occurrence of collective actions. Challengers seem to need opportunities more than power to get public discourses going.[10]

The second step in the process of cultural change concerned the ability to sustain the abolition discourse, at least long enough to accomplish the changes in meaning. The most important aspect in this respect was one that neither the abolitionists nor their adversaries could control, viz., maintaining the cultural conduciveness. The cultural climate remained conducive until 1792, when external events temporarily broke the volatile balance between the progressive theme of change and the regressive theme of order. This break, however, did not affect the change in defining slavery and the slave trade because it had by then become irreversible.

The role that both parties played in sustaining the abolition discourse was thus largely *circumscribed by the cultural conduciveness* of the action-structure within which both operated. *Within these restrictions*, both used—in the symbolic struggle that the abolition discourse was—the resources at their disposal and assembled new ones in attempts to gain the advantage over the other. This made sustaining the discourse and determining its course largely *a matter of power*.

Each contender used this power to push its interpretive package forward as the truth about slavery and the slave trade. Here, we arrive at the third element of the change process: which of its characteristics gave one package the edge over the other. In order to assess this, we have to look for the degree to which these packages succeeded in convincing people that the way slavery and the slave trade were defined was the right way to think about these phenomena.[11]

We saw that both contending parties structured their messages in the same way. With their packages both tried to appeal to (1) the cognition of people, and (2) their emotions. These lines in their respective approaches form the dimensions along which we will compare both packages to see why the abolitionist package was causally effective and the counter-abolitionist one was not.

We will call the first dimension *credibility*. We use this term because it designates those aspects of an interpretive package that are meant to convince people cognitively of the truth of what is put forward. Actors do this by making their packages resonate with existing cultural notions, empirically credible, and rhetorically convincing. We will call the second dimension *emotionality* as this points to those aspects of a package that are meant to either draw people to the cause depicted in a package or push them away from the contending package. Emotionality is thus a two-edged sword in discourses. It is, on the one hand, an indispensable complement to the credibility of packages, because emotional appeals may raise the empathy with a cause and, as a consequence, make people more ready to be convinced in a cognitive way. On the other hand, negative emotional depictions of the contender's cause and of the way contenders behave can effectively block the way for cognitive appeals.

When we compare both interpretive packages on the dimension of credibility, we see that:

(a)   The abolitionist package was clearly more *credible* in a *cultural* respect than the counterpackage because of its correspondence with the culture of late eighteenth-century Britain. The abolition package could be seen as a credible and plausible narrative because it pointed to a wrong and its remedy in a way that resonated with cultural themes on their way to dominance. The abolition narrative was conceived in such a manner that many late eighteenth-century British citizens could say, Yes, bondage is immoral because it is against the natural equality of all human beings and the natural justice reigning over them.

(b)   The abolitionist package was more *credible* in an *empirical* sense as well. The abolitionists could not only prove that their version of the slave trade (and of slavery) corresponded more closely to the harsh reality of this practice, but they were also better at presenting the "things" they could (and did) not prove as indisputable facts because their factual presentation concurred with important cultural notions. Credibility in this sense does not point to a necessary correspondence between an "objective" reality and the presentation of that reality in an interpretive package but to the way a package is constructed. Empirically credible packages are constructed as facts regardless of whether this construction could withstand a scientific empirical test. Empirical credibility is thus a matter of presentation and concerns, above all, a presentation of statements as facts that convinces people that these statements are experientially true.[12]

(c)   The abolitionist and the counterpackage were structured in a rhetorically logical way and were thus equally *rhetorically credible*. The abolitionist package had an advantage though, because it was linked with the then dominant Protestant rhetorical tradition, again a link with the culture of late-eighteenth-century Britain.

In the dimension of credibility, empirical and rhetorical credibility were conditions that were necessary but not sufficient for packages to be cognitively convincing. Cultural credibility was dominant. It appears to be a necessary condition as well and is sufficient as long as the two other aspects of credibility are at least present. Together, the three aspects form one dimension in which they can only be separated analytically.

The dominant position of cultural credibility concurs with the dominance Gamson attaches to cultural resonance (see, for example, Gamson and Modigliani 1989; Gamson 1988). This dominance, however, neglects somewhat the importance of empirical and rhetorical credibility. The efforts that the contenders in the abolition discourse put into "facts" and "rhetoric" more or less proves that these aspects of credibility must be important, too.

The second dimension, emotionality, was clearly present in both packages. The abolitionists used appeals on emotions, above all:

• To raise empathy with the dismal fate of the slave. They could do so because the appeals concurred with important traits in British culture.
• To underline factual statements and, thus, to enhance the empirical credibility of their message.
• To depict the slave trade, slavery and those involved in these practices in a negative way in order to make the counterpackage less credible.

The antiabolitionists mainly focused on this last aspect. They tried to discredit the abolitionists and through this to diminish the credibility of their package.

It is clear that the abolitionists succeeded in changing public thinking on slavery and the slave trade and that this was largely the result of the more credible way they framed their message. Although it appears that their appeal on emotions was also more effective, nothing definitive can be said about the place and role of emotionality in bringing about change in thought on slavery and the slave trade. This is largely the consequence of the way the emotional side of the abolition struggle is dealt with in historical studies. Ample attention is paid to emotional elements, but more as an illustration of what went on in the struggle than as a topic of research in its own right.

Benford and Hunt (1992) bring another, conceptual reason for this lack of attention forward. They point to the overwhelming influence of Resource Mobilization Theory with its emphasis on rationality. In a reaction to the earlier collective behavior tradition, the resource mobilization theorists brought the fiction of the "ultrarationalistic" movement actor to the fore. With it, they obscured the role of passions and emotions in the explanation of social movement processes. As Benford and Hunt show, passion and emotion are factors needed to explain the mobilization of constituencies because constituents "must be more than mobilized to act; they have to be inspired" (p. 50). The abolition case shows that emotions also deserve a place in the set of factors that explain the cultural effects of movement campaigns as they play an important role in public discourses. At this point, more work is needed and a "dramaturgical infusion" into movement theory, as Benford and Hunt propose, could be very useful in this respect. For the moment, it seems warranted to give emotions a place in the conceptual model.

8.4   THE REVISED CONCEPTUAL MODEL

The abolition case indicates that three elements were important in the processes leading to changes in the way slavery and the slave trade were collectively defined: *history, agency,* and the *collective campaign* resulting in a public discourse. In this subsection we will revise the conceptual model of Chapter 3 around the same elements. We begin by restating the model more elaborately and we will end by summarizing the model in text and with a figure.

Cultural changes effected by social movements depend, and this is the first element of the change process, on long-term historical processes and specific historical events, the episodic context of social movements. These processes and events affect the preconditions for every collective movement campaign: the set of collective actions that may actually bring about change. Moreover, they continue to affect the conditions of a campaign while it is going on. In our model, the processes and events are comprised under the term *history.* History produces, more specifically, an ever-shifting window for collective action that consists of a *potential cause*, the *propensity to act* on that cause, and a *conducive action-structure.*

The concept of window comes from Kingdon (1984), who uses it to refer metaphorically to moments in policy processes in which the opportunity arises for problems and/or solutions to enter these processes and to become part of the realm of politics (see also Tarrow 1994:179). Here we use it to denote the degree to which historical situations are more or less prone to collective actions. From time to time, history opens and closes a window for collective action. The opening and closing of the window of opportunity may be seen as a continuum. The opening pole accords more with the so-called grievance, political process, and new-movements theories in which collective action is viewed as more or less automatically proceeding from positive societal conditions. The closing pole corresponds more with resource mobilization theory. In this theoretical approach, collective action stems to a large degree from the efforts of the movement entrepreneurs.

History, however, is an element in change processes that must not only be thoroughly dealt with in historical cases but it needs to be attended to in contemporary sociological studies as well. For instance, the challenge of the establishment inherent in the youth movement of the sixties in the Netherlands and the resulting cultural changes are not fully comprehensible without at least taking into account the return of the prewar paternalistic social and political structure, the pillarization that was so typical for Dutch society, and events in the fifties such as the rock and roll revolution in popular music and the early challenges of the authorities by so-called maladjusted youths.

The second main element in the process of cultural change by social movements is *agency,* here the actual *decision to act* on a cause.[13] Agency is partially a matter of voluntary decisions and as such falls outside the causal relations in our model. In every specific campaign it is a given that makes that our model fundamentally underdetermined. It is also partially a matter of history. As we have seen above, history produces the *propensity to act* as well as several other elements of the situation in which *collective campaigns* arise. At this point the *opportunities* for collective action are particularly important and there are three types of these opportunities that make situations especially conducive to collective action:

1.   The *cultural climate.*   This is an "absolute" precondition for collective campaigns to arise. In this respect the *Zeitgeist,* dominant themes, or upcoming ones are of utmost importance in making a climate more or less conducive to collective action. The cultural climate of the eighties and the nineties in most Western countries with its emphasis on the benefits of the impersonal functioning of the free market, individual effort, and free self-interested choice is, for example, not very conducive to solidary collective actions. In this, it differs greatly from the climate of the sixties and seventies.

2.   The *movement potential.*   Every campaign depends on having leaders with their initial resources, such as social movement organizations, moral entrepreneurs, or sponsors of causes. It depends as much on the existence of constituencies, beneficiary and/or conscience ones,

that these leaders can mobilize into action. If the campaign is part of a series of consecutive campaigns waged by an ongoing social movement, the resources already mobilized—the *systemic power* of the movement—are important as well. A host of studies in the resource mobilization tradition make the importance of this potential sufficiently clear. It needs no further elaboration here.

3. The *political system*. Minimally, a political system must be partially open and partially closed to outside influences, have a measure of instability, and a workable format for contention. These characteristics are typical for Western democracies, although they differ from country to country and from period to period. These differences in political opportunities explain in great measure, according to Koopmans and Duyvendak, why the Chernobyl disaster of April 1986 only "caused" unrest and protest in some European countries and, more generally, why antinuclear movements were successful in some of these countries and not in others. As they state, "Social movements are sometimes victorious in their efforts to frame situations as problematic but only when they operate in a political context that offers them the opportunities to do so" (1995:249).

The conduciveness of a social situation to collective action also depends on the relative absence of countervailing forces, the *resistance in society*. If these forces are very strong, they may easily nip the upcoming campaign in the bud. However, these forces do not have to be totally absent in order for a collective campaign to arise; as long as they are not strong enough to effectively counter an arising campaign. The march on Washington of 25 April 1993 for gay and lesbian rights in the army illustrates this point rather well. There existed powerful countervailing forces concerning this issue, such as the Christian Right, the Republican party, and the army, but these were not powerful enough to prevent this form of collective action (Tarrow 1994:9–10).[14]

Agency in combination with the factors and conditions comprised under window of opportunity leads to a collective campaign because agency as a kind of catalyst enables the combined factors and conditions to work to their potential. The case of the abolition of the slave trade shows that agency does not work under all circumstances. Nothing, for example, happened when people called for action against slavery in adverse circumstances ("these first voices against slavery cried in the wilderness"; Rice 1975:154). Even when the situation is more conducive but still below the required degree of conduciveness, agency will not play its catalytic role. This was, for example, the case in 1783, when the Quakers launched their initiative. This shows, however, that in such suboptimal situations initiatives may not be killed on the spot. They may linger on and in this way offer opportunities for improving the situation as the Quakers did by allying with the Evangelical forces in British society.

With this, we arrive at the third element of the cultural change process: the *collective campaign*. The movement campaign in our model is the set of actions that may transform potential into actual change. It consists of two complementary parts: (1) the collective actions initiated by movement actors leading to an episode of sustained challenge of authorities, and (2) the reactions and actions of the authorities and other actors developing into a sustained argument, the public discourse.[15] Thus, cultural changes are only possible if the collective actions of movement actors result in a public discourse, in other words, if these actors succeed in opening a public discourse on the cause they are campaigning for (or entering an existing one) and are able to sustain it.

In this way of conceptualizing, a public discourse is the medium through which actors may bring about changes in the way people define situations, more specifically, in the way they think "things" are and ought to be. These definitions are shared views of social reality that comprise descriptions and interpretations as well as beliefs and valuations regarding this reality. They are both factual and normative. Collective definitions and changes therein come forth from these discourses because the actors involved succeed in convincing people that the views and definitions they put forward are true and right.[16]

Movement actors will succeed in bringing about cultural change if their power and the conduciveness of societal arrangements allow them to start a collective campaign, to turn it into a sustained public discourse, and to put convincing messages forward. Stated otherwise, it means that a number of conditions will have to be met. We will present these conditions below in three sets.

First, the opportunities for the collective campaign have to stay the way they were at the beginning of the campaign or even improve, or, in other words, the action-structure has to remain *culturally* and *systemically* *conducive*.

1. The *cultural climate*. This climate delimits the possibilities for a campaign and the related public discourse with its basic values, ideas, and themes. A clear example of this is the failure of the antiabortion activists in the Netherlands to launch a viable campaign on abortion. Their actions—with the exception of violence—do not differ much from those of their more successful American "brethren" but the cultural climate in which both operate is very different, particularly with regard to the place of religion in society. Religion plays a distinctively smaller role in Dutch society than in the United States and, thus, the Dutch public is far less receptive to an antiabortion message that is based on orthodox religious views and thus is less easily mobilized into action.

The cultural climate also provides the facilities for devising interpretive packages with which the battle is fought. The abortion case shows how crucial this tool kit role of culture is. Both the prochoice and the prolife packages draw on basic elements in American culture, viz., the right of freedom of choice and the right to life.

Finally, it sets the basic rules of the game of contention, especially the rules about which topics may be contended and which not. As Gamson (1988) shows, not all issues are always suitable for contention. This was, for example, the case with the civil rights movement in the fifties and sixties. The actors in this movement had to wage a hard struggle (not in the least on the symbolic plane; Harding 1984) to get a place on the agenda of the American society.

2. The presence of *systemic facilities* and the relative absence of *systemic constraints.* Setting the *societal agenda* plays an important role in processes of cultural change. The agenda may pose a formidable barrier for some causes against entering the public debate and thus form a constraint. An example in this respect is poverty and the need to do something about it. Other causes, such as cutting down welfare expenses, have at the moment far less difficulty entering the debate and for these causes the shape of the agenda is a facility. The societal agenda is, however, not strictly a systemic feature. It is a cultural one as well.

The basic cultural rules regulate the access to the agenda in a cultural respect. Often there is simply a bias against certain topics. Such is the case with prostitution. The persistent relation of prostitution with immorality and sin prevent organizations such as COYOTE in the United States or De Rode Draad in the Netherlands, both organizations of and on behalf of prostitutes, from getting the notion that prostitution is work on the agenda. At other times, discussions of certain topics are out of bounds. This has largely been the case (and still is in part) with the topic of immigration in the Netherlands. Discussions about problems and difficulties related to immigration, such as the number of immigrants, entry requirements and procedures, cultural differences, and the question of adjustment to Dutch society, were largely out of the question. Those who raised questions in this respect were almost immediately named racists or fascists and thus quite easily silenced.[17]

The agenda is part of the systemic side of the action-structure when we view at it from the perspective of the gatekeepers and the carrying capacity. Important gatekeepers are political parties and their representatives in parliament and government. They are often able to deny issues access to the agenda and may do so, in particular, when occupying a dominant position in the political system. The carrying capacity of the agenda is almost always limited, and issues must therefore compete for attention. Both elements were clearly visible in the discussion about health insurance in the United States. For years the issue of an adequate system of health insurance has been successfully kept from public discussion and once it reached the agenda, as it recently did, it was easily crowded out.

The presence of a system of and access to *media* is another essential systemic feature. Collective campaigns need media to succeed (see also Tarrow 1994:126–29). As the functioning of media is a topic of study in its own right, we will leave it at that and refer only to the short elaboration in Appendix A.

We dealt above with the other systemic elements of the action-structure that we discerned in Section 3.4, the *political system*, the *mobilization potential*, and the *resistance in society*. What was stated before about these elements remains valid and needs no further elaboration. Regarding the resistance in society, the situation at the beginning of a campaign is not the only important feature. If a campaign stimulates a large amount of counteractivities, its continuance and, with that, its cultural effects will be threatened. As we have seen in the abolition case, the movement-countermovement dynamics may easily augment the constraints for challenging actors and thus hinder their campaign.

Second, the campaigning actors must be successful in transforming the potential of the action-structure into actual resources and thus into *systemic power*. Conducting a campaign, particularly being able to open (or enter) a public discourse on the cause of the campaign and sustaining it, is largely a matter of systemic power. Here, the number of people mobilized into action and the amount of support that is organized determine (the other conditions in the model being equal) whether there will be a public discourse, whether it will last, and how forceful the message can be put forward. At this point, the movement entrepreneurs or social movement organizations play a pivotal role. They are the organizers of power and as such are the producers of change.

Third, the interpretive package (or packages) that campaigning actors put forward must be convincing; it must be culturally powerful. The *cultural power* of a package depends on:

- Its *credibility*, i.e., the measure in which it succeeds in cognitively convincing people that the content of a package, its message, is true and right. As we have seen before, this depends above all on its *credibility* in a *cultural* sense, provided that a package satisfies the minimal requirements of *empirical* and *rhetorical credibility*.
- Its *emotionality*, i.e., the degree to which emotional appeals couched in a package succeed in either attracting people to the cognitive content of a package or blocking the road to cognitively understanding contending packages.

Finally, there remains the way in which campaigns affect the culture of a society. Interpretive packages are directed at influencing this culture in a direct way. This was so in the case of abolition and, for the time being, we maintain in our model *direct influence* as the main channel of influence. *Diffusion* is self-evidently also an effect of public discourses, especially the widely publicized ones. Most probably, it only plays a subsidiary role. This will be different, however, in the periods that are characterized by gradual developments in the cultural sphere. Then diffusion will be more important. The *indirect* way of *influence* is most probably the main avenue for bringing about cultural changes when a campaign is primarily directed at bringing forth structural changes. This is, for example, the case if the cause of a campaign issue that is not directly relevant for many people and against which the cultural resistance is large. The gay rights movement that Weitzer (1991) describes may be seen as such an example. The campaigns of this movement succeeded in achieving structural gains such as judicial victories, passage of gay right ordinances, and repeal of sodomy statutes in many states, but not in changing the sentiment and perception of the public. In the longer run, these structural changes may affect the way homosexuality is collectively defined in the American society, because the movement organizations, as Weitzer points out, have already secured access to political elites, get sympathetic media coverage, and will continue to bring their case forward. This change in collective definitions will obviously take more than just time. Important contributing factors may be the "coming out" of popular public figures and the spreading of information by gay and lesbian organizations.

We may now summarize the foregoing in a slightly different way into a set of causally interrelated statements that represent the revised conceptual model in shorthand.

Social movements[18] will bring about cultural changes *if:*
1. The preconditions for collective actions are present: a *window of opportunities* shaped by *history*. A window of opportunities consists of:
   a.   a *potential cause;*
   b.   the *propensity to act* in a collective way on that cause;
   c.   a *conducive action-structure* (see also 3a). The main properties of conduciveness at this stage are (1) a positive *cultural climate*, (2) the existence of a *mobilization potential*, (3) a *political system* that offers opportunities and facilities for collective action.
2. Actors actually *decide to act* collectively on the potential cause—the *agency* aspect in social movement processes. Like history, agency is a determinant of collective action that as such is not determined by processes, factors, and conditions in the conceptual model.

Agency thus transforms the propensity to act (1b) into an actual *decision*. It also turns the potential cause (1a) into an actual *cause* by socially constructing it as a problem for whose solution collective actions are both necessary and possible. Both elements combined with the *conduciveness of the action-structure* (1c) have to be about right to let agency work as a catalyst so that

3. A *collective campaign* arises that leads to a *public discourse*. The campaign, discourse, and outcome depend, more specifically, on:

    a. The action-structure (see also 1c) remaining *conducive* (or even improving in this respect). Alongside the earlier mentioned properties others are important as well. Together:

        (1) A *cultural climate* with *basic values* and *themes* positive to the campaign, facilities in the form of *cultural tools*, allowing *basic rules*.

        (2) A set of *systemic facilities* and a relative lack of *systemic constraints*. These are (a) an accessible *societal agenda*, (b) a *media* system that is accessible for the campaigning actors and their cause, (c) the existence of a *mobilization potential*, (d) a *political system* with opportunities and facilities, (e) a relative absence of *resistance in society*.

    b. The campaigning actors, the movement entrepreneurs, succeed in transforming the action potential into *systemic power*. This power is needed to open (or enter) a public discourse on the cause the entrepreneurs are campaigning for and to sustain it. At this point, the number of people *mobilized into action* and the amount of *support* (in society at large) *organized* are crucial.

    c. The campaigning actors succeed in devising *interpretive packages* out of the cultural tool kit that can be used as weapons in the social struggle that every discourse is. These packages represent the *cultural power* of these actors and this power is large enough to bring about cultural changes *if* the packages are built in such a way that they are more convincing than existing interpretations and/or contending packages. This depends on:

        (1) the *credibility* of a package in a *cultural, empirical,* and *rhetorical* sense;

        (2) the *emotionality* of a package, i.e., to the degree to which the emotional appeals contained in a package are capable of enlarging the access of a package to the public or of blocking the entrance for a contending one.

The whole model is also represented in Figure 8.1.

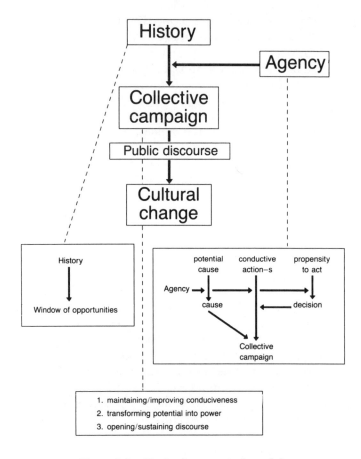

Figure 8.1. Revised conceptual model.

8.5   SOCIAL MOVEMENTS AND CULTURAL CHANGE

One of the notable characteristics of the study of social movements is, as Tarrow (1994) rightly remarks, its restriction to specific movements or to distinct elements of the movement process such as consensus mobilization, the organization of grass roots support, or the use of specific collective action strategies. This study is no exception in this respect; it limits the focus of attention even further by splitting the movement process into distinct collective campaigns. Yet it promises a wider look by taking as its subject matter the role social movements play in processes of cultural change. In this section, we will attempt to redeem this promise by placing the collective movement campaign as a unit of change in the more encompassing process of cultural change.

At the same time that we split the overall movement process into the units of collective campaigns, we enlarged the scope of attention by making history part of the explanation of cultural changes brought about by movement activities. History integrates collective campaigns into the stream of ongoing social processes. In this respect, our model fits in with a long-standing tradition in the study of social movements. Traditionally, particular movements were linked with conditions antedating those movements such as structural changes leading to strain and grievances or the extant conduciveness of the social structure to collective action. The value-added model of Smelser (1962) or the continental tradition regarding the so-called old[19] movements such as the labor movement are prime examples of this tradition.

This traditional attention to the preconditions of social movements has waned quite considerably with the advent of resource mobilization theory, in which the organizational aspects of social movements became the overriding focus of attention. This focus was ushered in by McCarthy and Zald's pioneering paper in the *American Journal of Sociology* of 1977. It gained ground rapidly in the study of social movements and almost swept away the traditional approach to the point that the old way was not done any more (for a revealing example, see Jenkins 1983, who nearly sanctifies resource mobilization theory).

In recent years, however, the preconditions of social movements have again advanced to a more prominent place in movement theory. Klandermans (1988), for example, acknowledges the importance of grievances and of the formation of consensus concerning the way in which "matters" are perceived and defined. Both form the stuff that movement actors use in their deliberate attempts to create consensus on the cause of a movement and on the need to act collectively on that cause. Grievances and consensus formation are thus conditions for consensus mobilization and collective action. Tarrow (1983) takes another tack and points to the importance of the political opportunity structure. In his view, extant and changing opportunities for movement actions largely determine the fate of social movements. This turn to external conditions—without, however, neglecting the movement process itself (see Tarrow 1994 for an excellent combination of both)—has proved to be very fruitful and has initiated a new and burgeoning line of research.

Social movements are not only part of ongoing social processes and not only rooted in systemic and cultural preconditions, but they are, as Tarrow (1983, 1994) shows, part of recurring cycles of protest. He contends (1) that extant political opportunities give well-placed contenders room to initiate collective actions and (2) that these actions in turn may broaden the opportunities for contention for less well-placed actors. This is, mainly, so because these well-placed contenders attempt to enlarge the opportunities for themselves, which then become latent possibilities for collective action for others. When the latter initiate actions for their own cause they turn these possibilities into manifest possibilities. In Tarrow's cycle concept, the latent-manifest dynamic we described in Chapter 2 is clearly visible. This way, protest begets protest, resulting in a cycle of protest that Tarrow describes as

> a phase of heightened conflict and contention across the social system that includes: a rapid diffusion of collective action from more mobilized to less mobilized sectors; a quickened pace of innovation in the forms of contention; new or transformed collective action frames; a combination of organized and unorganized participation; and sequences of intensified interaction between challengers and authorities which can end in reform, repression and sometimes revolution. (1994:153)

Tarrow's integration of social movements into more encompassing cycles of protest—especially when combined with the notion of history—lifts movements out of their conceptual isolation. With that, it makes possible the view of social movements as elements in processes of social change of the longer *durée*. If we take the abolition movement in Great Britain as an example, we see that it was part of a series of protest cycles that arose from the 1760s onwards. As we showed in Chapters 4 and 5, there existed in Britain in the second half of the eighteenth century a widespread discontent regarding the way society was organized. This discontent surfaced time and again in protest; examples are the support for Wilkes in his struggle with the authorities, Wyvill's Yorkshire Association demanding more political influence for the counties, and the later movement for parliamentary reform. When protest on a specific issue flared up, it often tended to spread to other topics as well, as was the case with the abolition of the slave trade, the repeal of the Test and Corporation Act, and the enactment of parliamentary reform at the end of the eighteenth century (Ditchfield 1980).

One of the important elements of Tarrow's cycle concept is that it links succeeding but distinct phases of collective activities. As he points out, the innovations of one protest period—new symbols, masterframes, or tactics—may become the dominating weapons of the next phase. Issue number 45 of the *North Briton*, the journal in which Wilkes denounced a speech of King George III, set off a prolonged dispute about civil liberties. In that dispute this number became a symbol of the struggle for liberty and reform. In following reform campaigns, the number 45 was used as a general symbolic device that made plainly clear to audiences what the campaign was about. It functioned in this manner as a powerful means to mobilize people into action. In this way, disparate periods of collective action are forged into chains, usually referred to as social movements.

Tarrow's concept,[20] however, does more than focus attention on the fact that societies regularly experience periods of protest and unrest. It implies as well that there are periods in between that are characterized by relative rest and stability. Collective movement campaigns and, for that matter, cycles of protest as well subside over time. The challenge of authorities is time and resource consuming and movement actors inevitably tire. The authorities respond to challenges as well. They may give in or—as they more often do—resort to compromise and therewith erode the support base of the campaigners. Authorities may also repress a campaign altogether (Tarrow 1994). Although collective campaigns and cycles of protest are only temporary affairs, they often have lasting effects. We have already mentioned that they may influence protest in the future. They also may, in intended or unintended ways, change society and sometimes do so in a relatively short span of time.[21]

As Tarrow (1994) emphasizes in his closing chapter, modern society has in an important measure become a movement society. In such societies periods of relative rest and stability alternate with phases of heightened conflict and protest. The periods of protest root in previous protest phases and form chains consisting of one or more social movements. They arise because developments and events in society, history, open the window of opportunities and some people seize the available opportunities to initiate collective actions and campaigns to remedy situations they find wrong. These phases of protest—often comprising several campaigns at one time—have a dynamic of their own and, what is more important, they may lead to relatively rapid and radical changes. This portrayal of social change in modern society as spasmodic is, however, one-sided and incomplete. The periods of rest are an essential part of the processes of social change because the seeds of change are often planted during the periods of so-called normal functioning of society. Below we will elaborate this relationship between periods of rest and stability and the cycles of protest by using notions of Weber described in Chapter 2.

We started our second chapter with Weber's famous switchmen metaphor, which so neatly captures his vision on social action and social change. It makes clear that people act in order to further interests and satisfy needs. People, however, do not act in a vacuum but do so within a pregiven action-structure that facilitates as well as constrains their actions. At the same time, through their actions people produce and reproduce the action-structure that makes their actions possible. Every actor acts within his own action-structure, which is linked to the action-structures of others. These links form networks that cluster into smaller and larger social systems, from small groups to societies. Through these links actions mutually affect the action-structures of the members of these systems and therewith produce and reproduce them. It is important to note that people may change their action-structure and those of others in these endless cycles of producing and reproducing.

Seen from an ideal-typical point of view, there are two types of processes through which changes are brought forward. First, social change may be the effect of slow and gradual—capillary (Tarrow 1994)—processes, which we have referred to as history. Second, social change may also be rapid and more radical. In this form it is the result of deliberate attempts to change society.

Gradual change, as we saw in Chapter 2, is sometimes the spinoff of normal day-to-day reproduction of action-structures in the form of imperceptible step-by-step changes. At other times, it is the often involuntary product of the activities of functionaries who "run" a societal order. For an example of this, see the gradual theological elaboration of the doctrine of Divine Providence in eighteenth-century Britain. Another example of this form of change may be found in the numerous bureaucracies, public as well as private ones, that run modern society and transform it toward the iron cage Weber envisaged ([1920] 1976). Their functionaries create rules and procedures in their attempts to guarantee the smooth running of daily life. In order to reach this goal they often have to adapt them or make new ones and thus bring about changes. Another form of gradual change arises from the activities of interest and lobby groups. These groups seek to adapt—often in a piecemeal fashion—existing institutional arrangements to make them more adequate to their needs and interests.

These gradual developments, as we also saw in Chapter 2, occur in different societal realms or institutional orders, each with its own dynamics. The autonomy of these orders is, however, relative, particularly because there often exist all kinds of relationships between these orders, and thus what is going on in one order may affect one or more of the other orders and vice versa. Chapters 4 and 5 abundantly illustrate the functioning of these orders, the gradual changes therein, and the relations of elective affinity between them. An example of this affinity is the relationship between Enlightenment thinking and the theological reaction to deism. In present-day society such a relationship is manifest between the economic and the political order. The paradigm of the economic order, the free market, which again became dominant from the 1980s onwards, in turn affects the political order to a great degree. The free-market recipe is transposed to the way political institutions are organized, to political relations, and to the behavior of politicians. This may be seen in the way politicians in all Western democracies adapt their policies and policy proposals to the preferences of the citizens as shown by opinion polls and (by-)elections, the political form of making free-market demand visible. The marked difference in the way President Truman and President Clinton reacted to the Republican victory in Congress is just one example out of many of this change in political behavior.

In this book the second type of change is represented by the abolition movement. Social movements and their campaigns are examples of how actors deliberately attempt to change society. In this they are sometimes successful, either in ways they intended or in ways they had never foreseen. Weber's analysis of the development of the spirit of capitalism is probably the most well-known example of such a deliberate attempt to change society that had enormous but unforeseen consequences ([1920] 1976). The religious innovation of the Puritans, the transposition of the monastic methodical rational way of life—*ora et labora*—into everyday worldly life, eventually led to the coming into being of a spirit that was particularly adequate for capitalist society. Their intention was strictly religious and directed at enabling laymen to become religious virtuosi without the necessity of leaving the world, but their success led inevitably to a secular economic ethic that is at least areligious [in this respect, see also Kalberg's (1980) illuminating paper].

As the history of the abolition of the slave trade in Great Britain shows, these deliberate and more radical changes are often not produced in one go. They generally take more than one cycle of protest and depend, moreover, on gradual changes in between. This can be seen in the abolition case, in which both types of change processes were interlocked. Abolition went from a movement campaign to a political lobby and then again to a campaign and so on.

What is more important, though, is the fact that the "normal" day-to-day functioning—in Weber's terms *Alltag*—sets the stage for the phases of protest with its—freely rendered from Weber—"charismatic eruptions." The gradual changes produce facilities and lift constraints for collective actions; they open the window of opportunities or, for that matter, close it. The demise of the cold war, for example, reduced the need for nuclear weapons in the eyes of many people and thus the necessity of developing and testing new ones. For many people nuclear tests are no longer a necessary evil that has to be accepted. This means that an important constraint on collective actions against those tests has largely disappeared. Stated otherwise, the opportunities for those actions are enlarged. This can be seen in the protests against the nuclear tests of France, particularly in the Pacific region where those tests took place. A contrary example can be seen in the absence of so-called poor movements. An important cause of this absence may be found in the gospel of the free market that dominates society today. This cultural filter effectively shuts the window for collective actions by or on behalf of the poor in spite of an abundance of reasons for those actions.

The gradual changes also shape the cultural and systemic resources that movement actors may use in their campaigns. The abolition case shows how important this effect of gradual changes is. Systemic changes in British society in the political, economic, and religious realms "produced" the leaders as well as the mobilization potential for the abolition movement. In time, all these gradual changes combined may lead to a situation prone to collective action, an action-structure that enables social movement actors more than it constrains them. Such a structure may become the point of departure of a movement campaign and possibly of more rapid and radical changes—the second type of social change.

Movement campaigns, whether they are successful in view of their stated aims or not, always imply symbolic struggles (Gamson 1988). As we have seen, movement actors develop interpretive packages with frames, symbols, metaphors, reasons, etc., to mobilize people into action, to organize support, and to convince people (authorities included) of the rightness of their aims. As social movements are at odds with society when they arise, their packages are at odds with the dominant cultural views and definitions of that moment. At the same time, movement actors draw on existing cultural notions when they devise these packages. When elements of these interpretive packages become part of the dominant cultural views and definitions, it means change on the one hand, while on the other it is change that potentially was already there. Movement actors thus realize the change potential of society through their movement campaigns and therewith link culture to culture—the *Eigengesetzlichkeit* or relative autonomy of the cultural domain Weber ([1920] 1986) emphasized so much. Movement actors create worldviews out of ideas and therewith help to determine the track that future action in society will take.

This Weberian view on cultural change combined with Tarrow's notion of cycles of protest reflects the spasmodic character of cultural change very well. Although the media and fashionable commentators try to convince us that society and the way people think change almost everyday, careful study gives us a different picture. This, for example, is the conclusion of Ester, who noted that there seems to be "a strikingly large gap between reality and all sorts of opinions aired by politicians, social scientists and journalists about the postmodern welfare state."[22] He and Halman (1994) were not able to find the changes "everybody is talking about" in their survey regarding values, norms, and opinions in the Netherlands. On the contrary, they found that the values and opinions of the Dutch did not reflect a drastic change toward a postmaterialist society.

The vision on cultural change as a spasmodic process resembles the evolutionary theory of punctuated equilibrium in paleontology. This theory seeks to explain one of the main features of the paleontological record, viz., "the concentration of major bursts interspersed with long periods of relative stability" (Gould 1994:164). Instead of assuming that this feature reflects the incompleteness of the record, the theory states that life developed and life forms diversified, above all, in relatively short periods of time that punctuated far longer periods of stability in which life changed only gradually. According to Gould, biological evolution is a highly irregular process.

Evolution has also always been popular in sociology as a theory for explaining social and cultural change. It gave the sociologist a tool for understanding the present as an indispensable part of processes leading to a better future. Evolutionist theory, and this is its major flaw, assumes progress and sees life as being directed to some higher end.[23] Gould has time and again crusaded against the concept of evolution as progress by pointing to the inherently contingent character of biological evolution. Dietz and Burns (1992) advance the same objection against evolutionist thinking in sociology. They propose instead an evolutionary approach concerning the dynamics of cultural change that takes contingency as a main feature of social life into account. At the same time they contend that special attention is needed for the role of agency in this respect: "We examine the confluence of three emerging streams in social theory. In recent decades, the concept of agency has received much attention. . . . There also has been a growing attention to culture. . . . In the last ten years or so the beginnings of a new theory of cultural evolution has begun to emerge" (p. 187).

The central points in Dietz and Burns's elaboration of a theory of cultural evolution are the idea of "contingent selection" and the notion of "population." Cultures in their view evolve and change because some elements are favored (selected) out of the set of cultural elements that make up a culture. Dietz and Burns use the term *rule* here but—as we already explained in Chapter 2—this is unnecessarily restricted. In our opinion, a culture comprises more than recipes and precepts for conduct (see also Sewell 1992 on this). Therefore, we use the broader and more abstract term *element* instead because this corresponds better with the variety in cultural life. A culture is thus a population of cultural elements that is subject to selection processes. This selection is contingent on social conditions and leads to changes in the frequencies of cultural elements that people hold in society and in the variation in these elements. As they contend,

Thus a culture can be thought as a population of rules, and for each rule there is a frequency of occurrence determined by the number of members of the population who hold that rule . . . culture change is a change in the frequency distribution of rules in the population. Cultural diversity is the variance in rule frequency in the population. (Dietz and Burns 1992:188)

Both notions—contingent selection and population—may be incorporated in the vision on cultural change elaborated above. In this way we arrive at an evolutionary theoretical view of cultural change in which the role social movements play in this respect gets its own important place. The first step in this incorporation regards the notion of culture as the population or set of extant cultural elements existing in society at a given point in time. First, a culture must not be viewed as a complete and definitive set that may be used in all kinds of situations by all members of society alike. There exist, on the contrary, several (sub)sets of cultural elements the relevance of which depends on the situation in which they will be used and on the actors that use them. Again, we see here the manifest-latent distinction of Chapter 2. Second, a culture comprises subsets that deviate from dominant and accepted standards. These subsets contain alternative views, rival definitions, and counterthemes that contradict the self-evident hegemonic culture of everyday life. Third, this whole of (partially different) subsets is also not always fully integrated (cf. Dietz and Burns 1992). Every societal culture thus displays a many-colored palette of variation.

This cultural variation may become a source of change because each of the sets may function as the toolbox out of which new schemata, meanings, definitions, rules, etc., are selected. Culture as the encompassing set of subsets may be the source of cultural change in another respect as well. People may combine elements of different subsets to arrive at new meanings and definitions. The abolition case, for example, shows that philosophical concepts, theological doctrines, economic theories, and literary themes were merged in the interpretive package the abolitionists used in their campaign. Tarrow illustrates this process of selection and recombination very well in his observation regarding the American civil rights movement as he states, "[T]he symbols of revolt are not drawn off the peg from a cultural closet and arrayed ready-made before the public. Nor are new meanings fabricated out of a whole cloth" (1994:130).

The culture of a society may thus be seen as a population of various cultural elements that are only partially integrated and often contradictory. Out of this population of culture elements actors select and recombine elements. In this way they create (partially) new meanings, schemes of reference, symbols, and collective definitions that are integrated into the sets and subsets that together make up the culture of a society. This notion of selection is the second element we incorporate in our overall view of social movements and cultural change. Hereby, it is important to note that these selection processes are contingent on the situation in society—the context—at the time of selection.

Generally, the selection takes place in two ways.

1. Actors select and recombine culture elements in executing their daily tasks and living their day-to-day lives, leading to gradual and often imperceptible changes. The already mentioned elaboration of the doctrine of divine Providence is a fine example of this type of cultural change.

2. Actors select and recombine culture elements in explicit attempts to change society. Here the changes are often rapid and radical although not always as intended. The collective movement campaign is a prime example of this type of selection.

The two different types of contingent selection processes are, moreover, interrelated. The gradual changes—the first type of selection—help to shape the action-structure of actors who seek to change society more thoroughly. As the latter attempt to do so and initiate a collective campaign, the second type of selection comes to the fore. In such a campaign they challenge authorities and thus the dominant meanings and definitions and therefore look for values, beliefs, views, and definitions that prove them right and the authorities wrong. If their—by definition nondominant—views prevail in the public discourse that their campaign entails, the culture of society changes. This changed culture will from then on again function as the source for day-to-day living and in the future as the source for new campaigns and change.

Together, social movements play a role in processes of cultural change because the actors involved in them radicalize and accelerate the extant possibilities for change and may even put society on a new track. They are able to do so, because:

1. *History* shapes the action-structure of change agents. Processes of contingent gradual social change of which cultural changes are part make this structure more favorable for collective actions. The cultural changes, more specifically, shape the potential for radical cultural change because they shape the population of cultural elements out of which the change agents select their "weapons."

2. *Agency* as a catalyst enables the action potential to be turned into an actual collective campaign and a public discourse on the cause of that campaign.

3. The *collective campaign and the related public discourse* functions as the interface between ongoing societal processes and cultural changes. In its functioning as an interface every campaign (a) is contingent on the action-structure as it is when the campaign starts (t_1), *and* (b) affects the same action-structure in the future $(t_2, t_3, \ldots , t_n)$ through which a campaign partially determines its own course. We have here the double contingency of collective action we brought to the fore in Chapter 2.

A campaign can function as such an interface because the actors who carry out a campaign compose their interpretive packages out of the existing culture and initiate discourses in which these packages with their collective action frames, symbols, metaphors, etc., contend. Out of these contentions new meanings and definitions may enter the culture of a society and therewith change it.

As we saw earlier, the intermediate period of collective action embodied in movement campaigns—often broadened to a cycle of protest—fades into a period of relative stability and gradual change. The routines of *Alltag* again take over and another round of *history* starts.

Diachronically, collective campaigns may be seen as parts of a spasmodic pattern of change and represent instances in series of challenges of authorities to which we refer—mostly with hindsight—as a social movement. Synchronically, campaigns tend to broaden into periods of protest and contention. In both ways, they play their role in bringing about cultural change through their challenge of dominant and authoritative societal arrangements. In these change processes, their role is, according to Sztompka, neither that of the ultimate change agent—in itself necessary and sufficient for change—nor that of the symptom of deeper-lying change processes. Instead, Sztompka describes

> social movements as mediators in the causal chain of social praxis. They are seen as both the products of earlier social changes and the producers (or at least co-producers) of further social transformations. Movements appear here as vehicles, carriers, transmitters of ongoing change, rather than either its ultimate cause or merely a surface manifestation. They do not arise in a vacuum, but at some historical juncture join the social process and attempt to affect its course. (1993:210–11)

NOTES

1. This opposition is, however, not a black and white one as shown by the example of Burke, who was both conservative and proabolition.
2. The fact that the slave interest did not make an organized attempt to counteract the earlier Quaker initiative illustrates rather well the fact that this

initiative on its own lacked the power needed for starting a public discourse on abolition.

3.   The opportunities and facilities, cultural as well as systemic, are naturally constraints for the opposing party. A comparison of the abolitionists with the antiabolitionists might easily leave the constraining elements of the action-structure on each of the contending parties out of the picture.

4.   As Davis (1975) shows, not every proponent of slavery based his argument on tradition. There were, for example, also "enlightened" planters such as Bryan Edwards. The "enlightened" proslavery argument remained marginal, however, in the abolition debate (see also Drescher 1977a:181–82 on the marginal position of the so-called moderate West Indians in the abolition struggle in Parliament).

5.   As Drescher states, "Both the racial and biblical lines of argument were burdened by an implicit delegitimization of contemporary metropolitan norms. Racial, biblical and classical Aristotelian proslavery arguments occupied a very subordinate place in British political discourse during the eighteenth and early nineteenth centuries" (1986:20).

6.   These were not only the seamen that Clarkson was able to produce as witnesses but important abolitionists, such as Newton and Ramsay, as well.

7.   See Griswold (1987) as well in this respect on the role of ambiguity in the construction of meaning in literature.

8.   The notion of problem refers to the perception of some "conditions as not only deplorable but as capable of being relieved by and as requiring public action, most often by the state" (Gusfield 1989:431).

9.   Davis (1975:148–51) comes to the same conclusion when he compares the antislavery struggle in France, Great Britain, and the United States. He finds that the political system itself was an important factor in this struggle because of the opportunities for action it offered.

10.   At this point it is wise to reiterate that the distinction between power and opportunities is an analytical one between aspects of situations that in reality are always related.

11.   Basically, changes in collective definitions, i.e., in the way people think about events and view them, cannot be forced upon them. That is what is meant here by stating that people have to be convinced.

12.   This way the unresolved conflict that Gamson (1992a:69) sees in the way Snow and Benford (1992) elaborated empirical credibility is solved. The presentation as facts complemented by the acceptance as facts by audiences suffices for empirical credibility. The degree to which statements may be proven is only an extra help in making them credible.

13.   We agree with Gamson (1992b) that agency needs a place in explanations of collective action. It encompasses more, however, than the conviction that something must and can be done about an identified wrong.

14.   This means physically as well as culturally. How important the constraining effect of this last factor can be is shown by Tarrow, who remarks that this issue "a few decades ago would have brought few people into the street" (1994:10).

15.   As Thompson argues, a discourse often takes the form of an argument,

which he describes as "a series of claims or assertions, topics or themes, strung together in a more or less coherent way and seeking, often with the aid of rhetorical flourishes, to persuade an audience" (1990:289).

16.   As we have seen, a public discourse is a very dynamic set of action and reaction in which all kinds of ideas, metaphors, and other symbolic devices are used. This may affect the societal stock of definitions in intended as well as unintended ways.

17.   These questions are naturally often voiced for racist/fascist reasons by political groups who try to use them as resources for political mobilization.

18.   Again, a warning is appropriate here. We use the shorthand notion of social movements in order not to complicate the model unduly, but what is meant is the challenge of authorities by or on behalf of outsiders.

19.   The depiction as old comes from the need to distinguish the traditional movements from the more recent ones. Old social movements are the movements that arose from the conflicts inherent in industrial society. The new ones come from conflicts typical of postindustrial society and thus should require another theoretical approach (Eyerman and Jamison 1991).

20.   Tarrow's cycle concept has its limitations as well. First, he unnecessarily restricts opportunities to political ones. As this study makes clear the window of opportunities for movements comprises more than chances and restrictions in the political realm. Second, cycles of protest are not only contingent on the actions of early contenders but on the actions of many others as well. The window of opportunities for repeal, abolition, and political reform was in important respects the same for each of these movements because this window was shaped by the same historical developments. Third, protest and collective action are more than a reaction to a changing political environment. They represent action, agency, as well. Man is more than an actor, rationally seeking the pleasure and avoiding the pain that his environment offers and is thus more than a Skinnerian or Homansian prisoner of his physical and social environment.

21.   For the purpose of this study, it does not matter whether changes were intended—and thus a campaign has been successful—or unintended. It also does not matter whether the changes are recognized at the time or become obvious at a later date. The only thing that matters is whether there have been changes and whether these would have occurred without the collective campaign(s) that is (are) studied.

22.   This is a translated quote of Professor Ester, who spoke these words on the occasion of the presentation of the results of a large survey of the values, norms, and opinions of the Dutch people.

23.   In biology, evolution runs from simple life forms to more complicated ones, culminating in the human life form, the goal of what life on earth is all about. In sociology, the same sequence is depicted, i.e., from simple family groups and clans through traditional societies to the complex industrial and postindustrial societies of today.

9

Epilogue

According to my lights, a last chapter should resemble a primitive orgy after the harvest. The work may have come to an end, but the worker cannot let go all at once. He is still full of energy that will fester if it cannot find an outlet. Accordingly he is allowed a time of license, when he may say all sorts of things he would think twice before saying in more sober moments, when he is no longer bound by logic and evidence but free to speculate about what he has done.

(Homans 1961:378)

Like Homans did in his last chapter, we return to our first chapter, in which we took the basic decisions that determined the scope of our study and the ways it was to be executed. We started our inquiry with two questions. The first is about the role of social movements with regard to the social construction of meaning and is as such part of the growing interest in the cultural aspects of social life. The second question concerns the best way to study this role and stems from the fact that social movements and construction of meaning, more generally cultural change, are very complex and elusive phenomena. As we have contended, it needs elaborate conceptualization that originates in empirical studies and is further tested in such studies. One needs, as Phillips (1990) emphasizes, to go up and down the ladder of abstraction time and again. This book contains, therefore, the report of a double exploration: one into the relationship between social movements and cultural change and one into the method of studying such "hard-to-get" phenomena. In this chapter we will reflect on the choices we have made in the first chapter and throughout the book in the relatively free manner that Homans demonstrated, and at the end we will attempt in the same manner to go beyond the questions of this book.

In this book, we took two basic decisions that run through it like continuous threads. We will reflect upon them successively. First, we chose a theoretical approach based on Weber and the more recent structurist view. This choice raises the question of what the position of our approach is vis-à-vis the other theoretical approaches that can be distinguished within the sociological discipline. We will therefore clarify our position in the scholarly debate on sociological theory, often in capitalized S and T to emphasize its status with respect to the theories that are applied in empirical studies. At the same time, we will delve into the problem of method, which occupies an equally high position on the scholarly agenda. Second, we chose to study social movements and cultural change as historical processes. A movement is not only seen as a stretch of consecutive, collective actions but also as a process embedded in history. Every movement is contingent on historical events and developments and together with cultural change movements are part of processes of the longer *durée*.

These reflections lead us to the end of the book, where we return to the topic of cultural change in modern society. Social movements are not the only agents of cultural change in modern society so we will look at those other agents and the way they operate. Another important point concerns the often made contention that modern society is undergoing a fundamental transformation and that therefore movements are changing, too. In this respect, the end of this century could resemble the end of the eighteenth century, in which society and the social movement as we know them were born and the way movements are changing now could be a signal of such a fundamental transformation.

The Scholarly Debate

This debate consists of several discourses on ontological, epistemological, and methodological matters, which have led to an impressive stack of books reflecting numerous differences of opinion [Lloyd pictures these differences rather well (see, for example, 1986:149, 194)]. It would obviously take us too far from our aims to attempt to clarify our position in all these discourses. There are, however, four interrelated pairs of oppositions that, in our view, are basic in the scholarly debate. Taking a position on each of them will suffice to make clear where we stand. The pairs are (1) man viewed as a self-sufficient unit or as a socially determined actor, (2) a vision of society in which human society is either seen as an aggregate of individuals or as a holistic entity sui generis, (3) social life as being basically characterized by integrative or conflictual processes, and (4) the perspective of the "social" as either an objective reality or a subjective construction.

The first pair of oppositions concerns the *view of man*. On the one hand, there is a long tradition in sociology (and other social sciences as well) in which man is viewed as a self-sufficient unit whose actions may be understood without explicitly taking society into account. On the other hand, there is an equally long tradition that takes the opposite view. Here, man is depicted as a being who is determined by society. Each view has two variants, which brings us to four basic views of man: two individualistic and two social views.

In the first view, man is seen as a pleasure machine, and in it human actors are depicted as active beings who are continually engaged in acts directed at fulfilling their needs. Actions and relationships with their fellowmen are governed by these needs and proceed from a combination of a hedonistic pleasure principle and rational calculation, which leads man to pleasure by the shortest way. It is Homans's view of man, which is also dominant in the rational choice tradition.

The second view portrays man as creator, and in it humans are seen as beings who use their capacity to create and use meanings and symbols in communicating with others. They use all kinds of symbolic devices to construct and reconstruct the world in which they live. This way they build their society, which is not seen as a lasting edifice but as a form of organization that is fluid, tenuous, and thus continually subject to change. This view is central to symbolic interactionism and constructivism.

The third view shows man as a cultural dope. Society, in this view, is a predominant fact of human life and it determines human action by shaping the intentions, preferences, and attitudes of the members of society. Cultural elements like prescriptions, recipes, beliefs, values, and definitions predispose human actors for certain kinds of actions and, with that, they put actors off behavioral alternatives. Durkheim and the later functionalists are important proponents of this view.

In the fourth view man is depicted as a position-bound actor. Here society seen as a system of hierarchical relations is also the predominant fact of life. In every society people occupy positions (structural locations) that give them access to power and other resources, and to the fruits these resources may provide them. Human actors act in order to maintain or improve their position and thus to further their interests. They do so by cooperating with others who have the same or similar positional interests. Workers join unions, representatives of large companies work together in their own employers' organizations, and small employers do so in the organizational vehicles of the petit bourgeoisie. We have here the view of man that is the core of Marxist social theory and of Weber's theory of class.

In this book, we chose a view that transcends the one-sidedness of each of these views. We do this because, in our opinion, none of these views is entirely wrong but each of them is incomplete. The view of man we propose incorporates important aspects of each of the four views but differs from each of them as well. Our view is that of man as an agent who is active and purposeful like the individualistic views state. Actors are seen as being creative and free to choose their line of action. They do not automatically follow the prescriptions of customs or the line of interests as the social views "dictate." But, as is contended in the social views, man is not completely free and his actions are not fully determined by rational calculations. His actions are, on the contrary, in part bound by the cultural and systemic context of the society in which he lives. In the agential view, humans are fundamentally seen as social beings.

As Lloyd (1986) states, only human actors have agency, which means that they can make choices, have intentions, and may reflect on both. But as Lloyd also points out, they do so within particular sets of relations in which they are guided by rules, values, and beliefs. This choice for agency, as the degree of freedom to act, brings a central element in movement processes to the fore. As we saw, the decision of movement entrepreneurs to wage a collective campaign is crucial in getting such a campaign going. Agency means, moreover, that these movement actors may use elements from the cultural and structural context in which they operate. The freedom and creativity of actors, which agency implies, make cultural change essentially human work.

The second pair of oppositions is about the *vision of society.* The visions of society that sociologists put forward correlate strongly with the way they view human actors. On the one hand, societies are depicted as aggregates of individuals and, on the other, as holistic entities that have a life and existence of their own. Again, each vision has two variants.

In the first vision society is viewed as the mere aggregate of its component parts, the human actors. This vision corresponds largely with the way the exchange and the rational-choice theories depict society. Human behavior is wholly explicable by looking at the properties of the individuals who make up society as self-sufficient units. Society and other macroscopic concepts like social relations or values are only used for heuristic purposes and may always be reduced to the properties of actors. As Lloyd typifies this vision, society is a taxonomic categorization of atomistic individuals who may form arrangements to further their individual goals but these are always loose and unstructured (p. 150).

Society is portrayed differently, and this is the second vision, in the other individualistic approaches in sociology like symbolic interactionism and constructivism. Here, the social aspects of human life are not so much absent but are given a minor place. They emanate from interactions that lead to sets of shared meanings and symbols and of meaningful interhuman relations. These sets are seen as intertwined patterns of action and interaction, in Blumer's language, joint actions, which together form society. The shared understandings and meaningful relationships remain, however, tied to the individual imagination and are conditional on further interactions in which they might be constructed quite differently. Society is thus fundamentally fluid and changeable. In this vision, society is no more than a residual category. We might describe both individualistic visions of society somewhat extremely by saying that in the first vision, there is no such thing as society while in the second society exists but not in a fixed form (Lloyd 1986).

According to the holistic visions of society, the social cannot be reduced solely to the properties of its members; it has properties and powers of its own. As we stated above, the holistic vision also has two variants. In the first variant, the third vision of society, society is seen as a cultural whole, an integrated set of ideas, symbols, worldviews, values, and norms. These cultural elements exist and function independently of individual actors, or more precisely as Durkheim describes them, "[T]hey consist of ways of acting, thinking and feeling, outside the individual, and are endowed with a coercive force with which they impose themselves on him" ([1895] 1967:5). The cultural thus guides actors through life and integrates them in society. We see here the Durkheimian vision of society which is also dominant in structural functionalism and more recent cultural theories (for examples, see Alexander and Seidman 1990).

In the other holistic conception, the fourth vision of society, the emphasis is placed on the systemic side of society. In this vision, society is seen as a structured whole of positions and relations that determine the lives of the individuals living in that society. It is, in this vision, a social organization with powers, needs, and goals of its own. The ideas of the later Marx depict this systemic vision quite well. As he contended, the relations of people as producers of commodities vis-à-vis each other and vis-à-vis the means with which these commodities are produced ultimately determine how people will act. The bourgeois of the *Communist Manifesto* could do nothing other than destroy the feudal order that restricted the pursuit of their interests. Marxist and conflict theories are clear examples of this variant of the holistic vision of society.

Again, we chose a vision that would transcend the one-sidedness of each of the preceding visions of society. This is the structurist vision of society, which differs from each of the visions mentioned above and corresponds with important aspects of them as well. It accepts the notion that people live and act within a pregiven social entity that consists of cultural elements like rules and collective definitions of the situation and systemic elements like social positions and the relations between them. Unlike the holistic vision, however, this pregiven entity is not seen as a reified whole that has a life of its own. As Lloyd (1986) contends, the holistic vision makes it very difficult to understand how a society functions and changes because the mechanism of its functioning, human action, has disappeared from it. In the structurist vision, society—its cultural arrangements and its systemic organization—is in turn the product of the actions of the human actors who live in it. People produce these arrangements and relate to one another in and through their actions and interactions. This picture of emergence corresponds with the atomistic and the symbolic interactionistic vision of social life, without at the same time accepting the indeterminacy and fluidity of the social arrangements. The latter is, quite obviously, difficult to square with everyday experiences such as shops opening every weekday at nine or trains running (approximately) on schedule. Structurists accept that social structures exist and have a degree of solidity and permanence.

In summary, the structurist vision conceptualizes society as an interactional network or structure that consists of sets of institutionalized rules, roles, positions, and relations that organize and guide behavior. This structure is only loosely integrated and emerges from the actions and interactions of the members of that society. People produce and, what is more important, reproduce the institutions and organizations of society in and through their actions. They are not able to do this as they like; their freedom of action is a conditional one. In the structurist vision, society is both the condition for and the consequence of individual actions, and individuals and society are related to each other in a dialectical fashion. They simultaneously constitute and affect one another. There has never been a time when society did not exist, nor a time when human beings lived entirely outside the social realm.

This vision of society is the complement of the view of man as agent and we agree with Lloyd when he states, "[S]ociety should be seen as a structured macroscopic totality that is determinate on both the micro and the macro levels. . . . Society must be continually reproduced through individual and collective action but it always pre-exists individuals. Any approach to explaining its structure and dynamics, or the actions of individuals within it, which concentrates only on micro or macro determination, would miss half the picture [and Lloyd also acknowledges that] society can only exist if collectively mediated by the minds of most of the persons that comprise it" (p. 163).

This structurist vision not only applies to the societal level but also to structures of the so-called lower-level. Social movements are an important example of these kinds of lower-level structures. They can be neither reduced to the partaking actors—the individualistic view—nor can they be treated as actors in their own right—the holistic vision.

Another topic in the scholarly debate is the discussion about which type of process may be seen as being fundamental to social life: *integration or conflict*. These processes form the third pair of oppositions. On the one hand, the notion of social life as an orderly process is emphasized. Order is the basic notion of structural functionalism and other theories that emphasize stability and social equilibrium. On the other hand, social life is, above all, depicted as being conflictual and contentious. This is the way life is seen in the conflict theories and in the theories of the related Marxist tradition. Functionalists see institutions and organizations as parts that contribute to the survival of society through their functioning. Human actors are integrated in the social whole and coaxed into activities that are positive and not negative to societal survival. Social life is portrayed as a well-integrated clockwork. Conflict theory reacted to the dominance of these theories with their emphasis on social stability and the permanence of the status quo by pointing to the ubiquity of dissension and conflict. In its view, social life could better be pictured as an arena full of contending actors whose actions often led to disintegration and change. Stability and order are only temporary. Order is just a phase in between periods of change.

For a study of social movements and cultural change the choice of either integration or conflict is a dead-end street. Choosing the "order" view inevitably means that conflicts, disorder, and contentious actions can only be seen as aberrations. Conflicts are irrational because they are contrary to the ratio of living together in society. The choice of the "conflict" view neglects order and stability that are also present. As every revolution and every social movement shows, people cannot endure the stress inherent in conflicts forever and they will eventually return to the orderly processes of daily life. An either-or choice is, for that matter, not necessary because both types of processes can well be seen as alternating phases in social life. To view social movements as series of interruptions in processes of the relatively stable functioning of society makes sense, as is shown in Section 8.4. Stability and conflict are two sides of the same coin: the one does not exist without the other. Moreover, as Coser (see Ritzer 1983) points out, conflicts—and thus social movements as well—may also have integrative consequences. The abolitionists, for example, made the dismal fate of the black slaves visible for everyone in British society and communicated their moral message to the public, the integrative communication function Coser distinguishes. In the course of time, abolition itself as an emblem of national virtue became part of the national myth concerning the heroic past of Britain (Colley 1992:354). The latter is preeminently an integrative device.

The last pair of oppositions concerns the *perspective of the social*. On the one hand, social reality is put forward as an objective reality that is "out there" and that sociologists can study with the "hard" methods of the natural sciences. On the other, sociologists contend that the social is fundamentally a construction made by people who live together. It is therefore a subjective reality that can only be studied through the "soft" methods of the cultural sciences. This opposition is partly related to the aforementioned oppositions. For example, Homans and Marx clearly belong to the camp of the objectivists, while Weber, Mead, and Blumer may be located in the subjectivists' camp. A clear division is, however, often difficult to make as, for example, is the case with Durkheim. His *Division of Labor* sets the standard for objective sociological studies, while his later *The Elementary Forms of Religious Life* tends more toward a subjective position.

Ritzer (1981) contends that it makes more sense to employ a perspective that treats the social as a continuum. Social phenomena, in his view, are more or less objective and thus less or more subjective. As we stated in Chapter 1, all social phenomena are social constructions: a church is more than an ordered heap of stones simply because we attach a specific meaning to that heap. Ritzer's point is that some phenomena are more visible and easier to get hold of—thus more objective—than other phenomena, which largely belong to the realm of the mind. In this perspective of the social as a continuum there are two extreme positions: the objective and the subjective poles, and several positions in between where social phenomena can be situated.

At the objective pole, one may put the physical entities that are part of the social world. An example in this respect may be found in the visible effects of World War II. In the Netherlands, one of the striking events of this war was the bombing of the center of Rotterdam in 1940. The social event "war" became immediately visible in this city in the form of burnt houses and debris. It remained visible for years as an open plain interspersed with an occasional building and, when the center was rebuilt, as a marked borderline that circled the center separating old buildings from new. Less objective but still relatively so are actors and their behavior, bureaucratic structures, and the law. These are "things" we still can (partly) see. The polity, the family, and religion are examples that occupy intermediate positions, while values, beliefs, and other social constructions are situated at the subjective pole of the continuum. The latter are predominantly "things" of the mind (for an insightful illustration, see Figure 3 in Ritzer 1981:26). Social movements straddle a large part of the objective-subjective continuum. Contentious actions like demonstrations, sit-ins, and blockades are very visible. This is, however, less so with the ideology and interpretive packages that movement actors employ. These must be predominantly situated at the subjective side of the continuum as, on the whole, is also the case with cultural change.

The position of the subject matter of one's study or its degree of objectivity or subjectivity has important consequences for the way a study is executed. It determines the degree to which this subject matter may be treated as consisting of objective measurable facts and may thus be subjected to exact, preferably quantitative methods. And, following from that, it determines to what degree of exactness causal factors and conditions and their effects may be located and with which degree of exactness it may be established what their relationships are. In other words, methods that are adequate for studying more objective phenomena are not fully suited for studying more subjective phenomena and vice versa.

We may illustrate this by looking at the abolition case. In this case, it is not too difficult to pinpoint the actors with power with respect to the decision to end or restrict the slave trade. In 1791 and 1792, for example, the West Indian Interest was capable of keeping the authorities on its side and preventing the ending of the slave trade. The polity, particularly Parliament, had the final say in this matter, and the West Indians who could persuade the authorities to decide in their interest thus had power. As Anstey's study (1975) shows, it can be rather exactly assessed who the powerholders were and on what their power rested. This is different when we look at the definition of slavery and the slave trade. In these matters, there is not a specific procedure by which or a specific moment when one can decide that these collective definitions have changed. The change itself can be assessed (see Section 7.4) as can the question of who struggled for and against change and who won. It is also possible to locate who had power in British society and to what degree, and who was in authority. But the decision itself and the decision-makers remain largely outside the picture. When studying subjective matters, it is apparent (as Tilly rightfully remarks in a personal comment) that it is hard to get powerholders and public authorities into the analysis. It is also not really possible to measure variables like cultural climate or collective definitions in the quantitative manner of "hard" sociology. These facts may be deplored but there is, in our view, no way around it other than to stop studying the subjective side of social life altogether.

We decided not to stop but to study the cultural aspects of social movements and their relationships with cultural change, phenomena on the subjective side of the objective-subjective continuum. This forced us to look at our subject matter from a subjective perspective. This choice has its drawbacks but as Lloyd (1986) states, a simple objectivism will not bring us much further. In our opinion, the best way to proceed in these matters is to keep as close as possible to the methods that are used to study more objective phenomena. We have attempted to do this by choosing the format of a conceptual model in combination with a qualitative case study. We are aware that the combination of a format that originates in positivistic sociology with a subject matter that is dominated by the apositivistic interpretive research tradition is tantamount to sacrilege. But we are not worried about traditions that much. Our main question is, Did it work?

Obviously, the reader will decide on this question in the end, but it will do no harm to look for an answer ourselves. The first point we assess in looking back at our study is that the constructivist position—social reality is basically a social construction—is maintained throughout the study. The abolitionist interpretive package, for example, is studied and presented as a temporary construct that could easily have been (and partially was) constructed differently. The second point we would like to draw attention to concerns the use of concepts. Concepts proved to be very useful, first of all, for sensitizing purposes. They guided our attention, for example, to the way the abolitionist and antiabolitionist interpretive packages were constructed as being culturally, empirically, and rhetorically credible. Further, the use of clear concepts coming from social movement theory structured the representation of the data a great deal and made for a better grip on the empirical material. Chapter 7, for example, shows the possibility of containing a multifaceted reality like the first abolition campaign without being unduly reductionistic. The third point we would like to make is that the conceptual model provided the possibility of going beyond Drescher's explanation of abolition as the result of popular mobilization. It pinpointed the focal role of specific conditions and factors, and showed how important the interplay of cultural and systemic factors has been without fading into vagueness. It also brought the indeterminacy inherent in social processes to the fore and showed that models in sociological research are inherently underdetermined due to the agency factor. Finally, our fourth point, the model enabled us to rise above the particulars of the abolition case and to insert our empirically based conceptualization into a more generalized theoretical line of thinking on cultural change. All in all, it proved to be possible—in paraphrasing Berger (1991)—to wrest some relatively simple generalizations from the infinitely complex data of the first abolition campaign.

The choice for the structurist vision of society and the related view of man as agent rests on the conviction that it is possible to transcend extant divisions in sociological theory. The path we have chosen does not reflect a mindless eclecticism but can, according to Sztompka, be seen as a "third sociology" that is opposed to both the sociology of action and the sociology of structures. More precisely, Sztompka sees the "structurist-agency" view as being "equally opposed to radical, extreme liberalism, atomism, personalism and individualism as . . . to radical, extreme historicism, totalitarianism, collectivism, holism. It presents the human world as two-sided, dualistic, and 'dialectical.'" He contends that the merger of opposed views gives a synthetic, more adequate approach to social reality (1994:277). This approach will, in our opinion, yield still better results when the dead-end street of the opposition of integration vs. conflict is avoided and the nature of social phenomena is taken into account more fully. This last point means, above all, that adequate methods are used.

History

It is clear that historical developments and events played an important role in bringing about the abolition movement in late-eighteenth-century Britain, and thus in changing the meaning of slavery. The abolitionists functioned as "signifying agents" (Snow and Benford 1988:198) by using the facilities at hand and by getting round the constraints present, which were both products of previous processes and events. The actions of the abolitionists were also affected by events taking place simultaneously with these actions. As part of the more encompassing abolition movement, the first abolition campaign was a definite historical phenomenon. All six ontological assumptions that depict historical phenomena (as Sztompka puts it) were met. It was (1) a dynamic process of becoming that was (2) part of a plurality of processes that together formed a (3) cumulating sequence of events. Abolition was (4) constructed as a process by human agents who acted within a pre-given structure that was at the same time affected by their actions. The dialectics of action and structure (5) were thus clearly present. Finally, (6) temporality was an essential element of the abolition process. This historical character (*coefficient* according to Sztompka) necessitates taking a historical perspective (1986a:332–33). The way we set up and executed our study shows that we cannot agree more.

Such a historical perspective is not only important in cases that like the abolition case are distinctly historical. It is—in many cases—the indicated format for the study of contemporary movements as well. As Shin shows, this perspective was important in the explaining of the 1946 uprisings in Korea and, more generally, "in explaining social protest movements." As Shin, moreover, contends, "[H]istory is not to be taken simply as a background for but as an integral part of collective action" (1994:1619).

Abrams (1982), Lloyd (1986), and Sztompka (1986a) go beyond the idea that sociological research sometimes ought to take the historical component into account. They state that sociology is fundamentally a historical science. In this they concur with Mills, who observed in *The Sociological Imagination* "that every social science—or better, every well-considered social study—requires a historical scope of conception and a full use of historical materials. [Sociology is] an attempt to write 'the present as history'" (1959:145–46). Sociology, in their view, is a historical science because sociologists like historians study processes of becoming, or structuring as Abrams calls it. Society is not just a state of being but is continually developing in ongoing dialectical processes of actors (re)producing structures while being affected by the same structures (re)produced in the past. In the words of Abrams, "The two-sidedness of society, the fact that social action is both something we choose to do and something we have to do, is inseparably bound up with the further fact that whatever reality society has is a historical reality, a reality in time" (1982:2).

This view of society as a set of processes and events stretched out in time, however, does not, as we see it, necessitate employing the historical perspective in all sociological research. Whether this is the case mainly depends on the questions sociologists pose and the strategy they choose to answer those questions. Ideal-typically, two sociological perspectives may be distinguished: a static and a historical one. If we take as an example the study of opinions about welfare, one might ask (1) which factors and conditions determine these opinions or (2) how these opinions evolved over time.

In the first case, one will be interested in factors such as social and/or economic position, education, age, political beliefs and ideological views. See, for example, Houtman (1994), who studied opinions regarding the right to unemployment benefits and the obligation to work. He used the static format of independent, intermediate, and dependent variables, and this "standard" format of sociological research was adequate and produced valid knowledge. There is thus a legitimate place for standard sociological studies in which history, at best, is the background of the subject matter that is studied.

In the second case, one may look for explanations of the changes in elite and/or public opinion about welfare in the eighties and nineties. Here, a historical perspective is indicated because—as Abrams rightly remarks—these opinions develop and evolve in a dialectic process of agency and structuring. The victories of conservative politicians like Thatcher in Britain and Reagan in the United States were outcomes of earlier developments in both countries. Both changed the political agenda of their countries and brought about systemic changes. This, among other things, created room for expressing extant discontent with the way their societies were organized. From then on, most dissension was set in the key of less government and more market, quite surprisingly, not only in their own countries but in many others as well. In this case, history must definitely be taken into account, as must be done in all those cases where agency, structuring, contingency, and chronology are explicitly involved.

As far as the study of social movements is concerned, both perspectives are used. The studies of Shin (1994) and Zaret (1989)—and of course this study—are examples of movement research in which the historical perspective is employed. In many other studies history is absent to a large extent, particularly in studies in the resource mobilization tradition, which according to Buechler (1993) is distinctly ahistorical. Although it is not always necessary to give historical developments and events a place in a study of a movement, leaving history out altogether may pose problems for understanding the movement process and its outcome. In order to give an idea of what these problems might be, we take the recent study of Koopmans and Duyvendak (1995) as an example.

In this study they tried to assess, among other things, what the effect of the Chernobyl disaster—the independent variable—was on antinuclear mobilization in some European countries—the dependent variable. They found, for example, a considerable rise in antinuclear mobilization in Germany. They attributed this rise to the fact that people in that country were already mobilized for antinuclear protest. Mobilization was thus contingent on itself, a result that does not fit in with an ahistoric format with variables that are either dependent or independent. It is, however, in line with the theory of structurism, in which history has its own explicit place. They also used some historical material to make sense of some of the results of their study. The main problem with the way they did this is that they employed this historical material only in an ad hoc fashion and not systematically. They conclude, for example, "that framing efforts by the anti-nuclear movement have had differential success across countries" (p. 244). Historical data about this movement and the framing efforts are, however, lacking and it is therefore not clear on which data they based their causal inference that the discourses in which the different frames were contested were not the cause of the diverging success of the antinuclear movements.

When we look more closely at the subject matter of the Koopmans-Duyvendak study, which, we reiterate, is only taken as an example of ahistoric movement studies, we see that the antinuclear protest in Western Europe has—in Sztompka's terminology—a high historical coefficient. It needs, therefore, a historical approach. More in general, we contend that studies of processes, like those of social movements, more often than not need to take history into account and that a historical perspective is required in far more cases than is done at the moment. With this conclusion we concur with Shin (1994), who states that history deserves its own place in the study of social movements and collective action, particularly, we would like to add, in those cases where movements are studied in relationship to social change. Employing a historical perspective does not mean, as Chapter 8 shows, that movement studies must use the format of the historical narrative, in which all events and actions are presented in a chronological fashion and are ordered according to criteria of logic and rhetoric. It only means that, one way or another, the factorial design of the standard sociological research format is combined with the sequential approach of the historical sciences.

Such a combination means, first of all, that the sociological way of studying social reality, i.e., the factorial design with its thinking in terms of variables and conditions and its emphasis on generalizing, must be upheld. This method may be applied as a means of structuring one's data, as we have done in Part II but it is above all the road to explaining what is happening in and with a movement (see Chapter 8 for the latter). In addition, social movement researchers must explicitly take the role and effects of historical events and developments into account; as Zaret (1989) states, one must not only look at the organizational context of movement processes but at their episodic context as well. Historical data may be used in the study of social movements in three main ways.

First, a movement is a historical process itself, even when it is split into discrete parts like campaigns, in which the collective actions of movement actors may enlarge or diminish the opportunities for collective actions at a later date. This means, as we contended in Part I, that movement actions may be contingent on themselves. The actions of the abolitionists in 1787 and 1788 awakened the slave interest and led to counteractions that circumscribed the possibilities of the abolitionists in the following years. In the variable language of sociology, a dependent variable on t_1 may, in the course of the movement process, become an independent variable on t_2 and again a dependent one on t_3.

Second, during the period in which movement actions take place, these actions may positively or negatively be affected by events and developments in society that occur simultaneously. The abolition movement gives examples of such effects. Abolition was, for example, positively affected by the support of actors who were involved in the movement for parliamentary reform. An example of a negative effect can be found in the Jacobin turn in the French Revolution in 1791–1792.

Third, the action-structure, with the opportunities, resources, facilities, and constraints for action within which a social movement operates, is itself the product of historical developments. As is concluded in Chapter 8, history may open or close the window for collective actions. This structure, its effects on the decisions of movement actors, and with that the course of a movement are often not really comprehensible without taking into account what happened before. For an example, see the active role of the Quakers in the abolition movement in Britain. Why they played this role and why they acted the way they did only becomes clear by going back into their history as Davis (1966, 1975) and Anstey (1975) did very competently.

Our plea for combining sociological and historical methods concerns the way sociologists should do this when studying social movements and change: no longer in an ad hoc fashion but in the systematic manner of the professional historian *at the same time* upholding the sociological way of doing things as well.

Beyond

The story of abolition is part of a more encompassing story: the story of the emergence of new social forms. The last part of the eighteenth century was very much the era of the advent of modern society. This emergence consisted predominantly of the scaling up of society. Less abstractly formulated, the England of regional communities gave way to the British nation comprising all the people living on its territory. A nation—the new organizational format of which Britain was the exemplar—organizes its members, the citizens, through a nationwide political system; regulates production, distribution, and consumption of commodities within a system of supraregional markets, the national economy; and provides means of nonpersonal communication via a system of media that covers the whole (or most) of its territory. This new national society is not only a systemic transformation but also the embodiment of the rising cultural current of the eighteenth century, the Enlightenment. This spiritual movement urged, among other things, the transcending of the boundaries of particularism and the move toward a universal community of all mankind.

Great Britain was not only the first to embark on the journey toward this new national society but also the first to experiment with the organizational forms belonging to this new way of living (see also Chapters 4 and 5). One of these experiments, as Tilly (1982) showed, concerned the new format of political protest, the national social movement. This new format was made possible largely via a new phenomenon, the nationwide public discourse, which was itself the product of the aforementioned scaling up of societal structures, particularly the emergence of a media system on a national scale. Examples are the discourses on the abolition of the slave trade, the reform of Parliament, and the repeal of the restrictions imposed on dissenters and Roman Catholics. The coming into being of the national social movement subsequently favored the spread of the national public discourse and the concomitant growth of a nationwide system of media; these developments went hand-in-glove. Like other elements of the nation-state, the national social movement, the omnipresence of media, and the large-scale public discourse diffused over much of the Western world. Together, they are central parts of the modernization process that later swept the rest of the world as well.

Tarrow (1994) is right to observe that modern society is very much a movement society. Collective campaigns waged by social movement actors and organizations are a recurrent feature of modern life and may be viewed as the expression of the modern enlightened idea of shaping a better society according to ideal and material interests. As we have already made clear, collective campaigns imply public discourses, which function as media through which societal changes are brought about. In our society, there are, however, far more public discourses than movements. The public discourse—as the necessary step toward desired changes—is employed by other actors and organizations as well. More accurately stated, modern society is more than anything else a discourse society in which all kinds of topics are discussed publicly. Examples of such topics are the family as keystone of society, the dumping of the oil-rig *Brent Spar*, abortion as either a woman's right or murder, the balanced budget as panacea for all social problems, acceptance of homosexuals in the army, legalization of marijuana, and the prohibition of smoking.

A closer look at what is going on in society reveals that there are not only discourses at the level of the general public but that society is full of discourses that do not reach the public level. The latter take place within distinct networks and arenas and only some of them may become public discourses. The debate on slavery as it took place within the Quaker community for decades is a fine example of such a nonpublic discourse. It remained a particularistic discourse until the cooperation with the Evangelicals gave it the momentum it needed to become a public discourse.

A more recent example concerns the way risks may become the subject of public discourses. Stallings (1990) examined this process and describes how the collapse of a bridge in the state of New York became a media discourse on the safety of bridges in the United States. Although all elements for a prolonged public discourse on the public safety of bridges were present—a triggering device, media attention, and claims-makers—it largely remained an "unconstructed" social problem (p. 92). He attributes this "failure" to a lack of resources on the side of the claims-making groups, i.e., social movement organizations concerned with highway safety and politically weak government transport agencies. Therefore, they could not bring the discourses going on in their own arenas, those of worried citizens and experts, respectively, to the arena of the public discourse.

The situation in the Netherlands in the winter of 1994–1995 concerning the safety of the inland dikes was quite different. Here, the claims-makers for a renewal program like the central government agency for Public Works—*Rijkswaterstaat*—and the local authorities charged with the safety of the dikes are not without power. This put these claims-makers in a position to profit from the threat of flooding, the massive evacuation of inhabitants of the threatened areas, enormous media attention, and a newly appointed minister of transport and public works who could use an opportunity to establish herself as a strong and capable minister. The combination of these conditions opened a window for them, enabling them to transform the discourses on dike safety going on in their own networks into a public discourse. The last made it possible for them to reach their goal: a crash program with lavish funding.

As we assessed in Chapter 8, the public discourse is an important condition for bringing about change (desired as well as unexpected changes). This assessment leads to the question of what may turn a private or particularistic discourse into a public discourse. In this book, we focused on the collective movement campaign as the means to transfer particularistic discourses to the public realm. There are other ways as well. Politicians, for example, often use events like the threat of flooding as an opportunity to bring one of their pet subjects into the public debate. The same is the case with special interest groups. Success in this respect generally depends on conditions similar to those we elaborated in Part I and in Chapter 8. Important in this respect, as the previous examples show, are conditions like triggering events and media attention, more generally, a relatively open window of opportunities. Most important, however, is the presence of claims-makers, or entrepreneurs as we called them before, with enough power to profit from the extant opportunities. Examples of such claims-makers are politicians and their parties, government agencies, special interest groups, social movement organizations, church leaders, and unions.

One of the remarkable features of contemporary public discourses is the extension of their scope across national borders that has occurred in recent decades. The decision of President Chirac of France to test nuclear weapons on the Pacific isle of Mururoa in 1995 not only led to protests and to explicit and tacit consumer boycotts in many countries, but it also invigorated the international discourse on a worldwide ban of the testing of nuclear weapons. Tarrow (1994) points to the same tendency when reviewing two hundred years of movement history. Movements spread faster and over larger areas (Tarrow specifically mentions the end

of Communism in Eastern Europe and the rise of militant Islamic funda-
mentalism) than two hundred years ago. In 1789 Clarkson was not able
to bring the abolition movement across the English Channel to France;
beginning in 1989 Communist regimes in all East European countries
were toppled from power at a very fast rate. As Tarrow states, "In 1789
antislavery advocates had difficulty crossing the English Channel. But in
1989 the democracy movement spread from Berlin to Beijing in a matter
of weeks" (p. 187).

Just as the nationwide public discourse and the national social movement arose in the context of the coming into being of the nation-state,
the transnationalization of discourses and movements takes place in a
comparably changing context. Without indiscriminately parroting all the
fashionable writing and talk about the world as a global village, a trend
toward globalization *is* clearly visible. This trend occurs in—at least—
three realms. First, the world of economics is enlarging at a rapid pace.
Companies transcend national boundaries more and more and the largest are now truly transnational. Capital moves over the globe more and
more quickly, at the same time causing the loss of economic independence of the separate states. Second, the realm of politics is enlarging as
well. Governments are cooperating more than ever and—though halt-
ingly—formal intergovernmental structures arise. The European Community is one of the foremost examples of this trend and the zigzag
pattern of its progress is exemplary for the experimental character of the
globalization of politics. Another example of globalization is the extension of human rights into constitutions and into the world of international politics (Berting 1990). Third, communication between people is
transcending national boundaries at an ever-increasing rate. Particularly
the advances in electronic and satellite technology have made it possible
to reach other people within seconds, either personally through fax or
e-mail or as audiences through worldwide broadcasting. Television
brought the shelling of Sarajevo, the final at Wimbledon, and Lady Di's
interview into living rooms all over the world and made Al Bundy the
world's most famous shoe salesman.

These and other trends toward globalization of the world in which
people live can be seen, in a sense, as the continuation of the direction
that Western societies took in the eighteenth century. It is still a process
in which boundaries around particularistic enclaves—first regional communities, later nation-states—are broken down. This has led to diminishing the direct social control of thought and behavior and to tolerating
diversity, distinctly one of the Enlightenment's ideals. At the same time,
the amount of manipulation and indirect control has increased, above
all, through the bureaucratization of daily life and the commercialization
of all societal realms, resulting in a new form of particularism: the worldwide uniformity of Mickey Mouse and the hamburger.

From the beginning, modernization has been characterized by this fundamental duality between universality and particularism. In the last part of the eighteenth century, this duality became visible in the "battle" between tradition and progress and, in the first half of the twentieth century, between nationalism and internationalism (for an example of the latter, see the Spanish Civil War, 1936–1939). Now it seems to be surfacing once again and is becoming discernible in the realm of culture, discourse, and movements in two distinct trends.

On the one hand, there is a trend to search for a new way of living based on a better self-understanding; a quest for identity. People exert themselves to realize the universal community of mankind in which every human being, regardless of skin color, ethnic background, class, gender, or other characteristics, can live in community with like-minded others while at the same time accepting and tolerating people who are or choose to be different. Openness, curiosity, and absence of radicalism are the hallmarks of this trend, which can be witnessed in some of the contemporary, or new, social movements, such as the peace, women's, and ecological movements (Cohen 1986; Melucci 1989).

On the other hand, there is a distinctive trend toward the comforting familiarity of one's "own tribe." This trend takes two main forms: (1) the yearning for bringing back the traditional community, mostly expressed by philosophers in their studies; and (2) the far more virulent form of actually creating exclusive in-groups. In the last case, biological and/or cultural characteristics are effectively used to determine who belongs and who does not and to grade people in terms of superior—the "ins"— and the inferior—the "outs." These characteristics are frequently derived from a distant (often reinvented) past and are as such part of the in-group's ideological package. They form the basis of mostly ethnic mobilizations and, in the worst case, as criteria for forcefully removing those who do not belong. Intolerance, exclusion, and exclusivity are the marks of these "tribal" movements, which, alas, can be witnessed all over the globe.

One of the central questions of modern—or, for some, postmodern— society is which of the two tendencies will dominate: the return to the safe womb of the in-group predominantly based on angst and uncertainty or the creation of a new way of living based on the belief in one's own potential? The first can only bring the loss of freedom for the insiders as well as the excluded; it divides the world into people who are locked in or are locked out. The second may make the ideals of the Enlightenment come true. This, however, will only be possible when the new nomads—as Melucci calls them—succeed in maintaining the principles of free choice and tolerance or, in other words, allow people to be different.

Appendix A:
News Production and Collective Campaigns

The production of news is not a neutral process in which media select items from a pool of "what is really happening." On the contrary, news involves the construction of occurrences into events and issues. It is a process in which media with their own needs and interests "mediate" between the needs and interests of the promoters of news and those of the news consumers (Molotch and Lester 1974). In a collective campaign, movement actors promote their ideas on the cause they are fighting for, their goals, their proposals for a solution, etc., and here they need the media to transform the "material" the movement actors promote into issues that necessitate attention by decision-makers, merit support by publics, and entice people to participate in an ongoing campaign.

Important in this respect is that the notion that media have powerful effects has regained ground in studies on mass communication (McQuail 1985). These effects are seen when researchers take a wider look by examining more than only direct exposure effects and take into account the role media play in creating symbolic environments and in unfolding major social and critical events. The results of Gamson's recent study point in the same direction. He observes that the effects of media "are effects *in use*" (1992b:180; emphasis in the original). Media are more important through the use people make of them as a tool or as a resource in their thinking and discussion on a issue than in directly changing their attitudes and cognition.

The transformation of movement material into issues by media implies the setting of the agenda, acting as one of the gatekeepers of the public discourse, contributing to the framing of issues, and supplying "news" on the campaign. Media may thus be an important facility or constraint for a collective campaign and as an establishment institution fulfill nonestablishment goals (Molotch 1979). In other words, media may have important effects on the impact of a collective campaign.

These effects depend on four interrelated sets of factors inherent in media processes.

1. The centrality of media in societal life or as Ball-Rokeach and DeFleur (1976)—looking from the other side—call it: the dependency of actors on media information. On the one hand, in their view this position depends on the complexity of society. In complex societies it is no longer possible to get all or most information directly. On the other hand, it depends on the existence of conflicts and change processes in society. In these situations the established institutions, beliefs, and practices are challenged and are no longer self-evident. This intensifies the dependence on media information, especially in view of the needed reconstruction of social arrangements.

2. Media routines. As McQuail states, media are "complex institutions whose theories, traditions, norms, practices, and self-chosen objectives all exert an influence on the messages they transmit" (1985:94). The way media work (e.g., actively looking for stories, accepting the newsworthiness and truth of copy coming from certain sources without much questioning, employing norms such as balance) enhance or diminish the chance that occurrences become issues and influence the way issues are seen. In general, media are, through their routines, biased against the stories and versions of challenging actors (Molotch and Lester 1974, 1975; Gamson and Lasch 1983; McQuail 1985; Gamson 1988).

3. The status of media. Media are not all seen as equally reliable by authorities, publics, and movement participants. Coverage in a newspaper "of repute" has, for instance, potentially more effect than coverage in a tabloid. The standing and the reputation of media will affect the trustworthiness of their accounts of issues and thus the impact of campaigns on those issues.

4. Control of/over media. This refers to the extent to which social movement actors are able to determine whether their activities are covered at all by the media, the content of that coverage (e.g., the agreement with their intent), and the way this is done (e.g., seriously and supportive, or characterizing the campaign as funny or way out). This control depends among other things on ownership, dependency of media on movement actors and their reports and stories, legitimacy of movement actors and their issues, and routine relationships between movement actors and the media.

Appendix B:
Scheme for Analyzing Interpretive Packages

In order to analyze interpretive packages and to assess their properties, an instrument is needed to expose the structure of these packages. An interpretive package is, as we have contended in Chapter 3, a set of ideas, metaphors, arguments, texts, symbols, etc., that is built and composed in such a way that it does the trick,[1] i.e., convinces people that something is problematic and has to change or convinces them of the opposite, viz., that everything is fine and has to stay that way. In other words, putting forward interpretive packages is a form of making claims, and thus interpretive packages involve the construction of a social reality that is (mostly in part) problematic and in need of change. The problematic part is constructed as an issue and consists of cognitive and moral elements. The cognitive elements are intended to highlight what the problematic situation is like, what its causes are, and how it may be changed. The moral element depicts how this situation (and society in general) ought to be and what and who are to blame for the negative situation (Gusfield 1981; Hunt 1992).

The preceding resembles the way Gamson and Lasch (1983) operate in developing an instrument for analyzing the political culture of contention (cf. the concept of issue culture in Chapter 3). Such a culture consists of interpretive packages in which framing and reasoning devices can be detected. The first functions as a means to cognitively organize the argument put forward, the second as a means to justify the argumentative position. These devices were brought together in a signature matrix that served as an instrument to analyze the political culture regarding social welfare policies and its different constituent packages. In this study, we have followed the lead of Gamson and Lasch supplemented by notions used by Gusfield and Hunt and tried to analyze the abolition discourse in this way [see d'Anjou (1992, 1994) for tentative results]. This approach proved, however, not to be wholly satisfactory and we have therefore adapted it on three points.

First, we have replaced the concept of frame or collective action frame with another concept, viz., *theme*. We have done so because the abolition discourse was much broader than a "standard" movement discourse. As is shown in Chapter 7, the abolition discourse blended, on the one hand, into the contemporary discourses regarding the religious, political, and social reforms in British society and, on the other, into a "to the point" political struggle between two pressure and lobbying groups. The interpretive packages and their themes thus did more than just play their part in "collective action" and thus their organizing core, the framing part, differs from a "standard collective action frame" in that it is less specific than such a frame.[2] Second, we discovered that pointing to the consequences of a problematic situation occupied a more important place in the packages than only being one of the several reasoning devices. It functioned, moreover, not as a justification of the issues. We have therefore given "consequences" a separate place in our analyzing scheme. Third, we found that the distinction between framing and reasoning devices, i.e., that metaphors, exemplars, etc., belong to the first type of device, and that roots, consequences, and appeals to principle to the second type, did not hold. For instance, a visual image—a framing device according to Gamson and Lasch—may equally well serve as a reasoning device, as is the case with the Wedgwood medallion with its stated principle of equality, Am I Not a Man and a Brother? We therefore decided not to use this distinction and left the signature matrix in its strict form out of the scheme.

This gives us a structure that, we assume, underlies all interpretive packages. Interpretive packages are sets of metaphors, exemplars, catchphrases, visual images, roots, principles, etc., that are used to function in an argumentative structure of the following three elements:

1. *Framing.* This pertains to the cognitive aspects of a package. These are directed at organizing the argument by telling what is going on and thus at organizing the perception, cognition, and views of those for whom the package is meant.

2. *Reasoning.* This element refers to the value aspects of a package. These are directed at telling people why the proffered frame (or better, the situation depicted) is the way it is. Value aspects are meant as reasons and justifications for frames.

3. *Consequences.* This part of a package contains the effects of what is being framed as an issue and thus indicates what will change if the sponsor or entrepreneur of a package is followed.

In Chapter 7, the results of the analysis of the arguments used by the abolitionists and antiabolitionists in the abolition discourse are presented, organized by the categories enumerated above.

NOTES

1. Thus the effectiveness of the properties may be inferred from the structure.

2. A "package theme" differs, however, also from the concept of "dominant and countertheme" as is used in elaborating the cultural conduciveness of the opportunity structure.

References

Abrams, Philip. 1982. *Historical Sociology*. Near Shepton Mallet, Somerset: Open Books.

Alexander, Jeffrey C. and Steven Seidman (eds.). 1990. *Culture and Society: Contemporary Debates*. Cambridge: Cambridge University Press.

Altick, Richard D. [1957] 1983. *The English Common Reader: A Social History of the Mass Reading Public 1800–1900*. Chicago/London: University of Chicago Press (Midway Reprint).

Amenta, Edwin and Yvonne Zylan. 1991. "It Happened Here: Political Opportunity, the New Institutionalism, and the Townsend Movement." *American Sociological Review* 56:250–65.

Anstey, Roger. 1975. *The Atlantic Slave Trade and British Abolition 1760–1810*. London: MacMillan.

———. 1980. "The Pattern of British Abolitionism in the Eighteenth and Nineteenth Centuries." Pp. 19–43 in *Anti-Slavery, Religion, and Reform: Essays in Memory of Roger Anstey*, edited by Ch. Bolt and S. Drescher. Folkestone/Hamden, CT: Dawson/Archon.

Anstey, Roger and P. E. H. Hair (eds.). 1976. *Liverpool, the African Slave Trade, and Abolition: Essays to Illustrate Current Knowledge and Research*, Occasional Series Volume 2. Bristol: Historic Society of Lancashire and Cheshire.

Archer, Margaret S. 1988. *Culture and Agency: The Place of Culture in Social Theory*. Cambridge: Cambridge University Press.

Aron, Raymond. 1965. *Main Currents in Sociological Thought*, Vol. 1. Harmondsworth: Penguin.

Ashley, Maurice. 1973. *England in the Seventeenth Century*. Harmondsworth: Penguin.

Ashworth, John. 1992. "The Relationship between Capitalism and Humanitarianism." Pp. 180–200 in *The Antislavery Debate: Capitalism and Abolitionism as a Problem in Historical Interpretation*, edited by Th. Bender. Berkeley: University of California Press.

Bachrach, Peter and Morton S. Baratz. 1962. "The Two Faces of Power." *American Political Science Review* 56:947–52.

Ball-Rokeach, S. J. and M. L. DeFleur. 1976. "A Dependency Model of Mass Media Effects." *Communication Research* 3:3–21.

Barker, Anthony J. 1978. *The African Link: British Attitudes to the Negro in the Era of the Atlantic Slave Trade, 1550–1807.* London/Totowa, NJ: Frank Cass.

Barry, Jonathan. 1991. "The Press and the Politics of Culture in Bristol, 1660–1775." Pp. 49–82 in *Culture, Politics and Society in Britain, 1660–1800,* edited by J. Black and J. Gregory. Manchester/New York: Manchester University Press.

Batiot, Anne. 1982. "The Political Construction of Sexuality: The Contraception and Abortion Issues in France, 1965–1975." Pp. 125–46 in *Social Movements and Protest in France,* edited by Ph. G. Cerny. New York: St. Martin's.

Becker, Howard S. 1963. *The Outsiders: Studies in the Sociology of Deviance.* New York: Free Press.

Becker, Howard S. 1970. "An Illustrative Case: The Marihuana Tax Act." Pp. 56–64 in *Crime and Delinquency. A Reader,* edited by C. A. Bersani. London: MacMillan.

Benford, Robert D. and Scott A. Hunt. 1992. "Dramaturgy and Social Movements: The Social Construction and Communication of Power." *Sociological Inquiry* 62:36–55.

Berger, Bennett M. 1991. "Structure and Choice in the Sociology of Culture." *Theory and Society* 20:1–19.

Berger, Joseph, Dana P. Eyre, and Morris Zelditch, Jr. 1989. "Theoretical Structures and the Micro/Macro Problem." Pp. 11–32 in *Sociological Theories in Progress: New Formulations,* edited by J. Berger, M. Zelditch, Jr., and B. Anderson. Newbury Park, CA: Sage.

Berting, Jan. 1990. "Societal Change, Human Rights and the Welfare State in Europe." Pp. 188–208 in *Human Rights in a Pluralist World: Individuals and Collectivities,* edited by J. Berting, P. R. Baehr, J. H. Burgers, C. Flinterman, B. de Klerk, R. Kroes, C. A. van Minnen, and K. Van der Wal. Westport, CT/London: Meckler.

Best, Joel. 1987. "Rhetoric in Claimsmaking: Constructing the Missing Children Problem." *Social Problems* 34:101–21.

Black, Jeremy and Jeremy Gregory. 1991. "Introduction." Pp. 1–13 in *Culture, Politics and Society in Britain, 1660–1800,* edited by J. Black and J. Gregory. Manchester/New York: Manchester University Press.

Blackburn, Robin. 1988. *The Overthrow of Colonial Slavery.* London/New York: Verso.

Blumer, Herbert. 1939. "Collective Behavior." Pp. 219–80 in *An Outline of the Principles of Sociology,* edited by Robert E. Park. New York: Barnes and Noble.

———. 1969. *Symbolic Interaction: Perspective and Method.* Englewood Cliffs, NJ: Prentice Hall.

Brand, Karl-Werner. 1990. "Cyclical Changes in the Cultural Climate as a Context Variable for Social Movement Development." Paper presented at the 1990 World Congress of Sociology in Madrid (Spain), July 9–13.

Briggs, Asa. 1959. *The Age of Improvement.* London: Longman, Green.

Brown, Vivienne. 1992. "The Emergence of the Economy." Pp. 127–77 in *Formations of Modernity,* edited by S. Hall and B. Gieben. Cambridge/Oxford: Polity/Open University.

Bruns, Roger (ed.). 1977. *Am I Not A Man and A Brother: The Antislavery Crusade of Revolutionary America 1688–1788.* New York: Chelsea House.

Buechler, Steven M. 1993. "Beyond Resource Mobilization? Emerging Trends in Social Movement Theory." *Sociological Quarterly* 34:217–35.

Cannon, John. 1973. *Parliamentary Reform; 1640–1832.* Cambridge: Cambridge University Press.

Cobb, Roger W. and Charles D. Elder. 1972. *Participation in American Politics: The Dynamics of Agenda-Building.* Baltimore/London: Johns Hopkins University Press.

———. 1983. *Participation in American Politics: The Dynamics of Agenda-Building.* 2nd edition. Baltimore/London: Johns Hopkins University Press.

Cohen, Jean L. 1985. "Strategy or Identity: New Theoretical Paradigms and Contemporary Social Movements." *Social Research* 52:663–716.

Colley, Linda. 1992. *Britons: Forging the Nation, 1707–1787.* New Haven, CT/London: Yale University Press.

Collins, Randall. 1980. "Weber's Last Theory of Capitalism: A Systematization." *American Sociological Review* 45:925–42.

Corrigan, Philip and Derek Sayer. 1991. *The Great Arch: English State Formation as Cultural Revolution.* Oxford: Basil Blackwell.

Coser, Lewis A. 1971. *Masters of Sociological Thought: Ideas in Historical and Social Context.* 2nd edition. New York: Harcourt Brace Jovanovich.

Craton, Michael. 1974. *Sinews of Empire: A Short History of British Slavery.* London: Temple Smith.

———. 1982. "Slave Culture, Resistance and the Achievement of Emancipation in the British West Indies, 1783–1838." Pp. 100–23 in *Slavery and British Society, 1776–1846,* edited by J. Walvin. London/Basingstoke: MacMillan.

Craton, Michael, James Walvin, and David Wright. 1976. *Slavery, Abolition and Emancipation. Black Slaves and the British Empire: A Thematic Documentary.* London/New York: Longman.

Curtin, Philip D. 1964. *Image of Africa: British Ideas and Action, 1780–1859.* Madison: University of Wisconsin Press.

d'Anjou, Leo. 1992. "The Movement to the Abolition of the Slave Trade in Great Britain: A Process of Constructing Social Meanings." Paper presented at the Culture and Social Movements Workshop, University of California at San Diego, June 18–20 1992.

———. 1994. "What Makes an Interpretive Package Successful? Gamson Revisited." Paper presented at the 1994 World Congress of Sociology, Bielefeld (Germany), July 18–23.

Davis, David B. 1966. *The Problem of Slavery in Western Culture.* Ithaca, NY: Cornell University Press.

———. 1975. *The Problem of Slavery in the Age of Revolution.* Ithaca, NY: Cornell University Press.

———. 1984. *Slavery and Human Progress.* New York/Oxford: Oxford University Press.

———. 1987. "Capitalism, Abolitionism, and Hegemony." Pp. 209–29 in *British Capitalism and Caribbean Slavery: The Legacy of Eric Williams,* edited by B. L. Solow and S. L. Engerman. Cambridge: Cambridge University Press.

———. 1992. "Reflections on Abolitionism and Ideological Hegemony." Pp. 161–80 in *The Antislavery Debate: Capitalism and Abolitionism as a Problem in Historical Interpretation*, edited by Th. Bender. Berkeley: University of California Press.

De Vries, Jan. 1976. *The Economy of Europe in an Age of Crisis, 1600–1750*. Cambridge University Press: Cambridge

Diani, Mario. 1992. "The Concept of Social Movement." *Sociological Review* 40:1–25.

Dickson, Donald T. 1968. "Bureaucracy and Morality. An Organizational Perspective on a Moral Crusade." *Social Problems* 16:143–56.

Dietz, Thomas and Tom R. Burns. 1992. "Human Agency and the Evolutionary Dynamics of Culture." *Acta Sociologica* 35:187–200.

Dijksterhuis, E. J. 1986. *The Mechanization of the World Picture: Pythagoras to Newton*. Princeton, NJ: Princeton University Press.

DiMaggio, Paul. 1991. "The Micro-Macro Dilemma in Organizational Research: Implications of Role-System Theory." Pp. 76–98 in *Macro-Micro Linkages in Sociology*, edited by J. Huber. Newbury Park, CA: Sage.

Ditchfield, G. M. 1980. "Repeal, Abolition, and Reform: A Study in the Interaction of Reforming Movements in the Parliament of 1790–6." Pp. 101–19 in *Anti-Slavery, Religion, and Reform: Essays in Memory of Roger Anstey*, edited by Ch. Bolt and S. Drescher. Folkestone/Hamden, CT: Dawson/Archon.

Drescher, Seymour. 1976. "Capitalism and Abolition: Values and Forces in Britain, 1783–1814." Pp. 167–95 in *Liverpool, the African Slave Trade, and Abolition: Essays to Illustrate Current Knowledge and Research*, edited by R. Anstey and P. E. H. Hair, Occasional Series Volume 2. Bristol: Historic Society of Lancashire and Cheshire.

———. 1977a. *Econocide: British Slavery in the Era of Abolition*. Pittsburgh: University of Pittsburgh Press.

———. 1977b. "Capitalism and the Decline of Slavery: The British Case in Comparative Perspective." Pp. 132–43 in *Comparative Perspectives on Slavery in New World Plantation Societies*, edited by V. Rubin and A. Tuden. New York: New York Academy of Sciences.

———. 1980. "Two Variants of Anti-Slavery: Religious Organization and Social Mobilization in Britain and France, 1780–1870." Pp. 43–64 in *Anti-Slavery, Religion, and Reform: Essays in Memory of Roger Anstey*, edited by Ch. Bolt and S. Drescher. Folkestone/Hamden, CT: Dawson/Archon.

———. 1986. *Capitalism and Antislavery: British Mobilization in Comparative Perspective*. Basingstoke/London: MacMillan.

———. 1987. "Paradigms Tossed: Capitalism and the Political Sources of Abolition." Pp. 191–209 in *British Capitalism and Caribbean Slavery: The Legacy of Eric Williams*, edited by B. L. Solow and S. L. Engerman. Cambridge: Cambridge University Press.

———. 1990. "People and Parliament: The Rhetoric of the British Slave Trade." *Journal of Interdisciplinary History* 20:561–80.

———. 1992. "The Ending of the Slave Trade and the Evolution of European Scientific Racism." Pp. 361–97 in *The Atlantic Slave Trade: Effects on Economies,*

Societies, and Peoples in Africa, the Americas, and Europe, edited by J. E. Inikori and S. L. Engerman. Durham/London: Duke University Press.

———. 1993. "Review Essay of 'The AntiSlavery Debate: Capitalism and Abolition as a Problem in Historical Interpretation'." *History and Theory* 32:311–29.

———. 1994a. "Whose Abolition? Popular Pressure and the Ending of the British Slave Trade." *Past and Present* 143:136–66.

———. 1994b. "The Long Goodbye: Dutch Capitalism and Antislavery in Comparative Perspective." *American Historical Review* 99:44–69.

Dubin, Steven C. 1992. "Bookreview of 'Symbolic Interaction and Cultural Studies edited by H. S. Becker and M. M. McCall'." *Contemporary Sociology* 21:719–20.

Durkheim, Emile. [1893] 1964. *The Division of Labor in Society.* New York/London: Free Press/Collier-MacMillan.

———. [1895] 1967. *Les Règles de la Méthode Sociologique,* seizième edition (The rules of the sociological method). Paris: Presses Universitaires de France.

Duyvendak, Jan Willem and Ruud Koopmans. 1992. "Protest in een Pacificatiedemocratie. Nieuwe Sociale Bewegingen en het Nederlandse Politieke Systeem" (Protest in a pacification-democracy. New social movements and the Dutch political system). Pp. 39–59 in *Tussen Verbeelding en Macht: 25 jaar nieuwe sociale bewegingen in Nederland* (Between imagination and power: 25 years new social movements in the Netherlands), edited by J. W. Duyvendak, H. A. Van Der Heijden, R. Koopmans, and L. Wijmans. Amsterdam: SUA.

Duyvendak, J. W., H. A. Van Der Heijden, R. Koopmans, and L. Wijmans (eds.). 1992. *Tussen Verbeelding en Macht: 25 jaar nieuwe sociale bewegingen in Nederland* (Between imagination and power: 25 years new social movements in the Netherlands). Amsterdam: SUA.

Eisinger, Peter K. 1973. "The Conditions of Protest Behavior in American Cities." *American Political Science Review* 67:11–28.

Eltis, David. 1982. "Abolitionist Perceptions of Society after Slavery." Pp. 195–214 in *Slavery and British Society, 1776–1846,* edited by J. Walvin. London/Basingstoke: MacMillan.

Eltis, David and James Walvin (eds.). 1981. *The Abolition of the Atlantic Slave Trade: Origins and Effects in Europe, Africa, and the Americas.* Madison/London: University of Wisconsin Press.

Ester, Peter and Loek Halman. 1994. *De cultuur van de verzorgingsstaat: Een sociologisch onderzoek naar waardenoriëntaties in Nederland* (The culture of the welfare state: A sociological study of value orientations in the Netherlands). Tilburg: Tilburg University Press.

Eyerman, Ron and Andrew Jamison. 1991. *Social Movements: A Cognitive Approach.* Cambridge/Oxford: Polity.

Ferree, Myra M. 1992. "The Political Context of Rationality: Rational Choice Theory and Resource Mobilization." Pp. 29–53 in *Frontiers in Social Movement Theory,* edited by A. D. Morris and C. McClurg Mueller. New Haven, CT/London: Yale University Press.

Fladeland, Betty. 1972. *Men and Brothers: Anglo-American Antislavery Cooperation.* Urbana: University of Illinois Press.

———. 1982. "'Our Cause Being One and the Same': Abolitionists and Chartism." Pp. 69–100 in *Slavery and British Society, 1776–1846*, edited by J. Walvin. London/Basingstoke: MacMillan.

Furneaux, Robin. 1974. *William Wilberforce*. London: Hamish Hamilton.

Gamson, William A. 1988. "Political Discourse and Collective Action." Pp. 219–44 in *From Structure to Action: Comparing Social Movement Research across Cultures: International Movement Research*, A Research Annual, volume 1, edited by B. Klandermans, H. Kriesi, and S. Tarrow. Greenwich, CT/London: JAI.

———. 1992a. "The Social Psychology of Collective Action." Pp. 53–77 in *Frontiers in Social Movement Theory*, edited by A. D. Morris and C. McClurg Mueller. New Haven, CT/London: Yale University Press.

———. 1992b. *Talking Politics*. Cambridge: Cambridge University Press.

Gamson, William A. and Kathryn E. Lasch. 1983. "The Political Culture of Social Welfare Policy." Pp. 397–415 in *Evaluating the Welfare State: Social and Political Perspectives*, edited by S. E. Spiro and E. Yuchtman-Yaar. New York: Academic Press.

Gamson, William A. and Andre Modigliani. 1989. "Media Discourse and Public Opinion on Nuclear Power: A Constructionist Approach." *American Journal of Sociology* 95:1–37.

Garner, Roberta A. and Mayer N. Zald. 1987. "The Political Economy of Social Movement Sectors." Pp. 293–317 in *Social Movements in an Organizational Society; Collected Essays*, edited by M. N. Zald and J. D. McCarthy. New Brunswick/Oxford: Transaction.

Gerhards, Jürgen and Dieter Rucht. 1990. "Unexpected Dissent: Micromobilization Contexts and Framing Processes as Conditions for Two Successful Protest Campaigns in West Germany." Paper presented at the 12th World Congress of Sociology in Madrid, July 9–13.

Giddens, Anthony. 1982. "Action, Structure, Power." Pp. 28–40 in *Profiles and Critiques in Social Theory*, edited by A. Giddens. London: MacMillan.

Giddens, Anthony. 1984. *The Constitution of Society: Outline of the Theory of Structuration*. Cambridge: Polity.

Gilbert, Alan D. 1976. *Religion and Society in Industrial England: Church, Chapel and Social Change, 1740–1914*. London: Longman.

Goodwin, Albert. 1979. *The Friends of Liberty: The English Democratic Movement in the Age of the French Revolution*. London: Hutchinson.

Gould, Stephen J. 1994. "The Evolution of Life on the Earth." *Scientific American* 271:62–70.

Granovetter, Mark. 1992. "Economic Institutions as Social Constructions: A Framework for Analysis." *Acta Sociologica* 35:3–11.

Griswold, Wendy. 1987. "The Fabrication of Meaning: Literary Interpretation in the United States, Great Britain and the West Indies." *American Journal of Sociology* 92:1077–117.

Gusfield, Joseph R. 1970. *Protest, Reform, and Revolt: A Reader in Social Movements*. New York: Wiley.

———. 1981. *Drinking-Driving and the Symbolic Order*. Chicago: University of Chicago Press.

————. 1989. "Constructing the Ownership of Social Problems: Fun and Profit in the Welfare State." *Social Problems* 36:431–41.

Hamilton, Peter. 1992. "The Enlightenment and the Birth of Social Science." Pp. 17–71 in *Formations of Modernity*, edited by S. Hall and B. Gieben. Cambridge/Oxford: Polity/Open University.

Harding, Susan. 1984. "Reconstructing Order through Action; Jim Crow and the Southern Civil Rights Movement." Pp. 378–402 in *Statemaking and Social Movements; Essays in History and Theory*, edited by Ch. Bright and S. Harding. Ann Arbor: University of Michigan Press.

Harley, C. Knick. 1993. "Reassessing the Industrial Revolution: A Macro View." Pp. 171–227 in *The British Industrial Revolution: An Economic Perspective*, edited by J. Mokyr. Boulder: Westview.

Haskell, Thomas L. 1992. "Capitalism and the Origins of the Humanitarian Sensibility, Parts 1 and 2." Pp. 107–61 in *The Antislavery Debate: Capitalism and Abolitionism as a Problem in Historical Interpretation*, edited by Th. Bender. Berkeley: University of California Press.

Heberle, Rudolf. 1951. *Social Movements; An Introduction to Political Sociology*. New York: Appleton-Century-Crofts.

Heller, A. 1978. *The Theory of Need in Marx*. London: Allison & Busby.

Hilgard, Ernest R., Richard C. Atkinson, and Rita L. Atkinson. [1953] 1971. *Introduction to Psychology*, 5th edition. New York: Harcourt Brace Jovanovich.

Hilgartner, Stephen and Charles L. Bosk. 1988. "The Rise and Fall of Social Problems: A Public Arenas Model." *American Journal of Sociology* 94:53–78.

Hilton, Boyd. 1988. *The Age of Atonement: The Influence of Evangelicalism on Social and Economic Thought, 1795–1865*. Oxford: Clarendon.

Hirsch, Paul M. 1986. "From Ambushes to Golden Parachutes: Corporate Takeovers as an Instance of Cultural Framing and Institutional Integration." *American Journal of Sociology* 91:800–37.

Holt, Thomas C. 1990. "Explaining Abolition: Review Essay." *Journal of Social History* 24:371–78.

Holz, Josephine R. and Charles R. Wright. 1979. "Sociology of Mass Communications." *Annual Review of Sociology* 5:193–217.

Homans, George C. 1961. *Social Behavior: Its Elementary Forms*. London: Routledge & Kegan Paul.

————. 1964. "Bringing Men Back." *American Sociological Review* 29:809–19.

————. 1974. *Social Behaviour: Its Elementary Forms*, revised edition. New York: Harcourt, Brace & Jovanovich.

Houtman, Dick. 1994. *Werkloosheid en sociale rechtvaardigheid: Oordelen over de rechten en plichten van werklozen* (Unemployment and social justice: Judgments on the rights and obligations of the unemployed). Amsterdam/Meppel: Boom.

Howse, Ernest M. 1952. *Saints in Politics: The 'Clapham Sect' and the Growth of Freedom*. Toronto: University of Toronto Press.

Hunt, Scott A. 1992. "Critical Dramaturgy and Collective Action Rhetoric: Cognitive and Moral Order in the Communist Manifesto." Pp. 1–18 in *Perspectives on Social Problems*, Volume 3. Greenwich, CT/London: JAI.

Hunt, Scott A. and Robert D. Benford. 1992. "Social Movements and the Social

Construction of Reality: An Emergent Paradigm." Paper presented at the Culture and Social Movements Workshop at the University of California at San Diego, June 18–20.

Hunter, J. Paul. 1990. *Before Novels: The Cultural Contexts of Eighteenth-Century English Fiction.* New York/London: W. W. Norton.

Hurwitz, Edith F. 1973. *Politics and the Public Conscience: Slave Emancipation and the Abolitionist Movement in Britain.* London: George Allen & Unwin.

Inikori, Joseph E. 1987. "Slavery and the Development of Industrial Capitalism in England." Pp. 79–103 in *British Capitalism and Caribbean Slavery: The Legacy of Eric Williams,* edited by B. L. Solow and S. L. Engerman. Cambridge: Cambridge University Press.

Inikori, Joseph E. and Stanley L. Engerman. 1992. "Introduction: Gainers and Losers in the Atlantic Slave Trade." Pp. 1–21 in *The Atlantic Slave Trade: Effects on Economies, Societies, and Peoples in Africa, the Americas, and Europe,* edited by J. E. Inikori and S. L. Engerman. Durham/London: Duke University Press.

Jenkins, J. Craig. 1983. "Resource Mobilization Theory and the Study of Social Movements." *Annual Review of Sociology* 9:527–53.

Jenness, Valerie. 1990. "From Sex as Sin to Sex as Work: COYOTE and the Reorganization of Prostitution as a Social Problem." *Social Problems* 37: 403–20.

Joppke, Christian. 1992. "Explaining Cross-National Variations of Two Anti-Nuclear Movements: A Political Process Perspective." *Sociology* 26:311–31.

Kalberg, Stephen. 1980. "Max Weber's Types of Rationality: Cornerstones for the Analysis of Rationalization Processes in History." *American Journal of Sociology* 85:1145–79.

Kingdon, John W. 1984. *Agendas, Alternatives and Public Policies.* Boston/Toronto: Little, Brown.

Kitschelt, Herbert P. 1986. "Political Opportunity Structure and Political Protest: Anti-Nuclear Movements in Four Democracies." *British Journal of Political Science* 16:57–85.

Klandermans, Bert. 1988. "The Formation and Mobilization of Consensus." Pp. 173–96 in *From Structure to Action: Comparing Social Movement Research across Cultures: International Movement Research,* A Research Annual, volume 1, edited by B. Klandermans, H. Kriesi, and S. Tarrow. Greenwich, CT/London: JAI.

———. 1992. "The Social Construction of Protest and Multiorganizational Fields." Pp. 77–104 in *Frontiers of Social Movement Theory,* edited by A. D. Morris and C. McClurg Mueller. New Haven, CT/London: Yale University Press.

Klandermans, Bert, Hanspeter Kriesi, and Sidney Tarrow (eds.). 1988. *From Structure to Action: Comparing Social Movement Research across Cultures: International Movement Research,* A Research Annual, volume 1. Greenwich, CT/ London: JAI.

Klandermans, Bert and Sidney Tarrow. 1988. "Mobilization into Social Movements: Synthesizing European and American Approaches." Pp. 1–38 in *From Structure to Action: Comparing Social Movement Research across Cultures:*

International Movement Research;" A Research Annual, volume 1, edited by B. Klandermans, H. Kriesi, and S. Tarrow. Greenwich, CT/London: JAI.

Klingberg, Frank J. 1926. *The Anti-Slavery Movement in England: A Study in English Humanitarianism.* New Haven, CT/London: Yale University Press/Oxford University Press.

Köbben, A. J. F. 1983. *De zaakwaarnemer.* Deventer: Van Loghum Slaterus.

Koopmans, Ruud. 1992. "Van provo tot RARA: Golfbewegingen in het politiek protest in Nederland" (From Provo to RARA: Waves in political protest in the Netherlands). Pp. 59–77 in *Tussen Verbeelding en Macht: 25 jaar nieuwe sociale bewegingen in Nederland* (Between imagination and power: 25 years new social movements in the Netherlands), edited by J. W. Duyvendak, H. A. Van Der Heijden, R. Koopmans, and L. Wijmans. Amsterdam: SUA.

Koopmans, Ruud and Jan Willem Duyvendak. 1995. "The Political Construction of the Nuclear Energy Issue and Its Impact on the Mobilization of Anti-Nuclear Movements in Western Europe." *Social Problems* 42:235–51.

Kriesi, Hanspeter. 1988. "Local Mobilization for the People's Petition of the Dutch Peace Movement." Pp. 41–83 in *From Structure to Action: Comparing Social Movement Research across Cultures: International Movement Research,* A Research Annual, volume 1, edited by B. Klandermans, H. Kriesi, and S. Tarrow. Greenwich, CT/London: JAI.

Lang, Kurt and Gladys E. Lang. 1978. "The Dynamics of Social Movements." Pp. 96–108 in *Collective Behavior and Social Movements,* edited by L. E. Genevie. Itasca, IL: F. E. Peacock.

Law, Kim S. and Edward J. Walsh. 1983. "The Interaction of Grievances and Structures in Social Movement Analysis: The Case of JUST." *Sociological Quarterly* 24:123–36.

Lewis, Gordon K. 1978. *Slavery, Imperialism, and Freedom: Studies in English Radical Thought.* New York/London: Monthly Review.

Lie, John. 1993. "Visualizing the Invisible Hand: The Social Origins of 'Market Society' in England, 1550–1750." *Politics and Society* 21:275–305.

Lloyd, Christopher. 1986. *Explanation in Social History.* Oxford/New York: Basil Blackwell.

Lukes, Steven. 1974. *Power: A Radical View.* London: MacMillan.

March, James G. and Johan P. Olsen. 1989. *Rediscovering Institutions: The Organizational Basis of Politics.* New York: Free Press.

Marshall, Gordon. 1982. *In Search of the Spirit of Capitalism.* New York: Columbia University Press.

Marwell, Gerald and Pamela Oliver. 1984. "Collective Action Theory and Social Movements Research." Pp. 1–27 in *Research in Social Movements, Conflict and Change,* volume 7, edited by L. Kriesberg. Greenwich, CT: JAI.

Marx, Gary T. and James L. Wood. 1975. "Strands of Theory and Research in Collective Behavior." *Annual Review of Sociology* 1:363–428.

Marx, Karl. [1869] 1968. *Der achtzehnte Brumaire des Louis Bonaparte.* Pp. 222–316 in K. Marx and F. Engels, *Ausgewählte Schriften in Zwei Bänden,* Band I. Berlin: Dietz Verlag.

———. [1887] 1965. *Capital: A Critical Analysis of Capitalist Production,* Volume I. Moscow: Progress.

Mathews, Donald G. 1980. "Religion and Slavery: the Case of the American South." Pp. 207–33 in *Anti-Slavery, Religion, and Reform: Essays in Memory of Roger Anstey*, edited by Ch. Bolt and S. Drescher. Folkestone/Hamden, CT: Dawson/Archon.

McCann, Michael W. 1991. "Legal Mobilization and Social Reform Movements: Notes on Theory and Its Application." *Studies in Law, Politics, and Society* 11:225–54.

McCarthy, John D. 1987. "Pro-Life and Pro-Choice Mobilization: Infrastructure Deficits and New Technologies." Pp. 49–67 in *Social Movements in an Organizational Society; Collected Essays*, edited by M. N. Zald and J. D. McCarthy. New Brunswick/Oxford: Transaction.

McCarthy, John D. and Mayer N. Zald. 1977. "Resource Mobilization and Social Movements: A Partial Theory." *American Journal of Sociology* 82:1212–41.

McQuail, Denis. 1985. "Sociology of Mass Communication." *Annual Review of Sociology* 11:93–111.

Mead, George H. [1934] 1962. *Mind, Self, and Society.* Chicago/London: University of Chicago Press.

Mellor, George R. 1951. *British Imperial Trusteeship 1783–1850*. London: Faber and Faber.

Melucci, Alberto. 1989. *Nomads of the Present: Social Movements and Individual Needs in Contemporary Society*, edited by J. Keane and P. Mier. London: Hutchinson Radius.

Mills, C. Wright. 1959. *The Sociological Imagination*. New York: Oxford University Press.

Mokyr, Joel. 1993. "Editor's Introduction: The New Economic History and the Industrial Revolution." Pp. 1–132 in *The British Industrial Revolution: An Economic Perspective*, edited by J. Mokyr. Boulder: Westview.

Molotch, Harvey. 1979. "Media and Movements." Pp. 71–93 in *The Dynamics of Social Movements: Resource Mobilization, Social Control, and Tactics*, edited by M. N. Zald and J. D. McCarthy. Cambridge, MA: Winthrop.

Molotch, Harvey and Marilyn Lester. 1974. "News as Purposive Behavior: On the Strategic Use of Routine Events, Accidents, and Scandals." *American Sociological Review* 39:101–12.

———. 1975. "Accidental News: The Great Oil Spill as Local Occurrence and National Event." *American Journal of Sociology* 81:235–60.

Morris, Aldon D. and Carol McClurg Mueller (eds.). 1992. *Frontiers in Social Movement Theory.* New Haven, CT/London: Yale University Press.

Nisbet, Robert A. 1966. *The Sociological Tradition*. London: Heinemann.

Nuttin, Joseph. 1984. *Motivation, Planning, and Action: A Relational Theory of Behavior Dynamics*. Leuven/Hillsdale, NJ: Leuven University Press/Lawrence Erlbaum Associates.

Oldfield, J. R. 1989. "Anti-Slavery Sentiment in Children's Literature, 1750–1850." *Slavery and Abolition* 10:44–59.

———. 1995. *Popular Politics and British Anti-Slavery: The Mobilization of Public Opinion against the Slave Trade, 1787–1807*. Manchester/New York: Manchester University Press.

Oliver, Pamela E. 1989. "Bringing the Crowd Back In: The Nonorganizational

Elements of Social Movements." Pp. 1–30 in *Research in Social Movements, Conflict and Change,* volume 11, edited by L. Kriesberg. Greenwich, CT: JAI.

Parsons, Talcott and Edward Shils. 1990. "Values and Social Systems." Pp. 39–46 in *Culture and Society: Contemporary Debates,* edited by J. C. Alexander and S. Seidman. Cambridge: Cambridge University Press.

Phillips, Bernard S. 1990. "Simmel, Individuality, and Fundamental Change." Pp. 259–83 in *Georg Simmel and Contemporary Sociology,* edited by M. Kern, B. S. Phillips, and R. S. Cohen. Dordrecht: Kluwer.

Phillipson, Nicholas. 1981. "The Scottish Enlightenment." Pp. 19–41 in *The Enlightenment in National Context,* edited by R. Porter and M. Teich. Cambridge: Cambridge University Press.

Plumb, J. H. [1950] 1968. *England in the Eighteenth Century.* Harmondsworth: Penguin.

Porter, Dale H. 1970. *The Abolition of the Slave Trade in England, 1784–1807.* Hamden, CT: Archon Books.

Porter, Roy. 1981. "The Enlightenment in England." Pp. 1–19 in *The Enlightenment in National Context,* edited by R. Porter and M. Teich. Cambridge: Cambridge University Press.

———. 1990a. *The Enlightenment.* London: MacMillan.

———. 1990b. *English Society in the Eighteenth Century; Revised Edition.* Harmondsworth: Penguin.

Porter, Roy and Mikulas Teich (eds.). 1981. *The Enlightenment in National Context.* Cambridge: Cambridge University Press.

Rice, C. Duncan. 1975. *The Rise and Fall of Black Slavery.* London: MacMillan.

———. 1980. "Literary Sources and the Revolution in British Attitudes to Slavery." Pp. 319–35 in *Anti-Slavery, Religion, and Reform: Essays in Memory of Roger Anstey,* edited by Ch. Bolt and S. Drescher. Folkestone/Hamden, CT: Dawson/Archon.

Ritzer, George. 1981. *Toward an Integrated Sociological Paradigm: The Search for an Exemplar and an Image of the Subject Matter.* Boston: Allyn and Bacon.

———. 1983. *Sociological Theory,* 2nd edition. New York: Alfred A. Knopf.

Rubinstein, W. D. 1993. *Capitalism, Culture, and Decline in Britain, 1750–1990.* London/New York: Routledge.

Schluchter, Wolfgang. 1981. *The Rise of Western Rationalism: Max Weber's Developmental History.* Translated with an introduction by Guenther Roth. Berkeley: University of California Press.

Schudson, Michael. 1989. "How Culture Works: Perspectives from Media Studies on the Efficacy of Symbols." *Theory and Society* 18:153–80.

Semmel, Bernard. 1970. *The Rise of Free Trade Imperialism: Classical Political Economy, the Empire of Free Trade and Imperialism, 1750–1850.* Cambridge: Cambridge University Press.

Sewell, William H. 1992. "A Theory of Structure: Duality, Agency, and Transformation." *American Journal of Sociology* 98:1–29.

Shin, Gi-Wook 1994. "The Historical Making of Collective Action: The Korean Peasant Uprising of 1946." *American Journal of Sociology* 99:1596–624.

Smail, John. 1992. "Manufacturer or Artisan? The Relationship between Economic and Cultural Change in the Early Stages of the Eighteenth-Century Industrialization." *Journal of Social History* 25:791–814.

Smelser, Neil J. 1962. *Theory of Collective Behavior.* New York: Free Press.

Smith, Alan K. 1991. *Creating a World Economy: Merchant Capital, Colonialism, and World Trade, 1400–1825.* Boulder: Westview.

Snow, David A. and Robert D. Benford. 1988. "Ideology, Frame Resonance, and Participant Mobilization." Pp. 197–217 in *From Structure to Action: Comparing Social Movement Research across Cultures: International Movement Research, A Research Annual,* volume 1, edited by B. Klandermans, H. Kriesi, and S. Tarrow. Greenwich, CT/London: JAI.

Snow, David A. and Robert D. Benford. 1992. "Master Frames and Cycles of Protest." Pp. 133–56 in *Frontiers of Social Movement Theory,* edited by A. D. Morris and C. McClurg Mueller. New Haven, CT/London: Yale University Press.

Snow, David A. and Susan E. Marshall. 1984. "Cultural Imperialism, Social Movements, and the Islamic Revival." Pp. 131–52 in *Research in Social Movements, Conflict and Change,* volume 7, edited by L. Kriesberg. Greenwich, CT: JAI.

Snow, David A., E. Burke Rochford, Jr., Steven K. Worden, and Robert D. Benford. 1986. "Frame Alignment Processes, Micromobilization, and Movement Participation." *American Sociological Review* 51:464–81.

Solow, Barbara L. 1987. "Capitalism and Slavery in the Exceedingly Long Run." Pp. 51–79 in *British Capitalism and Caribbean Slavery: The Legacy of Eric Williams,* edited by B. L. Solow and S. L. Engerman. Cambridge: Cambridge University Press.

Solow, Barbara L. and Stanley L. Engerman. 1987. "British Capitalism and Caribbean Slavery: The Legacy of Eric Williams: An Introduction." Pp. 1–24 in *British Capitalism and Caribbean Slavery: The Legacy of Eric Williams,* edited by B. L. Solow and S. L. Engerman. Cambridge: Cambridge University Press.

Speck, W. A. 1983. *Society and Literature in England, 1700–1760.* Dublin: Gill and MacMillan Humanities.

Stallings, Robert A. 1990. "Media Discourse and the Social Construction of Risk." *Social Problems* 37:80–95.

Stokes, Eric. 1975. "Foreword." Pp. xi–xiv in R. H. Anstey, *The Atlantic Slave Trade and British Abolition 1760–1810.* London: MacMillan.

Stolte, John F. 1983. "The Legitimation of Structural Inequality: Reformulation and Test of the Self-Evaluation Argument." *American Sociological Review* 48:331–42.

Swidler, Ann. 1986. "Culture in Action: Symbols and Strategies." *American Sociological Review* 51:273–86.

Sypher, Wylie. [1942] 1969. *Guinea's Captive Kings: British Anti-Slavery Literature of the XVIIIth Century.* New York: Octagon.

Sztompka, Piotr. 1986a. "The Renaissance of Historical Orientation in Sociology." *International Sociology* 1:321–37.

———. 1986b. *Robert K. Merton: A Intellectual Profile.* Houndsmills/Basingstoke: MacMillan.

———. 1993. *The Sociology of Social Change.* Oxford/Cambridge, MA: Blackwell.

————. 1994. "Society as Social Becoming: Beyond Individualism and Collectivism." Pp. 251–82 in *Agency and Structure: Reorienting Social Theory*, edited by P. Sztompka. Amsterdam: OPA/Gordon and Breach.

Tallman, Irving and Marilyn Ihinger-Tallman. 1979. "Values, Distributive Justice and Social Change." *American Sociological Review* 44:216–35.

Tarrow, Sidney. 1983. *Struggling to Reform: Social Movements and Policy Change during Cycles of Protest*. Ithaca: Western Societies Program Paper, Center for International Studies, Cornell University.

————. 1988. "National Politics and Collective Action: Recent Theory and Research in Western Europe and the United States." *Annual Review of Sociology* 14:421–40.

————. 1992. "Mentalities, Political Cultures, and Collective Action Frames: Constructing Meanings through Action." Pp. 174–203 in *Frontiers in Social Movement Theory*, edited by A. D. Morris and C. McClurg Mueller. New Haven, CT/London: Yale University Press.

————. 1994. *Power in Movement: Social Movements, Collective Action and Politics*. Cambridge: Cambridge University Press.

Tatalovich, Raymond and Byron W. Daynes. 1981. *The Politics of Abortion: A Study of Community Conflict in Public Policy Making*. New York: Praeger.

Taylor, Verta. 1989. "Social Movement Continuity: The Women's Movement in Abeyance." *American Sociological Review* 54:761–75.

Temperley, Howard R. 1965. "The British and American Abolitionists Compared." Pp. 343–62 in *The Antislavery Vanguard: New Essays on the Abolitionists*, edited by M. Duberman. Princeton, NJ: Princeton University Press.

————. 1977. "Capitalism, Slavery and Ideology." *Past and Present* 75:94–118.

————. 1981. "The Ideology of Antislavery." Pp. 21–37 in *The Abolition of the Atlantic Slave Trade: Origins and Effects in Europe, Africa, and the Americas*, edited by D. Eltis and J. Walvin. Madison/London: University of Wisconsin Press.

————. 1985. "Abolition and the National Interest." Pp. 86–110 in *Out of Slavery: Abolition and After*, edited by J. Hayward. London/Totowa, NJ: Frank Cass.

Therborn, Göran. 1991. "Cultural Belonging, Structural Location and Human Action." *Acta Sociologica* 34:177–91.

Thompson, John B. 1989. "The Theory of Structuration." Pp. 56–76 in *Social Theory of Modern Societies: Anthony Giddens and His Critics*, edited by D. Held and J. B. Thompson. Cambridge: Cambridge University Press.

————. 1990. *Ideology and Modern Culture: Critical Social Theory in the Era of Mass Communication*. Stanford: Stanford University Press.

Tilly, Charles. 1978. *From Mobilization to Revolution*. Reading, MA: Addison-Wesley.

————. 1981. "The Web of Contention in Eighteenth-Century Cities." Pp. 27–51 in *Class Conflict and Collective Action*, edited by L. A. Tilly and Ch. Tilly. Beverly Hills/London: Sage.

————. 1982. "Britain Creates the Social Movement." Pp. 21–51 in *Social Conflict and the Political Order in Modern Britain*, edited by J. E. Cronin and J. Schneer. London/Canberra: Croom Helm.

————. 1984. "Social Movements and National Politics." Pp. 297–317 in *Statemak-*

ing and Social Movements: Essays in History and Theory, edited by Ch. Bright and S. Harding. Ann Arbor: University of Michigan Press.

———. 1991. "Revolution, War, and Other Struggles in Great Britain, 1789–1815". Working Paper 127, New School of Social Research, New York.

———. 1993–94. "Social Movements as Historically Specific Clusters of Political Performances." *Berkeley Journal of Sociology* 38:1–30.

———. 1995. *Social Movements and (All Sorts of) Other Political Interactions.* Working Paper 207, New School of Social Research, New York.

Traugott, Mark. 1978. "Reconceiving Social Movements." *Social Problems* 26: 38–50.

Turner, Jonathan H. 1987. "Analytical Theorizing." Pp. 156–94 in *Social Theory Today,* edited by A. Giddens and J. H. Turner. Cambridge/Oxford: Polity/ Blackwell.

Turner, Ralph H. and Lewis M. Killian. 1972. *Collective Behavior,* 2nd edition. Englewood Cliffs, NJ: Prentice Hall.

Useem, Bert and Mayer N. Zald. 1982. "From Pressure Group to Social Movement: Organizational Dilemmas of the Effort to Promote Nuclear Power." *Social Problems* 30:144–56.

Van Praag, Philip, Jr. 1992. "De smalle marges van een brede beweging: Vredesprotest in Nederland" (The narrow margins of a broad movement: Peace protest in the Netherlands). Pp. 99–121 in *Tussen Verbeelding en Macht: 25 jaar nieuwe sociale bewegingen in Nederland* (Between imagination and power: 25 years new social movements in the Netherlands), edited by J. W. Duyvendak, H. A. Van Der Heijden, R. Koopmans, and L. Wijmans. Amsterdam: SUA.

Wallerstein, Immanuel. 1980. *The Modern World-System II: Mercantilism and the Consolidation of the European World-Economy 1600–1750.* New York: Academic Press.

———. 1989. *The Modern World-System III: The Second Era of Great Expansion of the Capitalist World-Economy, 1730–1840s.* San Diego: Academic Press.

Walvin, James. 1973. *Black and White: The Negro and English Society, 1555–1945.* London: Allan Lane: Penguin.

———. 1980. "The Rise of British Popular Sentiment for Abolition 1787–1832." Pp. 19–43 in *Anti-Slavery, Religion, and Reform: Essays in Memory of Roger Anstey,* edited by Ch. Bolt and S. Drescher. Folkestone/Hamden, CT: Dawson/Archon.

———. 1981. "The Public Campaign in England against Slavery, 1787–1834." Pp. 63–83 in *The Abolition of the Atlantic Slave Trade: Origins and Effects in Europe, Africa, and the Americas,* edited by D. Eltis and J. Walvin. Madison/London: University of Wisconsin Press.

——— (ed.). 1982. *Slavery and British Society 1776–1846.* London/Basingstoke: MacMillan.

——— (ed.). 1985. "Freeing the Slaves: How Important Was Wilberforce?" Pp. 30–47 in *Out of Slavery: Abolition and After,* edited by J. Hayward. London/Totowa, NJ: Frank Cass.

Watson, J. S. 1963. *The Reign of George III, 1760–1815.* Oxford: Clarendon.

Weber, Max. [1920] 1975. *Die protestantische Ethik I; Eine Aufsatzsammlung* (The protestant ethic I; a volume of papers). Hamburg: Siebenstern Taschenbuch Verlag.

———. [1920] 1976. *The Protestant Ethic and the Spirit of Capitalism*. London: George Allen & Unwin.

———. [1920] 1986. *Gesammelte Aufsätze zur Religionssoziologie*, Teil I (Compilation of papers on the sociology of religion, volume 1). Tübingen: Mohr.

———. [1921] 1976. *Wirtschaft und Gesellschaft* (Economy and society). Tübingen: Mohr (Paul Siebeck).

Weitzer, Ronald. 1991. "Prostitutes' Rights in the United States: The Failure of a Movement." *Sociological Quarterly* 32:23–41.

Wilkinson, Paul. 1971. *Social Movements*. London: MacMillan.

Willer, David E. 1967. *Scientific Sociology: Theory and Method*. Englewood Cliffs, NJ: Prentice Hall.

Williams, Eric. [1944] 1972. *Capitalism and Slavery*. London: Andre Deutsch.

Zald, Mayer N. and John D. McCarthy (eds.). 1987. *Social Movements in an Organizational Society: Collected Essays*. New Brunswick/Oxford: Transaction.

Zaret, David. 1989. "Religion and the Rise of Liberal-Democratic Ideology in 17th-Century England." *American Sociological Review* 54:163–79.

Index